P9-CMY-533

DISCARDED

GRACE WILL
LEAD US HOME

GRACE WILL LEAD US HOME

❋

The Charleston Church Massacre and
the Hard, Inspiring Journey to Forgiveness

JENNIFER BERRY HAWES

St. Martin's Press
New York

GRACE WILL LEAD US HOME. Copyright © 2019 by The Charleston Post and Courier. All rights reserved. Printed in the United States of America. For information, address St. Martin's Press, 175 Fifth Avenue, New York, N.Y. 10010.

www.stmartins.com

Designed by Susan Walsh

Library of Congress Cataloging-in-Publication Data

Names: Hawes, Jennifer (Jennifer Berry), author.
Title: Grace will lead us home : the Charleston church massacre and the hard, inspiring
    journey to forgiveness / Jennifer Berry Hawes.
Description: First edition. | New York, NY : St. Martin's Press, [2019] | Includes index.
Identifiers: LCCN 2018055446| ISBN 9781250117762 (hardcover) | ISBN 9781250163004 (ebook)
Subjects: LCSH: Emanuel AME Church (Charleston, S.C.) | African Methodist Episcopal
    Church—South Carolina—Charleston. | Hate crimes—South Carolina—Charleston—
    History—21st century. | Mass shootings—South Carolina—Charleston—History—
    21st century. | Racism—South Carolina—Charleston—History—21st century. |
    African Americans—Crimes against—South Carolina—Charleston—21st century.
Classification: LCC HV6773.54.C43 H39 2019 | DDC 364.152/3409757915—dc23
LC record available at https://lccn.loc.gov/2018055446

Our books may be purchased in bulk for promotional, educational, or business use. Please contact your local bookseller or the Macmillan Corporate and Premium Sales Department at 1-800-221-7945, extension 5442, or by e-mail at MacmillanSpecialMarkets@macmillan.com.

First Edition: June 2019

10 9 8 7 6 5 4 3 2 1

For the nine who died on June 17, 2015

CONTENTS

Preface   ix

PART I: *We Have Stared Evil in the Eye*   1

PART II: *Looking to Man for Comfort*   121

PART III: *What's Done in the Dark
                Comes to the Light*   179

Epilogue   285

Remarks by the President in Eulogy for the Honorable
Reverend Clementa Pinckney   287

Acknowledgments   295

Index   299

PREFACE

Like much of Charleston, I was at home preparing for bed when I saw my colleagues' first tweets about a shooting at Emanuel African Methodist Episcopal (AME) Church. Just two months had passed since our newsroom at *The Post and Courier* fanned out to cover the shooting death of Walter Scott, an unarmed black motorist killed by a white police officer. When I saw that this latest violence occurred in an AME church, I called a minister in the denomination who had been a helpful source in the past. He was at a hotel near the church ministering to survivors and other church members. The man could barely speak.

Mother Emanuel's rich civil rights history—its revered status as the South's oldest AME church, spiritual home to Denmark Vesey and his doomed slave rebellion—framed my first story. It was a brief one, written on late deadline that night as the first victim's name leaked out: Reverend Clementa Pinckney. A day later, I co-wrote the first detailed public account of what happened inside the fellowship hall, followed by dozens more stories over the coming months that allowed me to meet the survivors and many of the victims' family members. Almost four years later, I feel like I know all nine who died through the memories of those who loved them most. I wish that I'd gotten to meet them all.

I come "from off," as the white locals here call it when they want you to know they belong to the storied soil of the place more than you ever will. In fact, I have lived in Charleston for two decades. My children attended school right across the street from Emanuel. I once was employed at the public library two doors down. For nearly all my time in Charleston, I have worked as a journalist at the city's daily newspaper. Before June 17, 2015, I had written a lot about the city's troubled racial legacy, but I had never experienced it as closely as I did while reporting on this tragedy.

As a white woman, I've since thought a lot about the difference between empathy and shared experience. While covering Dylann Roof's trial, most of the black journalists sat together in the media courtroom's jury box. Over coffee, one described for me the particular shared pain they felt covering this massacre. Hearing the killer's racist rants and knowing he meant them for you and your family? I didn't experience his words the way that reporter did. But I could report and contextualize the roles of race, guns, and Christian faith in a state built upon the triumvirate of their influence. This is what I have attempted to do in the pages to come. I hope they provide a comprehensive picture of Charleston and the people who will live this story forever.

The adult survivors of this tragedy and many members of the victims' families took considerable time to sit with me and help to tell this story. I hope they feel that I have remained faithful to their experience and sensitive to their suffering. I also want to acknowledge my debt to the reporters, editors, photographers, designers, management, and countless others at *The Post and Courier*. This book could not have been written without their insistence on bearing witness to the shooting and its aftermath, events that forever changed our city and the nation.

Jennifer Berry Hawes

PART I

---　✻　---

We Have Stared Evil in the Eye

one

Sown Among Thorns

❋

I t would be a late night. That much Felicia Sanders knew when she gathered her worn Bible and headed out into the swampy summer heat of June. She had a 5 o'clock committee meeting at Emanuel African Methodist Episcopal (AME) Church, where her family had worshipped since the days when Jim Crow ruled the old slave city she still called home. First, she would attend two meetings, one small and one large, to handle routine church business.

Last would come Bible study, her favorite.

She slipped into her black Toyota 4Runner, where she kept an extra pair of flats in case she was called to usher at the last minute. A day rarely went by that didn't bring Felicia to the place that many folks called Mother Emanuel, given its revered status as the South's oldest AME church. Its members knew they could count on her to help with just about anything. Revivals. Mother's Day programs. Fundraising. Sunday school. Felicia, a fifty-seven-year-old grandmother and hairstylist, had served as a trustee, a steward, the usher board president. She even volunteered as Emanuel's chicken fryer, although she herself was a vegetarian.

Felicia did it because she loved God, and she loved the congregation. Mother Emanuel was home.

A handsome woman with soft hips and high cheekbones, she had grown up with her siblings in Charleston's downtown projects, attending church with her strict grandmother after her own mother died young. Felicia's husband, Tyrone, had also grown up among closely bound families in the working-class black neighborhoods near Emanuel. After years of hard work, however, they had been able to provide a suburban life for their own children, complete with a two-story house and the wide tree-draped front lawn that Felicia now drove past.

As she cruised along a winding road that led toward downtown Charleston, she wondered if her youngest child would make it to Emanuel that night. Tywanza also loved Bible study, but he was working a shift at Steak 'n Shake, one of his two jobs, and had warned her that he might run late. The thought meandered away as she crossed over a wide river, passed a marina adorned with gleaming white vessels, and merged onto downtown Charleston's thin peninsula.

Pedestrians crowded its thin streets, many lined with majestic old churches and finely restored antebellum homes. A few traffic lights stopped Felicia along a tourist-choked stretch of Calhoun Street, named after the country's seventh vice president and one of its most ardent defenders of slavery. A 115-foot monument to the man towered over a verdant city square that bordered the street Felicia, a black woman, now navigated. It was so much a part of the place that she scarcely noticed it anymore. One building beyond the statue, she eased into a lot outside of Mother Emanuel and strolled inside, as she had thousands of times before.

As Felicia made her way into the church of her ancestors, a young white man, lean of frame, with a mop of bowl-cut sandy brown hair, sat one hundred miles away pecking at a keyboard inside his father's house at the heel of a dead-end road. The young man sometimes slept overnight on the couch, although that wasn't his plan today. He was busy putting the finishing touches on his new website. Its subject: "issues facing our race."

A couple of years earlier, he'd Googled "black on white crime," mostly out of passing curiosity, and stumbled onto a surprisingly robust realm of white supremacist websites. There he'd discovered claims of grave threats to his race—an epidemic of violence against whites, the overlooked inferiority of blacks, and a vast conspiracy to cover it all up. Writings on the sites he'd plumbed after that search had fomented what he now considered his life's great epiphany: his racial awakening.

The young man's keyboard clattered in time with the words he'd read and now adopted as his own. "I wish with a passion that niggers were treated terribly throughout history by Whites, that every White person had an ancestor who owned slaves, that segregation was an evil an oppressive institution, and so on. Because if it was all it true, it would make it so much easier for me to accept our current situation."*

Instead, black people were slaughtering innocent whites, raping white women, and taking over the nation. Yet, nobody cared. The media ignored it. His friends didn't get it. Even his own family didn't see it. And the white people who did realize it—the skinheads, neo-Nazis, and KKK—just bitched about it online. Nobody was doing anything to change it.

"Well someone has to have the bravery to take it to the real world, and I guess that has to be me."

He apologized for not writing more. But he had to go.

His pale skin and rail-thin stature—though five-foot-nine, he barely topped 120 pounds—allowed him to move in a silence of unnoticeability. At 6:13 p.m., he slipped into his creaky old black Hyundai Elantra and steered it toward the city he'd visited a half-dozen times over the past six months, seeking his target. He'd selected a place that drew good people, the kind whose murders would garner notice and outrage.

The white stucco building, a Gothic revival style built back in 1891, stood grand as ever, though her paint crumbled in spots and termites chewed her frame. Gentrification and aging congregations hadn't been kind to many of downtown Charleston's black churches, including Felicia's beloved Emanuel. The collection plate just didn't go as far as it once did, given that neither the building nor the members were getting any younger. The church held just one service on Sundays now, and most of the pews still sat empty.

Two sets of stairs led to its front entrance and the crimson-hued sanctuary inside, a sacred space both for its tradition of worship and its role in America's civil rights history—the likes of Booker T. Washington and Martin

---

* Dylann Roof's writings are replicated as he wrote them, with spelling and punctuation errors intact.

Luther King Jr. had spoken here back when the congregation topped one thousand. Felicia didn't ascend those steps, however.

It was Wednesday, not Sunday, so she headed to the left side of the building, which bordered a neighboring church. This side of Emanuel had a narrow parking lot and two sets of doors that led inside to the fellowship hall, an open space that stretched across most of its ground floor. For the Bible study's regulars, this hall had been the site of hours upon hours spent studying the sacred text more closely than Sunday worship allowed. A core group of a half-dozen or so of Emanuel's most devoted members, including Felicia, showed up for the study every Wednesday evening.

Felicia entered one of the side doors, left unlocked for members and visitors alike. She associated the room with these intimate sessions but also with church meetings and special celebrations, like her Aunt Susie's big seventieth birthday. With its caramel-colored wood paneling, cushioned couches, and bulletin boards, it felt like a cross between a grandmother's living room and an elementary school classroom. The rectangular space was oriented around a small, slightly raised altar on one wall. Three ornate wooden chairs, cushioned in red velvet, sat perched on it near a hefty Bible on a lectern. The pastor's office door sat just a few feet to the altar's right. To its left, a short hallway led to the secretary's office and a second set of doors to the outside, the ones almost at the back of the church.

On both ends of the room, snug staircases allowed access to Emanuel's second-floor sanctuary, which slumbered above. The design necessitated the need for an elevator to serve its older members. Plans for that elevator brought Felicia to Emanuel now, early, before much of the congregation would arrive for their large quarterly conference meeting shortly after. Rows of empty folding chairs awaited larger audiences like that meeting would draw. On the other side of the room, away from the doors, four round foldable white tables stretched in a row. These hosted more intimate conversations, like Bible study.

The elevator committee members now gathered at one of them to check their progress after years of fundraising, planning, and building. Construction was almost done, a reason to celebrate. Felicia had a special place in her heart for the church's elderly congregants, including her beloved Aunt Susie, who had just arrived, walking with a cane.

conography intrigued the young man. His companions on the one-hundred-mile drive to Charleston included his new .45-caliber Glock and eight magazines with eleven hollow-point bullets in each. It made for a total of eighty-eight rounds. The number was a symbol for HH, based on the alphabet's eighth letter, a neo-Nazi favorite: Heil Hitler.

His fifteen-year-old Hyundai also bore a Confederate States of America license plate with three different Confederate flags, although its presence on the car wouldn't draw any particular attention. In much of the old Confederacy, battle flags still flew on porches and embellished pickup trucks, a symbol of white southern pride and a snub to elitist Yankees who flocked south for the strong economy and pleasant climate while deriding its heritage.

Without stopping, he cruised toward South Carolina's most historic city, where the first shots of the Civil War were fired in the first state to secede from the union. Charleston had once been home to the nation's highest ratio of enslaved black people to whites. An estimated 40 percent of America's slaves came through its harbor. That's why he'd picked it. Six times over the past six months, he had visited the city—and Emanuel—while devising his plans. Once he had chosen his target, he'd struck up a conversation with one of its congregants, who had provided a useful detail: The church had Bible study on Wednesday nights.

It was perfect. Bible study would draw a smaller crowd than Sunday worship. It surely wouldn't have any security. And a black church wouldn't draw any white people. He didn't want any of them to get hurt accidentally.

The young man drove down the same interstate that the church's senior pastor, Clementa Pinckney, had sped down just a couple of hours earlier. The traffic-choked road connected Charleston to Columbia, the state's capital, where Clementa lived not far from the young man, although they'd never met.

Clementa had just spent a hectic day embroiled in his other job, that of state senator. It was budget preparation season, an annual exercise in frustration given he was a black Democrat in a state where white Republicans maintained an easy grip on power. Over the two-hour drive to Emanuel, his cell phone rang incessantly. His immediate boss, the presiding elder, and about sixty members would arrive soon for the church's quarterly conference, and the evening's agenda wasn't quite ready yet.

His wife, Jennifer, and his six-year-old daughter had joined him for some family time given that he had been so busy lately. Little Malana begged him to stop for ice cream at McDonald's, but there wasn't time. He promised to take her on the way home.

As soon as they arrived at Emanuel, his secretary, Althea Latham, rushed to help him print off and copy the agenda. Their relatively new presiding elder, the Reverend Dr. Norvel Goff, would be there soon. When Althea finished, Clementa walked over and set his hand on her left shoulder. He thanked her.

"You know you're gonna owe me," she teased.

"When's your birthday?" he asked.

"Forget it," she answered dryly. "My birthday is in December when everybody is thinking about Christmas."

"You're going to have Christmas in July then!"

Althea tried not to smile. "I'm gonna hold you to it."

Clementa, she thought, looked unusually nice, even for him. Hair freshly cut, black suit fine, new shoes shining. When it was time for the quarterly conference to begin, she watched him persuade Malana to stay in his office with Jennifer. The winsome girl—Grasshopper, as he called her—clung to the smooth fabric of his pant leg until he gave her a parting hug and disappeared into the fellowship hall.

Presiding Elder Goff stepped in front of the group of almost sixty congregants. He and Clementa attended to church business, including the licensing of two new ministers, a first step in the long road to ordination. They also re-licensed a third, Myra Thompson. It promised to be a thrilling night for her.

In a few minutes, she would lead Bible study for the first time.

The young man reached Charleston at 7:48 p.m. and headed straight for the church. The parking lot, however, was full. Too full.

Something bigger than Bible study was going on.

Unhurried, he waited.

After the conference ended, Felicia watched most of those gathered stroll out into the waning sunset. The meeting had gone long, and the start of Bible study was now two hours behind schedule. Daniel Simmons Sr., a seventy-four-year-old retired minister who usually led the small group, wondered if they should postpone it. So did Reverend Pinckney, who faced an almost two-hour drive home.

They went back and forth. Stay. Cancel. Stay. Cancel.

DePayne Middleton Doctor, one of two women newly licensed moments earlier, spoke up: "Let's just do thirty minutes of it."

The group agreed and headed toward four round tables, the first one just outside the pastor's office door near the altar, then extending in a row down the length of the room. Five or six white plastic folding chairs waited around each.

DePayne, already an ordained Baptist minister, normally led her four daughters into Bible study like ducklings behind her, each with a milkshake in hand. Now, she headed for the second table from the altar alone.

"Where are your girls?" Felicia asked.

DePayne explained their busy schedules as Myra, a retired educator and head of the church's trustee board, joined them. Myra wore a classic black dress suit, her shoulder-length black hair smooth and dappled with gray, a headband holding it in place. Her face flushed with anticipation. This was her first time leading the Bible study, and she'd overprepared.

As the group settled in, Reverend Pinckney stood at the side door saying good night to the departing members, mostly older women whose skirts blew in the summer breeze as they headed out. He'd decided to stay.

Reverend Goff decided to go. He got into his black Cadillac, parked in the space closest to the side door where Clementa Pinckney bid people good night, and pulled out.

Cynthia Graham Hurd, a popular local librarian, had come to present a project about the church's history to the quarterly conference. Now, as she prepared to head out, Felicia greeted her. They'd grown up at Emanuel together and often sat beside each other during Sunday services. Felicia invited her to stay.

"No, I'm leaving," Cynthia demurred. She'd weathered an all-day managers' meeting at the Main Library a few doors down, in addition to the quarterly conference. She was exhausted.

"But I love you Felicia Sanders," Cynthia added.

"You love me, you'll stay to Bible study," Felicia teased back.

What could Cynthia say to that? She headed for the second table to sit with Myra, DePayne, and Sharonda Coleman-Singleton, another licensed minister who was a close friend of hers. Retired pastor Dan Simmons joined them, and soon their Bibles covered the table.

Susie Jackson shuffled toward the third table, pocketbook hanging from her cane. She was eighty-seven and wore a gap-toothed smile familiar to everyone at Emanuel. Hers was Emanuel's largest family, and Susie its matriarch. Felicia and her eleven-year-old granddaughter joined her. Aunt Susie was one of Felicia's closest friends and most dedicated prayer partners.

Earlier, at 6:50 p.m., Felicia had received a text from her youngest child, Tywanza. "You still at Bible study?" he'd asked. Since it was starting late, the twenty-six-year-old had figured he could make it after all. When he arrived, Felicia's granddaughter smiled big at her Uncle Wanza, a father figure, tall and hipster cool as he joined them at the third table.

Almost seventy years old, diabetic and hungry, Polly Sheppard had intended to skip this Bible study. A church trustee, she'd been in meetings all day. But she also had just run into Myra, one of her dearest friends, in the fellowship hall's ladies' room. Myra had begged her to stay. Now, Polly headed for the last of the four round tables, still tempted to duck out. If Myra looked away, she told herself, she still might, though it would be hard to get across the wide space to the doors without being spotted. Another old friend, Ethel Lance, the church's sexton, sat near her.

Across the room, the door to Reverend Pinckney's office stood open. He headed in that direction to check on his wife and daughter. Jennifer, an elementary librarian, had corralled Malana inside, on the other side of a thin wall from the fellowship hall, thankful that the normally energetic child was quietly eating some snacks and watching cartoons.

As Clementa turned to head back out for Bible study, she stopped him.

"Hold up, mister. I need your credit card." She needed to pay for their older daughter's dance class.

"Here you go, darlin'."

Clementa hugged and kissed Malana, then stepped through his office doorway and into the fellowship hall, where he sat alone at the first table. An empty chair sat beside him.

The young man waited until 8:16 p.m. By then, all but a dozen cars had left the church's parking lot behind the building. He pulled through an open gate in back and headed toward a narrow strip with a few parking spaces along one side. He wasn't certain which entrance to use; he'd never been inside. The front doors were way too conspicuous, elevated on the second floor and highly visible to cars and pedestrians on busy, four-lane Calhoun Street. The church had no back entrance, so he steered toward a set of double doors on one side of the building. They sat near the church's back corner, away from the street.

The parking space closest to them, where elder Goff's Cadillac had been, remained empty.

He eased into it and stepped out slowly. Despite thick humidity and temperatures that reached well into the nineties, he wore a long-sleeved gray shirt, dark pants, and Timberland-style boots, along with a black pouch that hung heavy on his waist.

It took him just ten steps to reach the tall wooden side doors, where he tugged first at the one on the right. It wouldn't budge, so he tried the left. It opened inward with an industrial clank. The church left it unlocked to welcome all who came seeking God's word. A narrow, wood-paneled hallway inside was made even more cramped by stacks of workbooks, a potted plant, and a console table. Along it, he passed an empty office on his left.

The brief hallway ended at a lobby with a red exit sign and an open doorway into a large room beyond it. Voices drew him forward. He flitted toward them, past a poster of the Ten Commandments, and stepped through the doorway.

two

The Visitor

✳

They'd barely opened their Bibles when the young white man entered the fellowship hall from the lobby.

"Pastor, we have a visitor!" Sharonda announced.

It wasn't unusual for strangers to venture inside, even white ones. Emanuel was a well-known church in the heart of a city that swelled with tourists during the summer months. The ever-growing College of Charleston's campus also sat just a couple of blocks away, sending forth thousands of mostly white young adults on foot and bicycles, including those who occasionally stopped in to pray or learn more about the church's important civil rights history.

Reverend Pinckney unfolded his tall form from his chair and strolled across the room to welcome their guest.

"Are you here for Bible study?" he asked, towering over the slight man before him, his baritone bridging the space between them.

The visitor nodded.

Reverend Pinckney handed the young man a Bible and a copy of Myra's study guide. Then, he pulled out a chair beside him and beckoned for the man to sit. There they settled in, just the two of them at the round table closest to the altar and pastor's office. The visitor stared silently at the table.

Polly Sheppard maneuvered her eyes toward their guest at the other end of the row of tables, trying not to be obvious. He looked like a college student, if an unusually docile and quiet one, with his boyish bowl haircut. The one thing that struck her was his eyes. They looked vacant and dull. Maybe he was just shy, she thought. Or hurting. Or on drugs.

In any event, if he'd come to Emanuel in search of God, they would guide him.

Outside, the summer sunset darkened, yielding to fluorescent lights hanging from the fellowship hall's low ceilings. Myra propped up her iPad to read the notes she'd prepared for several weeks. She had read tonight's text over and over, analyzing each verse until the minutes before she'd left home that afternoon.

Dan Simmons, a retired pastor, sat across from her. A tall and imposing former Army man with a deep knowledge of the Bible, he commanded respect from everyone he met. He'd been around the district for decades, and he'd run more than once for bishop. Myra knew that he did not brook laziness or ignorance and wanted to impress him. She knew too that he also lived for a good debate. She was ready.

They opened their Bibles to a passage in Mark 4 known as the Parable of the Sower, a story Jesus shared with his disciples about seeds cast onto ground ill-prepared to nourish them.

> Behold, there went out a sower to sow:
> And it came to pass, as he sowed, some fell by the wayside, and
>   the fowls of the air came and devoured it up.
> And some fell on stony ground, where it had not much earth;
>   and immediately it sprang up, because it had no depth of
>   earth:
> But when the sun was up, it was scorched; and because it had
>   no root, it withered away.
> And some fell among thorns, and the thorns grew up, and
>   choked it, and it yielded no fruit.
> And other fell on good ground, and did yield fruit that sprang
>   up and increased; and brought forth, some thirty, and
>   some sixty, and some an hundred.

The room became stuffy and they quickly exceeded the half hour they'd planned. Myra's enthusiasm carried them along. She described a world of sin in which hatred and worldly desires had hardened hearts, leaving too many people unable to nourish the seeds of God's grace within themselves. As Christians, they needed to provide that fertile ground.

Myra saw herself in the story. Once a single teenage mother, she had heeded God's call to become a teacher and guidance counselor for at-risk children and, now, to prepare for the ordained ministry.

Jesus told his disciples that even people capable of hearing didn't always comprehend what they heard. Similarly, Myra explained, people didn't always absorb or apply God's lessons to their lives. Like seeds that fell onto rocky ground or were choked by the thorns of sin, they often missed out on the redemption that God offered.

At the next table, Felicia listened with pride. She had known Myra her entire life. Like her, Myra was always at the church, always getting stuff done. She called Myra the "bugaboo" because she kept her nose in everything—and kept everyone else on task.

Reverend Simmons listened too, leaning back in his chair and grinning, arms spread widely as he jumped into the conversation. Felicia's son Tywanza opened the Snapchat app on his cell phone and recorded a few seconds of video, panning from the far right, where the visitor sat quietly hunched over a table, then stopping on Reverend Simmons—old "Dapper Dan"—wearing a button-down shirt and a wide smile. An imposing man, he'd once carried a bullhorn around his old church, blasting his commanding voice to chase criminals away. He also usually carried a gun and was trained to use it. At that moment, it sat beneath a towel on the front passenger seat of his Mercedes parked outside.

As Tywanza recorded his antics, Felicia shook her head. Tywanza had been nudging her to get onto social media, too, but she'd put him off. That was his world. A couple thousand people followed his life on his "freshwanza" Instagram page, where he posted inspirational memes and photos that showed off his stylish clothes and a smile so big it almost couldn't fit on his face. As Dapper Dan spoke, Tywanza typed across his Snapchat "Bible study knowledge planter" and then sent it.

Myra continued to plumb the passage for meaning.

"In like manner, the seed of God's word, falling upon a heart rendered callous by the custom of sinning, is straightway snatched away by 'the evil one,'" her notes read.

The visitor sat quietly as the study continued for almost an hour. At 9 o'clock, the group began a closing prayer.

They bowed their heads and closed their eyes.

The visitor did not close his eyes.

He'd later say that he had wavered. They seemed so nice. But his mission was too important, the moment too pivotal for the salvation of his race.

He reached a slender hand into his pack.

The cold grip of his Glock was scored, with indents that his fingers now grasped. He lifted its heavy weight in the quick motion he'd practiced and pointed the barrel at Reverend Pinckney, standing next to him. He pulled the trigger, shooting the pastor in the neck at close range. Pinckney stumbled toward the altar. The man fired at him again and then again, the weight of his pistol thrusting his thin wrist backward with each blast.

Reverend Pinckney fell onto the white linoleum floor.

At first, Felicia thought a transformer had blown from the elevator construction. Then she opened her eyes.

"He has a gun!" she shrieked.

The blasts exploded so quickly, so loudly, that she thought it was a machine gun. The women around her dove under their tables, cowering together, some praying. The doors to the outside felt far away, across an open space filled with folding chairs. Had this white man come to assassinate Reverend Pinckney?

They waited for the shooting to stop. They waited for the assassin to leave.

Across a table, Reverend Simmons stood up.

"Let me see my pastor. I need to check on my pastor!" he insisted. But the visitor turned the gun and pulled the trigger again. One hollow-point bullet pierced Simmons' chest, and then another. He spun away, stumbling past Reverend Pinckney's bleeding body and the poster of the Ten

Commandments. He staggered through the lobby and made it past the red exit sign.

He did not make it to the side door where the killer had entered or beyond to his car, where his own gun waited. Instead, Simmons collapsed at the side doorway's cusp, moaning outside the secretary's office door, now closed. The killer shot him again, at close range.

In the pastor's office, Jennifer Pinckney heard the gunfire explode on the other side of the wafer-thin wall between her husband's office and the fellowship hall. Someone grunted, *"uh!"* She heard chairs getting shoved around.

Jennifer got up and walked to the door, still cracked open, to see what was going on. But when gunfire blasted again, she eased it shut and locked it. She focused singularly on Malana, ferrying the terrified girl to another door, this one leading to the adjoining secretary's office. That room had a second door to the side hallway where Simmons had just collapsed, although she didn't know he lay there so grievously wounded. Jennifer quietly locked that door and shoved her daughter beneath a desk, scolding the child in terrified whispers to stay quiet.

Beyond the door to the hallway, she heard a groan.

Another voice said, "I'm not crazy. I have to do this."

Back in the fellowship hall, Felicia's granddaughter began to scream. Felicia grabbed the girl and yanked her to the floor beneath their table, whispering: "Just play dead, play dead, play dead."

"Granny, I'm scared!"

The killer began to fire down the row of tables.

"Don't say nothin'," Felicia ordered. She muzzled the girl tightly against her chest as shots rang out again, quickly coming closer and closer. Beside them on the floor, Aunt Susie lay motionless. Felicia wanted so badly to grab her too, but she couldn't protect everyone. She clutched her granddaughter more tightly, fearful she might suffocate her. Tywanza collapsed onto the other side of her.

"Momma, he shot me," he said.

A wound to his neck bled heavily. Warm blood seeped onto the bare skin of Felicia's legs. As the blasts continued, she had an idea. She dredged her legs through the blood. Maybe the shooter would think he had shot them all before he hurt the child, too.

The man reloaded, stalking around the linen-covered tables, firing over and over at the women cowering beneath them from just feet away. Shell casings clattered onto the hard tile floor. The bullets flew so close that heat from the gun's discharge seared Felicia's skin.

After every eleven shots, the killer paused again to reload. Again and again.

Felicia's Bible fell to the floor. A bullet pierced it.

Beneath the table next to her, she spotted her old friend Polly Sheppard cowering, as yet unhit. The killer's heavy boots marched toward her.

Felicia prayed silently. Polly prayed out loud.

The gunman stopped shooting when he reached Polly, dead eyes looking down at her, his heavy black pistol pointed at her feet.

"Shut up!" he snapped. "Did I shoot you yet?"

"No."

"I'm not going to," he said. "I'm going to leave you here to tell the story."

As he spoke, Felicia stayed perfectly still, comforted that Tywanza and her granddaughter still seemed to be alive. She whispered: "Just lay, just lay, just lay."

Tywanza, however, didn't just lay. As the gunman spoke to Polly, he struggled to prop himself up and distract the man.

"Why are you doing this?" Tywanza asked.

The killer turned to look at him, the only other young man in the room.

"I have to do this," he replied. "Y'all raping all our white women and taking over the nation."

Tywanza pleaded, "You don't have to do this. We mean you no harm."

"I have to finish my mission."

He shot Tywanza three more times.

A single word rolled through Felicia's mind: *Jesus. Jesus. Jesus.*

Polly, hiding beneath the other table, heard two clicks. Was he out of bullets? Reloading? When she heard him step farther away from her, she glanced around, desperate to summon help. Someone's cell phone, smeared with blood, had fallen near her. Grasping it, she punched in 911, and hit "OK."

Nothing happened.

She looked back at the phone. It was blinking now for some reason. She dialed 911 again.

"Please answer. Oh, God," she prayed aloud, moaning with terror into the phone.

A woman's perky voice answered.

"911. What's the address of the emergency?"

"Please, Emanuel church. There's plenty people shot down here. Please send somebody," Polly whispered, gasping for breath. "Right away!"

"Emanuel church?"

"Emanuel AME. 110 Calhoun."

"And there's people shot?"

Polly peered out from beneath the table. She wasn't sure if the man had fled or if he was still in the room. Near her, Tywanza tried to slide across the floor toward his elderly aunt lying still beneath a table. Was that a shadow of the gunman over near the hallway?

"Send someone down here, please!" Polly begged.

Don't hang up, the operator warned.

"He's coming. He's coming. He's coming!"

Polly tried to breathe.

"Help us, Lord, please. Help us, Lord. Please, Jesus, help us."

A few feet away, Tywanza moaned again, a desperate and primal sound filling the air.

The killer turned to leave. On his way out, he strolled past Clementa Pinckney's body. Then he unbuckled his belt and dropped his pouch, leaving the belt coiled like a serpent on the lobby floor. He popped an eighth magazine into the Glock, his final one. Stepping around Dan Simmons, still alive but bleeding heavily in the narrow hallway, he reached the side door he'd entered an hour earlier. Pushing it open a few inches, he peered outside in the dark night.

To his amazement, nobody was there.

He'd fired more than seventy shots inside a church just a couple buildings down from a major city park, a public library, school district offices, a three-story school, and a gas station. But it was nighttime on a weekday. The buildings sat empty, the streets quiet.

He eased out, glancing right, then left, the gun in his right hand pointed at the ground. Then he moved quickly to his car as the church door swung shut behind him. Cranking up the old Hyundai, he reversed out of his spot and drove quickly toward the lot's back gate. He turned left, not too fast, down a quiet side street, then right onto Meeting Street, a four-lane artery through downtown Charleston. One mile later, he merged onto the interstate and headed back the way he'd come.

three

What Is Hidden

✳

Still huddled under the table, clutching the phone connecting her with the 911 operator, Polly heard a voice. She wasn't certain the shooter had left, but the voice wasn't his anyway.

"Lord have mercy." It was Myra, her dear friend.

Polly scanned the room. Bodies lay motionless beneath the tables near her. Brass hulls littered pools of blood. Bibles, hymnals, chairs, and notebooks lay strewn about. The great-grandmother felt utterly alone in the room except for a strong and distinct sense of God's presence.

A moan broke the silence.

A few feet away, Tywanza tried to reach for his aunt Susie, who lay motionless on her side beneath the adjacent table. Blood from his wounds spilled onto his white T-shirt and smeared onto the white floor.

"Tywanza, calm down. Please calm down!"

It was her friend Felicia Sanders.

"Aunt Susie. Aunt Susie!" he moaned.

Beside him, Felicia begged. "Tywanza, lay still. Be still. Be still."

"I got to get to Aunt Susie."

But he couldn't breathe, he said. He needed some water.

"I love you, Tywanza. I love you, Tywanza," Felicia repeated.

"I love you too, Momma."

A police siren wailed in the distance. Polly crawled from beneath the table, still talking to the 911 dispatcher.

"Miss Polly, please help my son!" Felicia called to her friend, a retired nurse.

The church had two sets of side doors, including the one the killer used. Now, from the other, up closer to the front of the church, a door opened. The women fell silent again.

Officer David Stewart, a burly man with an AR-15 rifle, entered first. He'd been eating dinner five blocks away with Officer Edward Henderson, who rushed in behind him. A third officer, Andrew Delaney, closely followed. He was in only his second year on the force.

All three white men wore dark blue uniforms, their weapons drawn. They'd just received a call describing an active shooter, but they didn't know how many. Or how well-armed. They assumed all lives inside were in danger, including their own.

Their immediate mission: Locate the threat and eliminate it.

In earlier times, officers responding to an active shooter would have set up a perimeter and waited for the SWAT team to arrive. No more. Today's mass shooters try to kill as many people as possible as quickly as possible, so police officers are trained to enter a building immediately.

Stewart veered along one wall. Henderson hurried along the other. Felicia's granddaughter, a middle-schooler in a purple shirt, stood up in the center of the room near several bodies, brown eyes round with shock. On a table near her, a gun magazine lay beside an open Bible.

"Help! Help!" Felicia called from Tywanza's side. He writhed in pain.

But first the officers needed to discern if the killer was inside.

"Where is he?"

"I don't know," Felicia said. "He ran out that door, I think." She pointed toward the other side doors.

Delaney rushed by. From the floor, Tywanza groaned in pain.

"Please help me," he begged.

But Delaney couldn't help, not yet. First, they needed to secure the area to ensure they all survived these moments. Medical crews couldn't enter until they did so. The room was filled with doors and crannies.

"I'll come back to you," Delaney promised.

Sgt. Justin Kniess, a supervisor, slipped in next. Polly stood and walked toward him, dark eyes blank with shock. Felicia's granddaughter wandered among the bodies.

"Sweetheart, we're here to help," Kniess assured.

The officers hugged the walls, fanning out as they scanned the open space of the fellowship hall first. Later, even those long into their law enforcement careers would describe it as the most horrific crime scene they'd ever encountered. A handsome man in a black suit lay on his side in the middle of the room, blood flowing toward an altar. Women curled up, silent and still, beneath round tables. And everywhere bullets, shell casings, gun magazines. An iron scent clung to the air.

Polly struggled to recall what the gunman was wearing. A gray T-shirt. No, it was a sweatshirt. But it was gray. Yes, gray. Long-sleeved. And the gun. A handgun. Not a rifle. She was certain.

Just one killer. A white man, young and thin, like a college student, about twenty-one years old.

"Small, frail white boy," Felicia called out.

Sgt. John Lites, who had given the order for the officers to go inside, stepped in last and scanned the room. A middle-aged man with a fatherly manner, he had worked some of the city's most dangerous streets for years as part of an intensive community policing effort. As he entered the room, he hurried toward the child darting around, then spotted a young man sprawled on the floor bleeding heavily from a gunshot wound to his chest. An older woman stood over him.

"That's my son," Felicia said, her tone flat and distant.

At first, Tywanza lay motionless in a wide pool of blood. Then he moved, gasping for air.

"I got shot," he told Lites. The officer knelt beside him.

Across the room just then, Kniess spotted a foot sticking out from a short hallway near the other side doors and rushed over. Reverend Simmons lay on a green carpet runner, bleeding heavily from chest wounds. Four bullets were lodged in his body. He'd fallen at the side doors, as if he'd been trying to get out. He struggled to breathe.

"Hold on, buddy," Kniess said.

An officer summoned paramedics.

"How many victims do we have in this room?" Kniess shouted. "Give me a count!"

From across the fellowship hall, Lites counted aloud. "We've got one, two, three, four, five, six, seven." He couldn't see Dan Simmons from his spot kneeling beside Tywanza on the other side of the round tables. Lites would later realize he had blood all over himself, though he didn't think about it then. Tywanza's left hand reached out to touch the curly hair of his elderly aunt.

Lites clasped his other hand for reassurance, and Tywanza squeezed it tightly. Then, he looked up. Their eyes met in the chaos. When Tywanza focused on the sergeant, his expression slackened with relief. His grip softened. The young man's body relaxed, as if falling asleep.

Felicia hovered over Lites' shoulder. She had watched her baby boy come into this world. Now, she watched him leave it.

"Tywanza gone," she murmured.

Around them, officers still moved around the room. Radios barked. Felicia's voice rose.

"My baby gone. My baby gone," she cried. "Noooo!"

Lites knew there wasn't time to mourn, not now. The survivors needed to escape this horrific room—and quickly. The police needed to clear the place before paramedics could enter and help anyone left alive. He set Tywanza's hand onto his chest and stood, then asked Felicia to come with him. The officers had performed a quick search of the immediate space, but it wasn't enough to ensure everyone's safety. Gunmen could be hiding upstairs in the sanctuary, in a missed closet or corner, almost anywhere.

Felicia followed him, stepping past Susie Jackson, the eighty-seven-year-old now gone, too.

"This is my aunt," Felicia told Sgt. Lites, her voice flat as she glanced down at the elderly woman she'd prayed with and laughed with throughout her life.

As she walked away, Felicia clutched in one hand a cell phone that she'd found lying near her. It belonged to her beautiful friend, Sharonda Coleman-Singleton, the woman who'd first noticed their visitor and who now lay motionless beneath the next table over. Despite the commotion of officers around the room, Felicia managed to dial her husband, Tyrone, Aunt Susie's nephew.

His deep voice reached her through the phone.

"Tyrone, my baby's dead. My baby's dead. My baby's dead," Felicia repeated. "And Aunt Susie's dead . . ."

An officer approached her. "Ma'am, we're going to get you to safety."

Police escorted Felicia and her granddaughter away from the church, catching up with Polly Sheppard while heading toward Calhoun Street. Felicia still spoke to her husband on the phone.

"Susie, preacher gone. Everybody gone. Myra gone. Everybody gone . . ."

Back in the fellowship hall, Sharonda, a mother of three and beloved track coach, still had a pulse. Emergency crews pulled her from beneath a table, rolled her over, and hooked her up to an EKG machine. But they found no more signs of life. She, too, was gone.

In the side hallway, paramedics heaved Dan Simmons onto a stretcher and whisked him to a trauma center a few blocks away.

Amid the commotion, Lites took over supervision of the dead inside. He would remain with them in this room, all night and into the next morning, to ensure that no one disturbed them in any way. He also didn't want anyone else to see the horror before him.

Darkness covered the street out front and cloaked the surrounding buildings—the school, the bank, the Baptist church. Police led the survivors across Calhoun Street, where red and blue emergency lights arced over the trees, casting shadows of movement that could be anyone, anywhere. Felicia stepped across the warm asphalt, her stretchy black skirt weighted down with thick streams of blood, her feet bare, her shoes and Bible left behind in the fellowship hall.

As they crossed the street, an officer threw an older white man in a gray shirt to the ground.

"No, that's not the man!" Polly said, turning. "This boy looked just like a little child."

As the small group approached the Courtyard by Marriott hotel kitty-corner to the church, its glass front doors swooshed open automatically. They headed down a long hallway toward a conference room, where police pressed Felicia and Polly for a more detailed description of the killer. What kind of car was he driving? Which direction did he go?

What they all really wanted to know was: Would he kill again?

S till inside the church, Jennifer Pinckney continued to huddle with Malana beneath the secretary's wooden desk. They hadn't yet been found, and as far as they knew, the killer or killers were still in the building.

"Is Daddy going to die?" Malana whispered.

"Be quiet, Malana."

A phone receiver pressed to her cheek, Jennifer clung to the voice of a different 911 operator who had just answered her call. Jennifer had heard so many shots—it seemed like at least a hundred. A bullet had pierced the secretary's office wall a few feet from where they hid and sailed across the room but fortunately hadn't harmed either of them.

"911. What's the address of the emergency?"

Jennifer whispered in short, jagged bursts into the phone.

"I am at," she began. She could hardly speak. "I. Am. At. Emanuel. Mother Emanuel."

The operator, her voice tense with a deliberate calm, urged Jennifer to stay quiet and still until police came and got her. Jennifer did so, behind the doors she had locked while praying that Malana wouldn't scream out in terror.

Sgt. Lites rattled the knob of the pastor's office door in the next room over from her. It was, he realized, locked. He kicked the door, but it didn't break. Henderson kicked it next, and this time it opened.

Lites entered first. He felt certain the shooter was in there. It was the last place in the immediate area they hadn't checked. The first police responders had arrived so quickly after the call came in that there was a good chance the killer remained inside the church somewhere. Dispatch had said a woman and child were in the pastor's office. They hadn't yet emerged.

Deep down, Lites suspected the shooter had killed them, too—and now waited to ambush the officers. Gun drawn, he peered inside the study. It looked empty. He took one step in, then another, Henderson behind him. Glancing behind Clementa's desk, they saw no one. A dispatcher's voice spoke into Lites' earpiece. The woman and child were alive in the next room over, the secretary's office.

He saw a connecting doorway to that room, which sat in darkness.

The officers approached, weapons still drawn, and saw another wooden desk, then hurried over to peer beneath it.

Looking up at them, a terrified child sat in her mother's lap, clinging to her.

"Hey, sweetheart. How are you?" Lites asked.

"Good," a little voice answered.

From over the phone, the operator spoke to Jennifer again: "Okay, Miss Pinckney, I'll let you go, okay?"

"Come on, baby," Lites prodded.

To his fellow officers, he hollered, "I got 'em! I got 'em."

Jennifer and Malana eased out. Once she stood, Jennifer turned back toward her husband's office to get her purse. Lites stopped her.

"No, I don't want to go this way," he said. "Come on, sweetheart. Come this way."

He led them to the office's other door, the one leading out to the side hallway where Dan Simmons had just lay dying. A female officer approached, reaching her arms out for Malana. "Come here. I'm gonna carry you, and I want you to close your eyes, okay?" she said hurriedly.

"We'll get everything for you," Lites assured Jennifer. "Do me a favor and come this way, okay?"

"Thank you," Jennifer said.

She followed him into the side hallway. A thick pool of blood and paramedics' trash were all that remained of Reverend Simmons on the green carpet runner after medical crews hauled him into an ambulance. Jennifer stepped over it all. An officer stood between her eyes and the bodies, including her husband's, just beyond the hallway.

Pagers around Medical University Hospital rang with the distinct series of sharp, rapid-fire beeps that alerted the staff: incoming trauma.

ADULT TRAUMA A

GSW

BED 1 UNKNOWN

Medical crews streamed into the trauma bay. Attending doctors, residents, nurses, respiratory therapists, CT techs, pharmacy staff, until a good fifty people amassed in sky blue paper hospital gowns, heads covered in blue surgical caps, waiting.

Trauma A indicated the most severe trauma.

GSW stood for gunshot wound.

Unknown meant the hospital staff didn't know much else.

They yanked aside thick white curtains between rooms to open up the whole bay so that bright fluorescent lights illuminated the space. Others wheeled in hospital beds, squeezing six into a space normally used for three. They closed blinds in the ER lobby and pulled a metal detector around to guard the door. More public safety officers arrived. So did chaplains.

In a burst, a set of doors opened with a whoosh. Paramedics rushed in, one doing chest compressions on an older black man. They rolled Dan Simmons from the stretcher onto one of the six beds.

He had no pulse.

The retired pastor had suffered a massive wound to his chest. Medical crews inserted tubes and opened up his chest, massaging his heart, trying to do everything they could to jumpstart his life. They tried for thirty minutes before declaring that he was gone.

Earlier in the evening, Myra Thompson's husband, Anthony, had asked her if she wanted him to come watch her lead Bible study. They'd talked for hours upon hours about the parable and its message of tilling healthy spiritual soil.

"No," she'd said. "You're not coming."

"Yes, I am."

"No," she insisted. Anthony was a minister in another denomination, and he had duties that night at his own church where some drama had flared among a few women. Go, she said. Take care of your people. So he had.

Anthony's house of worship, Holy Trinity Reformed Episcopal Church, sat several blocks from Emanuel in the heart of the College of Charleston's bustling campus. After he'd finished up there, he had driven back to the brick house he and Myra shared, an easy five-minute trip up the city of Charleston's thin peninsula.

The house sat dark and quiet. Just as he walked in, Anthony remembered that he had promised Myra he would stop at a seafood restaurant to pick up dinner. It was a big night for her, and she'd be hungry when she got home.

He headed back out, then returned about thirty minutes later carrying a warm bag into their kitchen. She still wasn't home. He flipped on the lights. It was so hot and humid outside, he untucked his light button-down shirt and settled in, excited to hear how her Bible study had gone. She'd be home any minute.

Their home phone jangled.

"Hello," he answered.

"Reverend Thompson, put your wife on the phone. I got to talk to her!"

It was an Emanuel member he knew. She sounded curt, rude even.

"Anthony, put Myra on the phone!"

"She's not here," he said, a bit irritated.

Pause.

The woman's voice softened. "You need to go to the church."

"I just left my church."

"No, not your church. You need to go up to Emanuel."

"Why?"

"I heard some shooting is going on."

He dropped the phone and raced out the door.

When he reached a major intersection near the church, Anthony saw police barricades blocking access to Calhoun Street. A thicket of squad cars lay ahead, blue lights pulsating, officers swarming. Then he saw a row of ambulances parked along the street. Anthony had recently retired from a career as a probation and parole agent. He knew to ascertain certain details of a crime scene, things like how the ambulances all sat parked and quiet, no lights on, nothing indicating they might be heading someplace in a hurry.

Propelled by fear, he approached a policeman.

"Look, I got to get to the church. I heard some shooting is going on down there, and my wife's in church, and I need to get there!" The words gushed out with the rising tide of his panic.

"You can't do that," the officer said. "But don't worry because they took a lot of people out of the church and down to the hotel." He pointed at a Marriott across the street.

"Oh, thank God."

Anthony darted down the street and into the hotel lobby.

"Where's everybody at?" he asked the greeting staff.

Something about the way they looked at him seemed funny.

"They're all down there." A man pointed down a long hall past an area, quiet now, where guests normally gathered to eat.

"Oh God. Thank you, Jesus."

Anthony dashed down and stopped at the last door on his left. When he reached it, he paused and took several deep breaths to calm himself. If something just happened at Emanuel, Myra didn't need to see him all harried like this. Anthony always liked to keep his composure. His breathing steadied, he opened the conference room door.

He expected to see a roomful of people but instead saw only three. Felicia Sanders sat at a long table holding a child in her lap, their heads resting on one another's shoulders. Polly Sheppard, a close friend of Myra's, sat at the other end, her head down as if resting or deep in thought. Or in prayer.

Otherwise, the room sat empty.

He glanced back at Felicia. She and her granddaughter looked up and watched him approach. Felicia's normally warm brown eyes filled with tears. Before he could say a word, she spoke.

"Myra's gone," she said softly.

He absorbed this for a moment. But it simply couldn't be true.

Anthony bolted back outside and raced for the church. He would get inside and find Myra, no matter what. Police and emergency vehicles filled the street. Officers and FBI agents roamed. He ran past them toward Emanuel's iron side gate, ready to blast through it, anything to reach Myra, when someone snatched him back.

"Where are you going?" an officer demanded. Anthony tried to breathe, to speak, to sort his terror into words.

"I'm Reverend Thompson," he panted. "My wife's in that church. You need to let me go. I need to go on in and get her."

"No, no. You can't go in there."

Anthony demanded the man let him go. This time, the officer pulled him aside, his words gentler now. "Sir, you don't want to go in there."

Anthony paused.

"Are they in there?" he asked.

"I know there's some people in there, but I don't know who they are."

"Well, if you won't let me go in there, how about they come outside?" Anthony suggested. What if Myra was in there, hurt and suffering, and needed him?

"I don't think they can come out."

Anthony looked at the man. Horror filled his thoughts, threatening to overwhelm him. He mustered a single question.

"Just tell me this: Is anybody in there living?"

A t 9:25 p.m., Charleston police chief Greg Mullen's phone rang as he lay in bed watching TV with his wife. His deputy chief broke the news: a shooting at Mother Emanuel downtown. Multiple victims. The fifty-five-year-old police chief knew the house of worship and some of its historic past.

A black church, multiple people dead. Mullen immediately thought of what had been happening around the country, from horrific mass shootings to rioting after police officers killed black residents in cities like Ferguson, Baltimore, and New York. He thought of Walter Scott, a black man shot two months earlier by a white officer up the road in North Charleston, a killing that had left people on edge and police relations with the community at a particularly raw juncture.

A white man with gray hair and an even-keeled demeanor, Mullen had led the force for almost nine years. He was a big believer in community policing and had sought and achieved improved relationships between black residents and the police. Would they be tested in the hours to come?

Before racing out the door, he turned to his wife: "I'll see you when I see you."

After thirteen years of marriage and three decades in law enforcement, he'd uttered those words to her only once before. The last time was eight years earlier. On that night, Charleston firefighters had battled an inferno at a furniture showroom near his suburban home, five miles from Emanuel. Mullen had been on the job for only a few months then.

Nine firefighters had died in the blaze, shaking Charleston deeply. The anniversary would be the next day.

U nable to get into the church, Anthony collapsed onto the ground, overwhelmed by the notion that his wife lay dead inside. A car, the words FORENSIC SERVICES stamped on its side, sat parked between him and the white walls of Emanuel across the street. Everywhere, emergency lights circled through the darkness.

A gentle Presbyterian minister, Spike Coleman, was walking by with the city's fire chief when he spotted Anthony. Wearing a shirt that read CHAPLAIN, he approached and knelt, touching the tormented man's arm, then introduced himself. Slowly, Anthony stood up and let Spike lead him back into the Marriott's lobby, down the hall, and toward the conference room. Inside, Polly and Felicia and her granddaughter sat, still numb with shock, trying to answer the investigators' questions. Felicia's husband and sister had arrived and clustered around her. Anthony stumbled to an empty table in back and rested his head on its cool surface. In agony, he pounded his fists.

Outside, a massive manhunt gained momentum. Thanks to Felicia and Polly, the police now had a decent description of the killer: white male around twenty-one, roughly 130 pounds, sandy brown hair in a bowl cut. He was wearing jeans, Timberland-style boots, a gray shirt. Officers with police dogs scoured large buildings, thin alleys, and vast parking garages.

Emanuel sat on a business street normally choked with traffic. However, behind the nineteenth-century church building, antebellum homes tightly hugged narrow streets that concealed courtyard gardens, carriage houses, and parking spaces behind stone walls and wrought-iron gates. In midsummer's tropical heat, shrubs and vines grew into impenetrable masses. Majestic live oak and magnolia trees cast shadows into every corner.

The killer could be anywhere.

As the police scaled walls and knocked on doors, more Emanuel members and victims' relatives got word and rushed to the church and then into the Marriott. Investigators quickly realized a logistical challenge. Mother Emanuel had hundreds of members and was revered throughout the city of Charleston. Police couldn't have several hundred people swarm the hotel, possibly rushing frantically toward the church. It was too close. They needed to move the group to another hotel that would be near enough for easy access but not right across the street from the crime scene.

Felicia, her granddaughter, Polly, and the first family to arrive quietly left the Marriott and ventured back out into the dark night. In a line, they crossed Calhoun Street and headed up a sidewalk along Meeting Street toward an Embassy Suites on the other side of a public park that took up most of a city block. Sweat from fear and the night's stifling humidity made clothes cling to their skin. They passed the quiet side road that ran behind Emanuel as police dispatched rooftop surveillance and bloodhounds. Local officers, FBI agents, state law enforcement agents, paramedics, and coroners swarmed. Charleston felt like a war zone.

Felicia hurried with her husband and sisters near the front of the line. Spike, the Presbyterian chaplain, walked beside Anthony. Polly plodded along last in the group, low blood sugar making her feel woozy as she stepped along the sidewalk's uneven gray pavers, trying not to trip and fall. A police officer walked behind her.

"Take your time," he assured.

To the group's right, Mother Emanuel's steeple rose high into the dark sky, her body skirted with yellow crime scene tape. To their left, magnolias and live oaks draped in Spanish moss along the park, named Marion Square, cast shadows around them as they passed. By daylight, college students sunbathed and slung Frisbees in the park's grassy expanse while tourists strolled about admiring the lush landscaping. Now, the first curious onlookers trickled into it.

The small band of survivors walked, for now unrecognized, through a city whose streets the late southern writer Pat Conroy had once described as being "as haunted as time turned in on itself." Near the center of Marion Square, a pillar rose high above the group as they passed. Atop the pillar stood the bronze-cast image of former vice president John C. Calhoun. With a hand on one hip, the South Carolina slave owner who described the brutal institution as "a positive good" appeared to scowl at the survivors as they trudged past below.

four

Shadow of Death

❋

The survivors and their loved ones arrived at the Embassy Suites, originally built as an arsenal to protect the city's minority white population after a foiled slave rebellion in 1822. Denmark Vesey, a freed slave and class leader at Mother Emanuel, had masterminded the uprising and died for it. Even today, if one name evokes Charleston's racial tensions and the closely held fears of some white residents, it is Vesey's. Born a slave and married to one, the carpenter won a lottery at the age of thirty-two that enabled him to buy his freedom. He later plotted the massive revolt, ultimately planning to launch it at midnight on June 16, 1822, almost two centuries earlier to the precise hour.

Two frightened slaves, however, betrayed him. After a secretive "trial," Vesey was hanged, as were nearly three dozen co-conspirators. Unlike many of the others, whose executions were announced publicly beforehand, the place of Vesey's execution remained a secret. Some black residents maintained he was killed at the Hanging Tree on the city's peninsula, long the storied site of lynchings. White residents then torched the church and instituted ruthless measures to subdue the black population with terror. Emanuel members were forced to worship underground until after the Civil War.

City leaders built the arsenal. Whites controlled the halls of power back then, but enslaved people comprised almost two-thirds of Charleston

County's population. The arsenal building later became the first home of
The Citadel, a public military college whose cadets fired the inaugural shots
of the Civil War. Today, the four-story structure's stucco walls and turrets
are painted pale pink, lending it a fairy-tale effect.

The band of survivors filed through the grand hotel's front entrance and
toward a cavernous atrium where water danced down a tiered fountain amid
palm trees and handsome planters. Just before reaching the atrium, a vast
space encircled by five floors of guests' rooms, most full of tourists, the survivors plodded up a spiral staircase to the second floor. Green carpet led to
a hushed wing of conference rooms where they arrived at the Colonial Ballroom, a spacious area with arched windows and white plantation shutters.

As Polly sank into a plush chair, a small group of church members already waiting there hurried over. Was she okay? Who did this? Were people
really shot?

Was anyone dead?

Polly tried to describe the unspeakable through the fog of trauma and
her ebbing blood sugar. She struggled to remember who exactly had been
in the Bible study. She also wasn't certain who had died and who had lived,
if anyone.

Meanwhile, Felicia sat with a group of police and FBI agents, trying to
give them information to help locate the assassin. She rattled off the names
of everyone in Bible study, although through the shock she forgot to name
Cynthia, who wasn't normally there. Anthony sat by himself, silent. He
didn't know most of the people arriving in the ballroom given that Emanuel was Myra's house of worship, not his, and his own church members
hadn't heard the news yet. Neither had the Thompsons' three grown
children, none of whom lived nearby. After retiring, Anthony had sworn
off carrying a cell phone, so he couldn't call any of them. His thoughts were
too overwhelmed to think of what to do next anyway as the ballroom filled.

Emanuel members, friends, relatives of the Bible study regulars, nearby
AME ministers, victims' advocates, crisis chaplains, more FBI agents, and
more local police flowed into the space, several hundred people in all. Some
cried, some prayed, some paced. Another church sent pizza. Hotel staff
brought hot coffee, cold water, and sweet tea. Two employees would later

learn they were related to people who'd been at Bible study that night. Despite a tidal wave of recent growth, Charleston remained at its heart a small town.

On Meeting Street outside, bundles of local police and FBI agents clustered and roamed. The ballroom had to be the safest place in all of Charleston in those moments. But was it?

A woman in the ballroom scrolled through social media searching for the latest news. Then she stopped and turned the screen of her phone toward Charleston police lieutenant Jennie Antonio, who was serving as a conduit between police and those gathered. A post described a bomb threat to Mother Emanuel, which sat just on the other side of a large building from the hotel.

"Is this real?" she asked.

Antonio, a seventeen-year police veteran, tempered her voice.

"Yes, ma'am." She added that the woman was free to leave, if she was afraid. She would understand. "But I am not leaving."

The woman nodded. She too would stay.

At 10:30 p.m., someone claiming to be the killer had called a local TV station. The man gave his name and, in calm tones, said he'd placed a bomb near the church in a plastic container with handles like a toolbox. It would detonate at 11 p.m.

Jennifer Pinckney arrived at the hotel shortly after the rest. Without her husband, she'd been uncertain whom to call and chose Kylon Middleton, a close friend of Clementa's and a fellow AME minister. Clementa had always called Kylon when he needed help.

Kylon was leaving his own Bible study when his cell phone rang.

"Pinckney's been shot!" Jennifer hollered into his ear, using the name Kylon called her husband.

Kylon paused. Shot? Where would Clementa Pinckney be on a Wednesday night to get shot? Jennifer liked to play pranks on him. So did Clementa. He hung up.

She called back, hysterical.

"Clementa. Has. Been. Shot!"

Her voice made it clear that this was not a joke.

As he sped toward Charleston, his phone began to buzz with calls. He answered one from his mother, who lived in the city.

"Kylon, I don't want to be the one to tell you."

"Tell me what?"

"Something terrible happened at Mother Emanuel."

Kylon had known Clementa since they were skinny, awkward little boys. Even back then, they busied themselves making plans that stretched well beyond their years. Clementa began pastoring when he was thirteen. Kylon graduated from high school at sixteen, college at eighteen. Clementa became a state legislator at twenty-three. Back and forth, a deep friendship built on common faith, love, and competition.

Kylon reached the hotel and found Jennifer huddled in the ballroom with Malana. The normally rambunctious little girl now looked mutely at him, her eyes wide in shock. She and Jennifer both wrapped him in ferocious hugs. Nobody had ever clung to him so tightly.

He glanced around, finally asking, "Where's Pinckney?"

"I think he's gone," Jennifer mumbled.

"Gone where?"

He heard someone else nearby say that a person from the Bible study was at the hospital. Why aren't *we* at the hospital? Kylon wondered. If Clementa was there, injured, they should go.

One of Clementa's legislative colleagues arrived with the pastor's older daughter and Jennifer's mother, who was battling cancer. Clementa's father, sister, and other family arrived, too.

As 11 p.m. approached, an FBI agent arrived with an update. The coroner would come soon. Kylon leaned forward to hear.

"And meet with all of the families."

All of the families?

Eight thousand miles away in another port city, this one in Oman on the Arabian Sea, Arthur Stephen Hurd lay in bed. The ship on which he worked as an engineer, maintaining the massive vessel's refrigeration system, sat dry docked as the sun rose. Steve, as many people called him, had departed Charleston in November, leaving his wife Cynthia, the popular librarian, for what was supposed to be a six-month job. But it had taken longer, and so he still found himself across the world. Because of the nine-hour time difference, he made a point of calling her every morning from Oman to tell her good night in Charleston.

He checked his email as he did every morning and was surprised to find that no messages had arrived from her overnight. He wrote to her instead.

"What?" he teased. "No email?"

No response.

When he'd said good-bye to Cynthia in November, leaving her standing on the platform as his train pulled away, he had an unsettling feeling that he might not see her again. But if tragedy struck, he figured, he'd be the one gone—lost to a train crash, lost to a plane crash, lost to the sea. Cynthia would be at home or the library or church, always safe.

The previous day, she'd texted him: "Call me."

He'd lit a cigarette and dialed.

"I just wanted to hear your voice," she said.

Unable to reach her now, Steve called his mother, who lived downtown not far from Emanuel and just blocks from the house he and Cynthia shared. The elderly woman had been helping him secretly plan gifts for Cynthia's fifty-fifth birthday celebration, just four days away.

"Where's Cynthia?" he asked.

His mother paused. "There's been a shooting at the church."

She told him that Reverend Pinckney had been killed, and possibly others too. Everyone was heading to the Embassy Suites. But Steve could think only of the words his wife had spoken to him after he'd vented about problems he was having with the ship's machinery, just before they'd last hung up.

"I'm your number one fan," she'd said. "I love you."

Nadine Collier and her husband were driving home to North Charleston after eating dinner downtown when her left eye began to twitch.

"Something's wrong."

"Oh, every time a vein pop in your eye—"

"No, something is wrong!"

Shortly after they arrived home, her phone rang. She wasn't thrilled to see it was her oldest sister Sharon Risher, a minister and trauma chaplain who worked at a big hospital in Dallas. The two hadn't spoken much over the past two years, ever since a big blowout they'd had right after the painful process of burying their middle sister, claimed by a terrible cancer.

"Nadine, you talk to Momma?"

"Earlier today."

"Well, Jon Quil just called Aja and tell Aja, and Aja called me and tell me that there was some shooting at the church . . ."

"Shooting at the church? What church?"

"Momma church!"

Nadine stopped. Why would Sharon, way off in Texas, hear about something like that before her? Nadine attended Emanuel with their mother, Ethel Lance. She sang in the choir and knew way more of its business than Sharon. She was the one who'd stayed in Charleston and helped their mother and other siblings. Surely she would hear any news like that first.

"I didn't hear anything about that."

Just then, a girlfriend texted: "Call me. It's an emergency."

Nadine knew that her mother faithfully attended Bible study every Wednesday evening. Ethel had joined Emanuel back in the 1970s and worked as its custodian. If the church was open, she was sure to be found inside, ready with a joke and a hug.

Nadine and her husband soon sped back downtown. He turned down one of the many side streets into a neighborhood near the church where black families once raised their children but now wealthier whites spruced up the houses into pricey investment properties. She spotted police and emergency lights ahead. Before her husband could pull up near Emanuel's back parking lot, Nadine leapt from the car and sprinted toward the church.

A police officer stopped her. "Ma'am, I can't let you go back there."

She tried to sound calm, like a lady. Like her mother taught her.

"Why is that? My momma's in that church."

The officer didn't answer. Instead, he directed her toward the Embassy Suites hotel across Meeting Street. The families were gathering there, he explained. But going to a hotel made no sense to Nadine. She jumped back into the car, and they rushed to the city's major trauma center just a few blocks down Calhoun Street.

Inside Medical University Hospital's trauma bay, nearly forty medical workers stood shoulder-to-shoulder awaiting more casualties from the church. If the first patient had been that bad, what did the rest of the night hold? A physician stood outside in a horseshoe where ambulances pulled in, clipboard in hand, readying himself to triage multiple injured people.

Forty minutes ticked by. Pagers beeped with other patients' needs. Lines formed in the emergency room as sick people waited to be treated.

Finally, the charge nurse walked in. She was young, her tone flippant, a defense against the unsettling realities of life they handled here.

"We're done," she said. "No one else is coming. They're all dead."

With the victims still lying in the fellowship hall, not yet identified, the bomb threat had forced crime scene investigators to halt their work. Chief Mullen and other law enforcement leaders launched a second investigation into the bomb threat.

Identifying the dead would have to wait.

Adding to the tension, police still didn't know where the killer was, or whether he'd had accomplices. Was he planning more violence? Modern law enforcement procedures required that police watch their backs while investigating the crime scenes in front of them, always anticipating secondary attacks.

Police set up a command post down a few doors from the church in the Charleston Gaillard Center, an ornate $142 million concert hall in the later stages of construction, a grand and much-anticipated addition to the culturally rich city. Its big inaugural event was supposed to feature cellist Yo-Yo Ma and the Charleston Symphony Orchestra. Instead it would house police trying to respond to the worst mass killing in modern South Carolina history.

In those early hours, process overtook everything. Chief Mullen focused on making sure the crime scene was secured, the area around it safe, a traffic perimeter established. He paired his detectives with the State Law Enforcement Division (SLED), FBI, and ATF agents to coordinate everyone. They established a unified command. Mullen had spent three decades in law enforcement but never handled a crime of this magnitude. Two years earlier, however, he had attended an executive training program put on by the FBI to discuss mass casualty events in the wake of the Sandy Hook Elementary shooting in Connecticut. Mullen took away several key things. In the coming hours, he would use them all.

Among them, he focused on two critical challenges: finding the killer and nurturing the traumatized families. To help, he summoned a network of victim advocates and others from different agencies to form a family assistance center that would care for the hundreds of people amassing at the Embassy Suites. One of the ironies of the spate of mass killings in recent years was the training it had given law enforcement. An FBI team that had aided families of the Sandy Hook and Boston Marathon massacres soon arrived, bringing invaluable lessons learned. They would form a bridge between the devastated families and law enforcement, a connection that would prove critical later on.

But for now, the fear that invariably attends the early, confused hours after an event of this scale spread through the Embassy Suites ballroom, to the handsome homes beyond it, and across the entire city Mullen was charged to protect. Rumors flared. One person had been taken to the hospital alive. No, it was two. The pastor was dead. So was his sister. There was a bomb threat at Emanuel. No, it was at the Embassy Suites. Outside, more and more local residents arrived at Marion Square to pray and await news.

To provide what basic facts he could, Mullen had called a press briefing for 11 p.m., now delayed given that it was the precise time the threat had claimed a bomb would explode. Instead, as the crime scene sat quiet, bomb investigators and bloodhounds searched for explosives—but found none.

By 11:30 p.m. investigators were cleared to go back inside.

Mullen left that scene to walk across Meeting Street to the Embassy

Suites. Before addressing the press, he needed to talk to the families. He'd toiled in a bubble of process since arriving on the scene. He hadn't seen the look of terror in people's eyes yet or heard their desperate prayers. Now, it was time.

When Mullen arrived at the hotel just after midnight, about three hundred people were packed into the ballroom, with dozens more spilling out into the hallway. Some sobbed, some prayed silently. The city's longtime mayor Joseph Riley Jr. arrived too, along with the FBI's agent in charge, the State Law Enforcement Division chief, and an AME Church leader. The coroner also joined them.

Chief Mullen had no idea what to expect.

Fortunately, from the start of his tenure, he had worked to build bridges between the police department and African American residents in town. When black-on-black violence spiked in the early 2000s, his predecessor, the charismatic and controversial Reuben Greenberg, had famously said it wasn't his fault "every time one black son of a bitch kills another." Greenberg, who was black himself, had struggled to contain a violent, open-air drug market that festered along America Street, a main passageway through Charleston's predominantly black East Side just a few blocks away from Emanuel. When Mullen assumed the job, he installed special police teams in the area and clamped down on the drug trade. However, he also spent a great deal of time walking the area's streets, chatting with people during his weekends and spare time. Quietly, without publicizing it, he forged friendships and bonds while encouraging others in his department to do the same.

Nonetheless, as Mullen headed for the mass of anguishing people at the Embassy Suites, he knew that some members of the city's black community remained suspicious of the police, particularly after the shooting death of a nineteen-year-old named Denzel Curnell during an encounter with a Charleston officer a year ago almost to the day. The officer had stopped Curnell after spotting the young black man walking through a low-income apartment complex wearing a hooded sweatshirt on a warm day, a sight the officer apparently found suspicious. They struggled, gunfire crackled, and

Curnell died. Though a state investigation had determined that Curnell shot himself during the struggle, one question remained: Why had he been stopped in the first place?

Now at the ballroom, pressure enveloped the chief. Pressure to find the killer. Pressure to care for the families. Pressure to keep everyone safe. Pressure to say what would reassure and inform, not inflame or distract.

As he and the other leaders waded together into the thicket of tormented people to stand before them, all heads turned. Silence fell. A sea of people looked at them, waiting and expectant. Many wept. Some stared with blank eyes of shock. Others scowled, irritated by the wait for answers.

Mullen began with explaining that he was very sorry. This was personal to him, too. The police didn't know a whole lot yet, but many skilled people were working very hard. They would find the killer and bring him to justice.

He paused, and answered the question hanging in the air.

"Nine people are deceased."

A collective gasp rose from the entire crowd, a gale of disbelief. Then came the wailing. Chaplains and advocates hurried to those collapsing onto the carpet.

Mullen stepped aside so that the coroner could address the group. She explained that she was returning to Emanuel now that the bomb threat investigation was cleared. Thankfully, it had been a hoax. She did not mention that Sgt. Lites had refused to leave the fellowship hall during the bomb scare or that he remained there now, still guarding the bodies of their loved ones.

The coroner would continue her work identifying the victims. She promised to return as soon as possible to talk with them again.

The Reverend Norvel Goff Sr. spoke last. Having made the fateful decision to skip Bible study after the quarterly conference, he'd returned to pray with survivors and family members.

Speaking to the entire crowd, Goff reminded them of their faith. He reminded them of the salvation God promised his faithful. But faithful they must remain, even in the face of fear and evil. Then he asked people to gather and hold hands. For those too overcome to stand, people knelt to wrap them in arms of comfort. Goff's voice rose in prayer, then in song. He began the first lines of an old Christian hymn, and the group joined him.

> *My hope is built on nothing less*
> *than Jesus' blood and righteousness;*
> *I dare not trust the sweetest frame,*
> *but wholly lean on Jesus' name.*

The people sang together, hundreds of human voices converging in a somber river of shock and grief. Mullen, a Christian man, breathed a thank you to God. The spirit seemed to move through the crowd, a reminder to believers of God's call to faith, even in the dark shadows of death.

Chief Mullen and the mayor now left to get on with the business of finding the killer. A cluster of reporters and photographers awaited them on a corner of Marion Square across from the Embassy Suites. The journalists' ranks swelled larger than usual. The presidential primary campaigns were in full swing, and political reporters from across the country happened to be in town following candidates.

Chief Mullen and Mayor Riley approached the group. Black community leaders, pastors, and worried residents had gathered in Marion Square as well. Mullen wasn't sure what to expect. Other American cities facing racially charged violence had erupted in riots. Would Charleston?

As Mullen and Riley stepped to microphones, a group of a dozen ministers and prominent black community activists approached, all wearing tense and somber expressions. Sweat beaded on his forehead. Mullen knew many of them personally and hoped they would trust him now. But he also was keenly aware that they were angry and hurting—and needed answers.

As he glanced around and prepared to speak, the group of pastors and activists formed an arc behind him. Mullen said a silent prayer of thanks.

They all faced the cameras together.

Mullen started right in. Nine people were dead. He described the killer, reminding people that the man was at large and obviously very dangerous. Then he turned to the shooting itself.

"This is a tragedy no community should have to experience," he said, the firm tone of his words edged tightly with sorrow. "It is senseless, and it is unfathomable that somebody in today's society would walk into a church when people are having a prayer meeting and take their lives."

A local TV reporter asked bluntly: Was this a hate crime?

Mullen hadn't expected to address that right then. But the words just came out:

"I do believe this was a hate crime."

Emanuel had several security cameras. However, only one of them was trained on a door. It happened to overlook a set of side doors, the ones near the back of the church. The images were stored on a computer in the secretary's office. When police reached her at home, Althea Latham quickly offered to come and help.

No thank you, the officer said. The church was a crime scene.

Althea gave them the computer password.

Police soon entered her office, found the surveillance equipment, and removed it. Chief Mullen leaned hard on them to get a "Be on the Lookout" report out to the public ASAP. Dawn approached with the killer still at large.

The young man had brought with him the leather-bound journal where he'd stored his thoughts about race. He'd also brought along two notes that he had written to his parents. One was to his father, who had been riding him hard to get a job. Over a brief few lines, he told his dad that he loved him.

He'd written a longer note to his mother, who had tried to understand him and assuage his anxieties over the years. She had known that he did not like to be hugged or tell other people that he loved them. But he would tell her so now.

> Dear Mom,
> I love you.
>   I'm sorry for what I did, but I had to do it.
>   This note isn't meant to be sentimental and make you cry. I just want you to know that I love you.
>   I know that what I did will have repercussions on my entire family, and for this I truly am sorry.
>   At this moment I miss you very much, and as childish as it sounds I wish I was in your arms.
>   I love you

He didn't explain his mission to either of his parents. They wouldn't understand.

Most people didn't get it.

Just last week, he had told someone about his plans—an old middle school skateboarding buddy whom he'd lost track of a half-dozen years earlier, around the time his dad and stepmom got divorced. He had found the guy, Joey Meek, on Facebook a few weeks earlier. They'd started hanging out again, partying at Joey's trailer with his brothers. He lived in Red Bank, a fast-growing suburb south of Lexington that was, like most of the county, largely white and once haunted by white supremacists.

One night, he and Meek had gotten wasted swilling vodka and using cocaine, and he'd mentioned his idea of killing black people at a church. He'd mentioned starting a race war.

But Meek hadn't seemed to get it. Maybe he would now.

Several hours had passed since the young man had walked out of the church and headed northwest across South Carolina. He'd briefly stayed on the interstate, then cruised down a string of country roads that passed by farm fields, country churches, and the small-town gas stations that also served as general stores. As he cruised toward the North Carolina border, he figured it unlikely that anyone had detected his absence or connected him with the crime. He had no cell phone, no job, wasn't in

school, and floated between his divorced parents' homes, sometimes staying with Meek, other times sleeping in his car.

Just after 2 a.m., as he approached Charlotte, sleep began to nudge. He
could doze in the car—he'd brought with him a beige bath towel, a trunk
full of clothes, a roll of toilet paper, and his black toiletry bag. A bed pillow
in the backseat hid his loaded gun. On a floorboard behind him, next to his
tripod, a gray plastic Walmart bag held two more boxes of bullets next to
a rolled-up Confederate flag, the smaller kind on a stick. On the front console, beside the emergency brake, he'd set down the laser attachment for
his gun. The car was a mess. All around it, he'd strewn crumpled napkins,
scraps of papers, an empty Smirnoff Ice bottle, a box with scraps of cold
French fries. Nonetheless, he would find space to sleep.

He pulled over and parked his car.

Not everyone in the ballroom would remember what happened that night
exactly the same way later. Some would recall the coroners coming in
and, one by one, calling out the names of the victims to summon each of
their families from the crowd. Others would remember them coming
around to tables where tormented relatives and friends gathered together.
All would remember the terror of wondering if their loved ones were among
those killed.

The Reverend Herbert Temoney pastored another downtown church
and worked with the crisis chaplains now assisting law enforcement. Like
the other AME ministers gathered, Temoney had held Bible study that night
at his church, too. What if the killer had walked in there instead of Emanuel?

The coroner asked him to find Reverend Pinckney's family first. He had
seen Jennifer and her little girl sitting quietly off to themselves earlier that
night and stopped to greet them. Malana, an adorable six year old wearing
a pretty floral dress, had looked up at him with eyes that he felt certain he
would never forget.

"Is my daddy alright?" she had asked.

What could he say?

"Baby, when I get more information about his condition, I'll let you
know."

Now he went into the ballroom to find Jennifer sitting with her mother, her two daughters, Kylon, and other family and friends.

"The coroner would like to see you," said Temoney, a large man speaking softly.

Jennifer stood up to learn what, by then, she already knew. She left her daughters with her mother and, along with several other adult family members, followed Temoney out of the ballroom and into a narrow conference room one door down. Brown leather office chairs surrounded a dark wooden oval table where several strangers sat with heavy expressions.

One of them introduced herself. She was the coroner and needed to ask Jennifer about Clementa's clothes, jewelry, any identifying birthmarks. Jennifer nodded. She wasn't sure she could speak. Yet, when she closed her eyes and thought of Clementa, and his image filled her mind, she realized that she could. He was with her. He would want her to help these people.

So, she forced words to come from her mouth.

The woman quickly offered her sympathies. Then she confirmed that Clementa was among the dead. Shock still kept the worst of the grief at bay. Instead, Jennifer's thoughts flew to her girls, waiting in the ballroom just a few steps away. She needed to speak with them. She needed to do it before anyone else could, before they overheard anything in the commotion around them.

She summoned them—her tall and poised older child and her chubby-cheeked little girl. They would hear this news only from her. When they arrived in the room, she seated them in front of her.

"Malana," she said to the younger one, "you were there, and we heard gunshots."

Round eyes of innocence answered her.

The next words were the hardest ones Jennifer had ever spoken. She looked at Eliana, who idolized her father, who emulated him in so many ways.

"Daddy got hurt," she said. "Daddy was killed. He will always be with us, and we're going to make it."

Back in the ballroom, Temoney next found the family members of Susie Jackson and Tywanza Sanders, two large and intertwined families, among them Felicia Sanders. She, too, already knew what the coroner would tell them.

Anthony Thompson was standing alone when he heard someone call his wife's name.

"Anyone from the family of Myra Thompson?"

In spite of what Felicia had told him, Anthony held out some hope as the coroner closed the conference room door behind him. She began by asking a few questions. Could he describe what his wife looked like? What she was wearing?

"These questions you're asking me—you're trying to identify a body!" he blurted out.

The coroner confirmed it.

Numb, he left the conference room and lingered in the hallway with a bunch of strangers. What should he do next? He was too overwhelmed to re-enter the ballroom where people waited to see the next family summoned. His grown children, who lived a couple of hours or more away, hadn't arrived. He wanted to tell them the news. Anthony didn't know that Facebook already had done that for him.

All he knew was that he couldn't imagine driving home to an empty house yet.

Back in the ballroom, Polly heard a voice. And yet another name.

"Anyone from the family of DePayne Middleton Doctor?"

N adine and her husband had waited at Medical University Hospital, the nearby trauma center, for hours. They knew that her mother, Ethel Lance, was among those who had been shot and that one person had been brought to the hospital. One of Nadine's girlfriends who was stationed at the Embassy Suites called her as the coroner began to summon individual families. "Dine, Reverend Pinckney was one of the persons that got shot."

"Oh my God."

Then Nadine's niece, also at the hotel, phoned.

"Auntie, the coroner wants to know what Granny had on."

Nadine didn't think about why the coroner would want to know what her mother had been wearing. Or maybe she just couldn't think about it now. "Tell her she had two knee replacements, got a lot of rings, she got a gash on the side of her forehead, on her arm, her hair is salt and pepper, it's curly. She wears a lot of jewelry . . ." Nadine rattled off.

She hung up and turned to her husband.

"I'm tired of waiting. Come on, we're going to the hotel. Somebody's got to tell me something." As they drove the few blocks back to the Embassy Suites, her niece called back.

"Auntie?"

"Yeah, Najee."

"Auntie, you driving?"

They were on Calhoun Street, almost at the hotel.

"Auntie, Granny gone."

As they pulled into the Embassy Suites, Nadine started to scream.

Still stuck in Oman, Steve Hurd had continued to call his wife Cynthia's cell phone, leaving messages until her voicemail filled up. The son of a career Navy man, brother of a Marine, he wasn't a laid-back person under the best of circumstances. His mind often veered along his crisp, unwavering notions about things.

And right now he needed to know what happened to his wife.

He dialed Cynthia's brother Melvin, who just then was walking into the Embassy Suites where people from the church had gathered. He, too, had waited at the hospital for several hours before finally figuring that Cynthia wasn't there. With the phone line connecting them, Steve could hear Melvin talking to people he passed, trying to find out who was in charge, until he located a deputy coroner. Melvin explained to the woman who he was. And who Cynthia was.

Steve listened intently on the line. The woman's voice emerged gently, and he strained to hear her.

"I can't tell you anything definitive, but based on the reports we've gotten, she's in there." A coroner had just spoken to another one of Cynthia's brothers who'd described a lanyard his sister usually wore, a clump of keys dangling from the end that clinked as she walked.

Steve's self-control slipped.

"Check under the pews!" he yelled into the phone. "Check in the restrooms. Check in the closets. She's hiding. She's waiting for me to come get her."

Melvin handed the phone to the coroner so she could talk directly to Steve. She described the clothes the one still-unidentified victim was wearing: black loafers, black slacks, white blouse, lime green sweater.

A lime green sweater? No, Steve thought, that didn't sound like Cynthia.

five

Hate Is Grown

❈

The computer screen showed a black 2000 Hyundai pull into an empty parking spot near the church's side door. From it emerged a slim white man with a bowl haircut wearing dark jeans and a long-sleeve gray shirt. He also wore a dark tactical pack and reached to tuck something into the back of his waistband. Fifty minutes later, he emerged, a large pistol in his right hand, entered the car, backed up, and drove away.

The city police officer reviewing the footage snapped several still shots. They would be turned into wanted posters.

Chief Mullen could not get over how young the man looked, practically indistinguishable from any other skinny, shaggy-haired guy walking around downtown near the College of Charleston's campus. One thing was for sure. The images were about as clear as Mullen could have hoped for.

They would find the killer.

But what would it take to capture him? Would an armed man depraved enough to go into a Bible study and kill nine people, mostly middle-aged and elderly women, have qualms about firing at police officers?

Mullen knew calls would pour in immediately after disseminating the images. Using lessons learned from other mass casualty events, he helped to set up a call center with twelve phone lines, each of which went to a state trooper who would be responsible for sifting the real tips from the disturbed and attention-seeking. Twelve investigative teams, consisting of members from local, state, and national agencies, would have the jurisdiction to follow the leads wherever they led.

They were ready.

At 6 a.m., Mullen released a Need to Identify sheet to the media. The world would finally see the killer's face.

Morning news programs across the nation followed roughly the same formula, starting with images of the young man reaching for the church's wooden side door, a shot of the black Hyundai, vehicles racing through the darkness to reach the grand church. Then the authorities' ominous warning: "The suspect is considered armed and dangerous."

Mother Emanuel had officially assumed its unwanted spot among places known for the country's deadliest mass shootings: Columbine High, Sandy Hook Elementary, Virginia Tech, a Colorado movie theater. A church in Charleston.

Just after 6 a.m., the gunman pulled out of a Shell gas station near a big shopping center in south Charlotte. He had rested for three hours. Soon after hitting the road again, he had stopped for gas, then went inside to buy Doritos and a drink. But he didn't have enough cash to pay. So he'd used his debit card to get cash. Though he figured the police could track it, he had no choice. He paid without incident and quickly returned to his car.

Where should he head next? Maybe to Nashville. Why not? He'd never been there. He could listen to some music, maybe hide out in the country. He steered the car toward the rolling Blue Ridge Mountains, in the direction of a small town named Shelby.

Late the night before, in the quiet of her bedroom, South Carolina's governor had peered at the glowing face of her cell phone. Nikki Haley's chief of staff had texted her first that there had been a shooting. Then her phone buzzed with an incoming call from Mark Keel, the State Law Enforcement Division's chief. The shooting was at Senator Clementa Pinckney's church.

However, the notion that Clementa might have been in Charleston hadn't crossed her mind right then. He'd been in the capital all day working on the budget. Surely, he hadn't then driven the two hours from Columbia to Charleston afterward.

Haley had quickly hung up and dialed Clementa. They weren't especially close—she was a Republican, he a Democrat; he believed in gun control, she did not; he wanted to expand Medicaid, she refused—but she knew and admired him. Though they fell on different sides of the political divide, she respected him for his determination to improve the lives of his constituents.

Haley, the state's first female governor and a staunch fiscal conservative, also shared Clementa's deep Christian faith. The daughter of Indian immigrants, she'd grown up in a Sikh household but converted to the Methodist denomination of her husband, Michael, as an adult.

She thought about Clementa, a towering but gentle man who'd been a fixture in the General Assembly since he was barely an adult. He represented a sprawling rural and mostly black district the size of Rhode Island that included some of the state's poorest counties. They were among the state's forgotten places where "segregation academies," private schools that allowed white flight during integration, still left public schools mostly black and often struggling.

At forty-one, Clementa had served in the Senate since he was just twenty-seven and had spent that time pushing for more economic opportunities in his district, though he served in a party with little power. White Republicans overwhelmingly dominated the halls of both the state's House and Senate. In that world, Clementa wasn't known for pontificating, although in the wake of the Walter Scott shooting, he'd taken to the Senate floor to deliver an important call for mandating that police officers wear body cameras. The legislation had passed, and Haley had signed it.

Now, she reached Clementa's voicemail. He must be busy ministering to his flock, she figured, and left a message.

"This is Nikki. I've heard about the shooting. I'm sending my full SLED team down there. Call me."

She soon learned her assumption had been wrong. He'd left the Senate early and gone to Emanuel. Increasingly tense, she awaited more news.

Throughout the night—at 11:15 p.m., 11:25 p.m., midnight, 1:20 a.m., 2:45 a.m.—she spoke with the SLED chief as sickening details emerged. Each call, each new death count and detail, felt like another kick in the gut.

By sunrise, when Chief Mullen called a press conference to release images of the killer, she knew that nine people were dead. Pinckney. An elderly woman. A young man. Three licensed ministers. A retired pastor. She also knew the killer had spewed racial hatred while gunning down innocent Christians gathered to study the Bible.

Haley's husband was out of town for military training, and she didn't want to leave her children, who were seventeen and thirteen. But she had to get to Charleston. She dressed and then stepped into each of her two children's bedrooms. It was supposed to be a carefree day of summer for them, and she preferred to keep it that way. But she also didn't want them to hear about the shooting from anyone besides her. So, she told each that she was leaving—and why.

Her thirteen-year-old son had the most questions, ones about his own safety at church and whether they'd caught the killer yet. He wanted to know how someone could be so filled with hate. Haley explained as best she could, "Hate is taught. Hate is experienced. Hate is grown."

At about 8 a.m., she boarded a state airplane to fly to Charleston.

A few hours before Governor Haley departed for Charleston, Jennifer Pinckney and her two daughters arrived home in Columbia at around 3 o'clock in the morning. Given Jennifer's Highlander was part of the crime scene where her husband lay dead, the keys on his body, Clementa's legislative colleague had driven them. Jennifer had put the girls to bed and tried to sleep herself, although she could not. As the sun rose, she remembered that her older daughter, Eliana, was supposed to attend a dance camp at 9 a.m.

She ventured into Eliana's bedroom and sat beside the eleven year old, who reminded her so much of Clementa. Eliana had his focus, his innate poise, his hungry curiosity about history and culture.

"You know you have a dance intensive . . ." Jennifer began, struggling to keep her composure.

"Yes, Momma. I want to go."

Jennifer insisted that it was okay to cry, to stay home and rest.

"I don't want to cry. I know my daddy is with me. I know my daddy will always be with me. I want to go."

With Eliana's words, she realized something. She needed to keep things as normal as she possibly could for her girls in this maelstrom of shock and grief. They would all need it in the coming days and weeks. Clementa wasn't only their father and her husband. He also was Emanuel's pastor and a state senator, a very public person, though Jennifer herself had lived her own life quietly beyond that spotlight. Given how Clementa died, all their lives were about to turn even more surreal.

Jennifer stood up and went to get herself ready. Eliana needed to get to dance camp.

Almost 8,000 miles away from Charleston, Steve Hurd still had no official notification of whether his wife, Cynthia, was alive or dead. She didn't own a lime green sweater. Or so he desperately hoped. Maybe she'd just gone someplace and not told anyone. Maybe she was at the hospital with someone who'd been injured. Maybe her phone had died.

Steve stared at a picture of his wife's sunshine smile, his clock ticking in slow motion as he waited for the Charleston library to open halfway around the world. Maybe he could reach Cynthia's boss or someone, anyone who would know what she'd worn last night.

Just before 9 a.m. in Charleston, Steve dialed the county's Main Library, where he knew Cynthia had gone for the monthly branch managers' meeting before going to Emanuel. He reached Doug Henderson, the library system's executive director.

"I'm 8,000 miles from home," Steve blurted out. "I need someone who sat by Cynthia or who was at the meeting with Cynthia who knows what she had on—"

"I sat next to her," interrupted Henderson, a no-nonsense man. But much as he tried, Henderson couldn't remember for certain what she was wearing. Who else was there? Who else might remember? Wait. The library had a surveillance system. An employee called it up. He found the right time. Henderson found Cynthia.

"She's smiling. She's laughing," he relayed to Steve.

"What is she wearing?"

Black loafers, black slacks, white blouse, and a lime green sweater.

six

The Blood of Life

❋

Felicia Sanders trudged up the front steps of the two-story home where she and Tyrone had raised so many children. Their own children, grandchildren, children of friends, nieces, nephews. Felicia still wore the clothes she'd put on the day before. She still smelled of blood.

She hadn't slept all night. She hadn't eaten.

Shortly after she walked inside, her telephone rang. Behind her, the doorbell rang. A reporter showed up. Children of family and friends soon ran around the house playing, unaware of the historic tragedy unfolding. Normally, Felicia loved the sound. But now, she wasn't sure how much more she could take.

She slipped upstairs to her bedroom, desperate for a moment to breathe. Behind her, the doorbell rang again. She could hear the telephone ringing. In a delirious rage, she dialed an old friend, attorney Andy Savage, the city's most prominent criminal defense attorney and the man who happened to be representing Michael Slager, the white police officer charged with murdering motorist Walter Scott two months earlier.

Andy had gone to bed sick the night before. Now, he answered groggily, unaware of the shooting at Emanuel. As Felicia tried to explain the horror of what had happened, her phone beeped incessantly with incoming calls.

"Andy, it's too much. I can't take it!"

"Don't worry. I'll take care of it."

Andy's mantra.

"I'll be right there," he added.

Felicia hung up. Mats of blood crusted on her calves and weighed down her springy black skirt as she walked to her bathroom. In the mirror she saw the same clothes she'd worn when she left this house yesterday, none of which she wanted to take off. They were her final connection. To Tywanza. To Aunt Susie Jackson. To cousin Ethel Lance. To old Reverend Simmons. To beautiful Sharonda. To them all.

How could they be gone?

She removed the clothes and folded them into a careful, sacred stack. She would keep them forever and never wash them. In the shower, water flowed over her skin, transforming the layers of crust back into something warm and fluid. The blood of her son and aunt swirled into the water and then vanished down the drain.

For the first time since the gunman stood to kill them all, Felicia sobbed.

About 250 miles away in western North Carolina, a florist was running late for work. The night before, after leaving her Southern Baptist church, Debbie Dills had watched the news out of Charleston with deep sorrow. A highlighted blonde with blue eyes and a sunny smile, Debbie believed deeply in her Christian faith. She'd gone to bed last night praying for the people in the AME Church.

Debbie still prayed now while cruising westbound through the small town of Kings Mountain on U.S. 74, a busy four-lane highway along the mountainous border between North and South Carolina. At a stop light, her eyes wandered to an older model black Hyundai pulling up next to her. Something about the car looked familiar. Was it someone she knew? Her eyes settled on the driver, a young white guy with a bowl haircut.

Her eyes jerked away. She'd seen a picture of the killer on the news that morning. Could it be him?

She waited for the light to turn green and eased off the highway to call her boss and good friend Todd Frady. As she did, Debbie felt God nudge her. If she'd just been near the man who had gunned down nine people in a house of worship, she couldn't let him just drive away. What if he planned to hurt other people? She pulled back onto the highway, caught up with the little black car, and followed it toward the next town, Shelby. When she got close enough, she noted the car's license plate number.

At 10:32 a.m., with Debbie on one line, Todd dialed police on the other.

A woman answered, her voice pleasant. "Shelby Police Department."

"Hey, this is Todd Frady from down at Frady's Florist in Kings Mountain," Todd began quickly. One of his drivers was possibly behind the shooter from Charleston. He rattled off Debbie's location and the license plate number to the car she still followed.

"And the boy has a bowl-lookin' haircut," Todd added.

As Debbie tracked the suspected killer, Chief Mullen ran a manhunt. Four hours had passed since they released the killer's image to the public at 6 a.m., and tips had poured in ever since.

Mullen knew that it wasn't unusual for someone in the suspect's family to recognize him and call in. Often, families did so, worried about their loved one or the possibility of someone else getting hurt due to their inaction, or both. Sure enough, an hour after releasing the shooter's picture, several key people had called the hotline—first a friend of the killer, who identified him as a twenty-one-year-old named Dylann Roof. Then, in quick succession, Roof's uncle, one of his sisters, and his father.

Roof's sister told police that he'd been living out of his black Hyundai. His father said Roof owned a .45-caliber handgun. A friend said Roof drove a car with a Confederate vanity plate and had talked about segregation and another civil war. They sent pictures to investigators that matched images from the church's camera.

Later that morning, a bank employee also called the hotline. She too recognized the suspect. Dylann Roof frequented her branch. His account showed he had withdrawn cash at 6:15 a.m. from a location near Charlotte.

It was the first tangible evidence of the killer's whereabouts.

Shelby police sergeant Michael Myers had started work at 6:45 a.m. that morning after a pre-shift staff meeting to catch everyone up on the town's happenings. For some reason, while Roof's name and image had gone out in news reports at 6 a.m., they hadn't been shared at the meeting.

A tall man with a heavy drawl and a laid-back demeanor, Myers knew every corner of Shelby. Born and raised there, he'd joined the police force as a young man, and nineteen years later, knew most of the town's roughly 21,000 people one way or another. He'd been out cruising for two hours when his command center radioed him—a caller thought the Charleston killer's car was nearby. Myers was just a couple of miles away from its location, so he headed that way.

When he reached U.S. 74, he threaded through traffic to catch up with the black Hyundai, finding two patrol cars already lurking behind it. With the three of them in place, and other officers nearby, one squad car eased in right behind the Hyundai and called in the plates.

Someone didn't enter the tag number correctly, however, and the report came back for a Mazda.

As they approached, the Hyundai shifted to the right lane and drove close behind a big tractor trailer. Its driver didn't appear to be trying to flee. Myers blocked in the car from the left lane. They had nearly reached a busy intersection with a big Kangaroo gas station and a traffic light ahead when the officers flipped on their blue lights.

Immediately, the Hyundai's driver put on his turn signal, crossed an empty right turn lane, and eased into the gravel driveway of an abandoned house. The three white squad cars followed, blocking him in, his right turn signal still flashing. So far nothing but calm, methodical actions. Could this actually be the shooter?

Myers wasn't sure. People often called in tips that turned out to be nothing. However, he and his officers still approached this traffic stop as an unknown threat. The police emerged from their vehicles into the late morning sun and walked toward the car from behind. Officer Dan Bernat approached the car's open driver's side window, his gun drawn. He peered into the car and saw a skinny young guy in the driver's seat and told him to place his hands on the steering wheel. The man complied. Bernat holstered his weapon and sidled to the driver's side door, looking for a weapon but seeing only a GPS in the driver's lap.

Bernat's partner, an African American officer named Joe Burris, slipped around to the passenger door. Officer Scott Hamrick trained his weapon at the rear window. Myers, the supervising officer on scene, had worked with the men around him for years. He walked up behind Hamrick and peered through the back windshield. The driver stared out the front window with his hands visible on the steering wheel, what police wanted to see, especially if they suspected somebody might have a gun.

"Slowly take your right hand and turn off the ignition," Bernat commanded.

The young man obeyed. Hamrick holstered his weapon as it became clear the suspect was cooperating.

"Step out of the vehicle."

The driver emerged slowly with what looked like deliberate acquiescence, wearing a plain loose-fitting white T-shirt and black Dickies rolled up to just below his knees. Skinny calves stuck out of black socks and brown Timberland-style boots. His clothes and hair looked slightly rumpled, like someone on a long road trip or just getting out of bed.

Bernat, at the driver's door, placed a hand on the suspect's shoulder and directed him to face the car, then patted him down with the other hand. The other officers fanned out across the rear of the vehicle. Traffic bustled along behind them. Myers approached.

"What's your name?" he asked.

"Dylann Roof."

Myers asked if he had ID on him. The man indicated he did, in his back pocket.

A voice came over the police radios. "Be advised, that will be the correct vehicle, per the news agencies."

Bernat informed Roof that he was under arrest and pulled one of the man's thin wrists, then the other, into handcuffs behind his back.

Myers asked Roof if he knew what the stop was about.

Roof nodded, expressionless.

"Is there something in the car we need to worry about?" Explosives or weapons that could hurt someone?

"Yeah, the gun is under a pillow in the backseat."

Myers couldn't believe this guy had killed nine people in a church just thirteen hours ago. He didn't seem nervous or agitated at all. In fact, he mostly just looked relieved and a little tired. Myers led Roof to Hamrick and asked the officer to transport their suspect to the police station. As they drove away, Roof stared blankly ahead saying nothing.

The remaining officers searched Roof's car, finding the heavy Glock pistol right where he said it was, beneath a soft bed pillow on the backseat.

With the suspect gone, and this final confirmation that they had their man, the officers exhaled. They smiled and high-fived each other. Burris, the black officer, smacked his hands together hard three times with triumph.

seven

Love One Another

❋

Governor Haley and her staff had landed in Charleston a few hours earlier, visiting Mullen and his colleagues at the command post and then touring the Embassy Suites. Afterward, they had stopped for an early lunch to regroup when her phone rang with a call from the chief of SLED.

"We think we've got him," he told her.

She ushered the group back out into the heat. She needed to get to a joint press conference where officials would announce the killer's capture—and provide residents relief from the fear. Her car followed a black police vehicle, its blue lights swirling to caution drivers who, although it was late morning on a Thursday, weren't there. Downtown streets normally jammed with cars, bicyclists, and pedestrians this time of day stretched eerily quiet and empty.

By 11:45 a.m., Haley stood in a stiflingly hot warehouse with a group of men including Chief Mullen, Mayor Joseph Riley Jr., and the Reverend Norvel Goff from the AME Church.

Heat swelled in the cavernous room as reporters set up and dignitaries gathered before a light-drenched lectern filled with microphones. Sweat glistened on their faces and dripped beneath suit coats and police uniforms.

Chief Mullen spoke first.

"I am very, very pleased to announce we have made an arrest in this case."

As the chief described the arrest, Haley realized that the hardest part of this ordeal now lay ahead. Even before the shooting, she'd been alert to the fraught state of race relations after Ferguson and the shooting death of Walter Scott just miles from where she stood. She now had to lead a grieving state in the wake of a historically tragic act of violence with the potential to boil over into even more violence. A practiced and polished speaker, she typically stood confident before microphones. She'd developed a tough exterior as a woman leading a state that, in spite of progress, still clung to its share of patriarchy and good old boys.

But now, as her turn to speak approached, Haley's thoughts went blank. What could she possibly say to ease the pain and prepare the public for the details that would soon come out about Roof's racist agenda?

When Mullen finished, she stepped to the microphones and looked at the wall of journalists.

"We woke up today . . ." she began. Her voice quivered, and she paused. The room fell silent. She glanced down as if looking for notes that weren't there. Across South Carolina, the public saw their governor, normally so controlled, fighting back tears. After a moment, she continued.

"And the heart and soul of South Carolina was broken. And so we have some grieving to do. We've got some pain we've got to go through. Parents are having to explain to their kids how they can go to church and feel safe— and that's not something we ever thought we'd deal with."

She immediately felt irritated by her momentary display of emotion. She'd been raised by a tough mother, a lawyer from India who couldn't take a judgeship position because her family considered it inappropriate for a woman. Raj Randhawa had taught that there were no tears when kids in tiny Bamberg, South Carolina, had teased the town's only Indian family. Get things done, she chided. Don't cry about them.

Working in a man's political world had only reinforced Haley's awareness of the importance of appearing strong and determined at all times. Yet, here she was getting emotional as the world watched. She felt she'd let the state down. She'd let herself down.

There was no time to think about it. The group of dignitaries was anxious to head out to a large prayer vigil at another historic AME church nearby. As Haley focused on getting there, her aides watched social media light up with approval. They weren't surprised—they knew Haley beyond the cameras could be an approachable boss who asked how they were doing when things got stressful. But for a public accustomed to seeing her polished veneer, this was a new Haley. They saw a vulnerable and very human governor, one who felt their fears and pain.

As police in Shelby arrested Dylann Roof and Haley addressed the nation, investigators arrived at Roof's father's mustard-colored home in Columbia. Benn Roof lived at the end of a dead-end street in a middle-class neighborhood of eclectic homes and shady trees not five minutes from the South Carolina State House. A Confederate flag flew on a pole in front of the Capitol. However, Benn didn't fly it on his property. He flew an American flag from the front porch, where several beach towels also hung to dry. His was the only house on the street that faced inward, giving it a feel of seclusion.

When police arrived, Benn was expecting them. He'd already called the authorities to identify the shooter as his only son. At home with his two daughters and parents now, he explained that he didn't know where Roof was; his best guess was with a friend named Joey Meek. He told them Dylann slept on the couch some nights and showed up on weekends to do his laundry when it suited him. He also left a few items around the place.

Investigators wanted to see them.

Leading them inside, Benn pointed to a tall black filing cabinet with a Hello Kitty drawing on it where he had stuffed his son's black jacket. When an agent pulled it out, he noticed two patches on the right chest, both of them flags, one from South Africa and the other from Rhodesia, among the last holdouts of apartheid. Benn didn't indicate that he had a problem with the message, or if he understood it. He said only that he'd gotten sick of seeing the jacket thrown on his floor.

As investigators began poking around the place, they soon found a copy of the movie *Made in Britain*, about a teenage skinhead, and several pictures of Dylann Roof glowering at the camera wearing all black in front of an ancient live oak in Charleston. In the pictures, he wore the black jacket. Investigators quickly realized that they had a young man with a penchant for white supremacist symbols. However, their main concern at this stage was determining whether Dylann Roof was the killer—and whether he had acted alone or had accomplices planning to enact more atrocities.

Nothing they found indicated he had a whole lot to do with anyone outside of his parents and perhaps this friend Joey Meek. The picture emerging was that of a lone wolf type of killer. But the agents still weren't sure why a twenty-one-year-old, even one who adhered to white supremacist ideology, would walk into a church and gun down nine people at a Bible study.

Among those searching was FBI agent Craig Januchowski, a special agent with a Chicago accent, who soon emerged with a birthday card that Benn had given to his son a few months earlier. It featured a cute brown otter on the front. Inside of it, Benn had penned a note to his son.

Happy 21st b-day! I love you buddy!
I.O.U good for up to $400.00 toward pistol and CWP
I love you!

Dad

(Based upon job!)

Januchowski knew the acronym CWP in the note stood for "concealed weapon permit," and indeed Benn Roof said that his son had purchased a Glock. A father giving his adult son money to buy his first gun didn't raise many eyebrows in South Carolina, and it appeared that Benn Roof had tried to use it as leverage to ensure his son was on the road to employment. Besides, what mattered now was that the suspect appeared to own the same type of gun used in the massacre.

Soon after Januchowski left the house, he took a call: Dylann Roof had been arrested without incident.

Roof hadn't said a word to Shelby police officer Scott Hamrick on the drive to the police department. When they arrived, several officers together deposited Roof into "the library," a smallish conference room with an oval table surrounded by six leather office chairs.

"Sit in that chair." An officer gestured to one side of the table. Roof did so, then leaned forward slightly given his hands were cuffed behind his back. His legs also were shackled.

Two other officers approached to unlock and remove the shackles and waist chains, filling the room with the sound of metal clanking and twisting. Then they switched the handcuffs so they locked in front, more comfortably, and left Roof alone with Detective Matt Styers, a white man with a shaved head dressed not in a uniform but rather a buttoned-down shirt and slacks. Styers set a plastic bottle of water on the table in front of Roof.

"That water's for you, man," Styers said. Everything about his tone, manner, and facial expression communicated trust and compassion.

"For me?" Roof asked, the first words he had spoken since arriving at the station. The monotone that emerged sounded oddly thick-throated given his slight build and youthful haircut.

Styers would guard Roof until two FBI agents driving up from South Carolina arrived. His job was to make the suspect feel at ease and ready to talk. He scooted the water bottle closer to Roof.

"When's the last time you ate?" he asked.

Roof leaned forward. "Well, I had a bag of chips this morning."

It was just after 11 a.m., fourteen hours since he left Emanuel.

"You hungry?"

Roof smiled slightly, as if humored by the offer, but didn't answer.

"We're probably going to be here a while. You want a burger or something? We can grab you a burger."

This time, Roof leaned back in his chair and grinned with disbelief, perhaps aware that the offer was tactical rather than a sign of concern for his welfare.

"Okay," he chuckled. "I'll take a burger."

Styers sat at the head of the table in a chair pulled out a few feet so he could directly face the young captive. Roof stared at the table. The leather chair dwarfed his slender frame. He spoke no more.

Thirteen minutes passed this way until another officer walked in and dropped a Burger King bag in front of the prisoner. The smell of a Whopper plumed out of the paper sack. Roof devoured it, still in silence.

When he'd finished, he sat back and resumed staring ahead. For two hours and thirty-seven minutes, Styers marveled at how a man who might have killed nine people just last night could sit so still and emotionless. He didn't seem high or drunk or medicated. He didn't seem agitated or worried or remorseful. He seemed simply blank, as if he wasn't thinking about anything at all.

Finally, at 1:38 p.m., the silence broke when Januchowski walked in with FBI agent Michael Stansbury. Both had been chasing down leads in South Carolina when they had received word of Roof's capture and hurried to Shelby to interview him. Stansbury, in a black golf shirt and khaki slacks, shook the Shelby detective's hand first and then, with the casual demeanor of someone meeting a new friend at a bar, shook Roof's hand and introduced himself. Januchowski, his buttoned-down shirt untucked, followed suit. The three men stood over Roof, making every effort to appear calm and unhurried.

Stansbury, acting assistant special agent in charge of the Columbia field office, had spent the previous decade investigating gangs, drug dealers, and violent crimes. As he and Januchowski entered the conference room in Shelby, Detective Styers collected Roof's Burger King trash before heading for the door.

Januchowski handed Roof another water bottle, "nice and cold," as he put it. Stansbury gently unlocked the handcuffs in Roof's lap. It was time to see if they could get him to talk.

"Would you like to have some privacy or . . ." Styers asked from the doorway.

"Yeah," Januchowski said.

The door closed, leaving only Roof with the two agents. Both strolled to the oval table and sat down, Stansbury at the head, Januchowski across from Roof.

"We want to talk to you about some stuff. I'm sure you probably already know that," Stansbury began. He went through Roof's rights, using a form on the table to explain them. Roof leaned forward, suddenly attentive. He initialed and signed, as if eager.

"Having all these rights in mind, do you wish to speak to us?" Januchowski asked.

"Oh sure." The epitome of a willing, helpful subject.

First, Stansbury started with small talk to get the suspect warmed up and comfortable. Where was he from? Roof said he was from South Carolina, that he'd dropped out of high school, dropped out of online school, got his GED, was unemployed, had worked in lawn maintenance, his only job. He sounded intelligent enough. He explained that he lived mostly with his mom at her boyfriend's house in Eastover, a more rural area not far from downtown Columbia, where he sometimes stayed at his dad's house.

Stansbury rarely questioned a suspect who seemed this eager to talk, so he decided to jump right in.

"Well, can you tell us about what happened last night?"

Roof looked off to the side and paused. The agents leaned forward.

"Well, um, yeah, I mean, I just, I went to that church in Charleston and, uhhh, you know, I uh." He stopped for a second or two. "I did it."

"Did what?"

Roof exhaled loudly and grinned, as if embarrassed, like a kid caught stealing or cutting class.

"I know it's tough sometimes to—to say it," Stansbury assured.

Roof groaned lightly. "It's not that I don't want to say it because I don't want to make myself seem guilty. I just don't really like saying it, you know."

"Sometimes we have to face those things, the realities, you know?" Stansbury angled his chair so that his knees were only a couple feet from Roof. As if they were friends, confidants.

Januchowski backed him up. "We don't want to put any words into your mouth . . ."

"Well," Roof admitted, "I did. I killed them."

The interrogation lasted two full hours, eliciting, in addition to the confession, that Roof had deliberately targeted innocent black people and had acted alone. When they were finished, there was the matter of extradition, the legal process of handling someone charged with committing a crime in one state, then fleeing to another. Some defendants fought extradition, but Roof, ever compliant, opted not to fight being sent back to South Carolina.

Less than twenty-four hours after he had joined Bible study, Dylann Roof landed at Charleston International Airport, twelve miles from Mother

Emanuel. At 7:28 p.m., he became inmate #0001518680 at the Charleston County detention center, a concrete fortress that housed almost 1,400 inmates. The jail's tactical team escorted him to a segregated unit where he would live alone in a cell, for his own protection from the other inmates, most of whom were black.

Inside those impenetrable concrete walls, in a unit for inmates kept in solitary confinement, word of the church shooting had spread quickly. Inmates who had radios listened to coverage of it.

Can you believe it? This is crazy!

Then the talk changed:

They got him!

He's coming here.

When he arrived on the unit, Roof shuffled through a door, his body bound by leg irons, a waist chain, and handcuffs. The officers walked him along one edge of the unit, past the guard desk and into the first cell, in a corner. Faceless inmates behind the white doors catcalled slurs as he emerged into their view. He turned into his new home, a cell roughly six feet wide and eight feet long. Across a hard, white floor, his cell contained a twin bed with a gray metal frame, a slender mattress, and a thin blanket. It took up half of the room. A metal stool sat bolted to the floor next to it near a small platform affixed to the wall, a makeshift desk. A single metal contraption near the door served as both sink and toilet.

Guards closed the heavy door to his cell with a loud clank. Like in the movies, he would get his meals through a rectangular slot. Peering through the narrow window in the door, Roof could see a common area beyond with only a few square tables in the big, open space ringed with cells. Given his was in a corner, he had just one neighbor.

In that cell lived Michael Slager, the former North Charleston police officer who faced a murder charge after gunning down Walter Scott, a black man he'd stopped for a broken brake light. The two inmates' proximity in jail marked an early union of two local stories of race and gun violence that mirrored a national storm raging over both issues.

eight

God Forgives You, and I Forgive You

❋

Set in an industrial area north of Charleston, bond court was a place of routine business where offenders were paraded before a magistrate tasked with setting bail. It seldom drew spectators beyond lawyers, police, and the occasional victim. But now, two days after the shootings at Emanuel, TV trucks lined the parking lot, and the small courtroom swelled with police and loved ones of those killed, who arrived still deeply in shock.

"All rise!"

The black-robed magistrate, an older white man with silver hair, walked through a door behind the bench and sat down, peering over his glasses to scan the crowd.

"Bring him on in, sir," a voice said. "Roof."

On a large screen hanging at the front of the room, the crowd saw a heavily armed black detention officer appear through a steel door, followed by a shackled young man in a striped gray jail jumpsuit, then a white officer. Roof stood in front, filling the screen's foreground. His face looked longer, his hair flatter and greasier than in the surveillance images. He licked his lips and looked down.

Cameras clicked. Papers shuffled.

"Today is June 19, 2015. Charleston County Bond Court. I'm James Gosnell, the chief magistrate of Charleston County. This is the case of the State versus Dylann Roof."

Across the globe in Dubai, Steve Hurd hustled down metal stairs to the tarmac and headed into the airport terminal. After the horrible confirmation that his wife, Cynthia, had in fact been at Bible study, he'd spent two days desperately trying to get home. After a six-hour car ride through the desert with nothing but camels, donkeys, and sand passing him by, he'd caught an hour-long flight to Dubai, where, with fifty-five minutes until his connection to Atlanta, he now sat at a bar and nursed a beer. His eyes settled on a TV, where the news showed a young white guy in jail stripes.

"What did this kid do? Huff some paint and drive through Walmart?" he thought.

Then words streamed across the screen.

"Bond court in Charleston, South Carolina."

Steve stood and pointed.

"That!" he shouted. "That thing killed my wife?"

Dylann Roof stood staring at the courtroom from a TV screen mounted on one wall beside Gosnell, the black-robed magistrate presiding over the bond hearing, as the world watched.

"Ladies and gentlemen, before we get into the hearing, I'd like to make a statement, please," Gosnell said.

"We have victims, nine of them. But we also have victims on the other side. There are victims on this young man's side of the family. Nobody would ever have thrown them into the whirlwind of events that they have been thrown into."

Roof faced the camera, his expression blank.

The magistrate went on about Roof's family, speaking emphatically, even angrily. Both his words and tenor felt hugely insensitive, given the magnitude of injury to the survivors, shooting victims, and their families, all barely mentioned yet.

When Gosnell finished, he praised the police and lawyers involved before asking Roof some basic questions. The man on the screen answered with soft "yes, sirs."

Finally, Gosnell began calling the victims' names, one by one, and invited their family members to speak. When he got to the third, Ethel Lance, the seventy-year-old's youngest daughter stood. Nadine Collier was sitting in the back and hadn't planned to say anything. Yet, she felt herself rise and move toward the front of the packed room. As she walked forward, she heard her mother's voice warning, "I don't want any fast talking out of you today. Don't be a smart-ass today."

The church's longtime custodian, Ethel had known her youngest daughter's nature well and loved her for it. Nadine was strong-willed and passionate with a spicy edge of humor. She could let words fly, truth be told. But in the bond courtroom, with every step she took forward, her sage summer dress swirling around her ankles, Nadine felt certain that her words would be her mother's. Ethel Lance's warm, gospel-loving spirit filled her so much that when Nadine stepped to the microphone, at first she couldn't remember her own name.

"And you are whom, ma'am?" the magistrate asked.

"Her daughter."

"Her daughter," Gosnell repeated. "I'm listening. And you can talk to me."

Instead, Nadine looked toward Roof.

"I just want everybody to know, to you, I forgive you! You took something very precious away from me." Her husky voice cracked with a muffled sob. "I will never talk to her ever again. I will never be able to hold her again. But I forgive you! And have mercy on your soul. You. Hurt. Me! You hurt a lot of people." Beneath her spiky black hair, long gold earrings swung with each emphatic statement.

"But God forgives you. And I forgive you."

With those words, Nadine turned away and returned to her seat.

Roof stared down impassively.

Gosnell read the next name: Myra Thompson.

Myra's husband, the Reverend Anthony Thompson, hadn't planned to speak, either. A retired probation and parole agent, he'd seen his share of bond hearings and knew they were routine affairs. He had warned Myra's two grown children not to say anything, either. It wasn't necessary, and it might upset them.

But now, hearing Myra's name, he rose. Their children looked at him questioningly.

"I'll tell you later," he whispered. His slender frame strode to the lectern, where he stopped and, for a moment, looked at Roof. In his mind, everyone else vanished, as if Anthony were standing in the killer's cell, the two men alone. Anthony's voice emerged so softly that Gosnell asked him to speak up.

"I forgive you," Anthony said more loudly. "And my family forgives you. But we would like you to take this opportunity to repent. Repent. Confess. Give your life to the one who matters the most—Christ—so that he can change it, can change your ways no matter what happens to you."

Anthony peered at the screen, trying to catch Roof's eye, to get him to stop for a minute and think about those words. Redemption. For a quick second, Roof's glance indeed shifted a bit, and Anthony wondered if he'd caught his eye. As he turned to go back to his seat, he hoped that somewhere deep beneath the vacant gaze, there was hope—hope that Roof would repent and be saved.

Felicia Sanders heard her son's name called next.

She too hadn't planned to speak. But when she heard Tywanza's name, she too changed her mind. Felicia thought of places like Ferguson and Baltimore. She thought of someone else's son dying. God nudged her forward, so she stood and walked to the microphone, one hand clutching a ball of folded-up tissues. She heard the sound of her own voice.

"We welcomed you Wednesday night in our Bible study with open arms. You have killed some of the most beautifullest people that I know. Every fiber in my body hurts!" she cried. "And I'll never be the same. Tywanza Sanders is my son, but Tywanza was my hero. Tywanza was my hero! But as we say in the Bible study: We enjoyed you, but may God have mercy on you."

Her voice broke with sorrow, but she sounded warm and strong. Roof's destiny was in God's hands now. Her destiny remained in her own. What if she didn't forgive this killer? She wouldn't go to heaven, and that's where she would find her baby boy. She had to get there.

Other family members spoke after her, echoing similar themes, those at the heart of Christianity: repentance, love, mercy, forgiveness. Sobs filled the background. Chief Mullen sat in awe. The bond hearing lasted just thirteen minutes, but it had only begun to reverberate across Charleston and the nation.

M arine One thundered over California. President Barack Obama and four staffers discussed gun violence statistics that he hoped would harness the public's attention to the prevalence of mass shootings, most recently at the black church in Charleston. There had been twenty-three of them, with at least four people killed in each, over the five years of his presidency so far.

Shortly after the bond hearing ended, Obama's deputy press secretary thumbed through breaking news on his cell phone and came across a headline about the families' forgiveness. He read their words out loud.

"God forgives you, and I forgive you . . ."

Everyone paused, the chopper's blades thumping over their sudden silence.

Obama spoke first.

"Hold off on the statistics. That's what I want to put the spotlight on."

nine

Not So Fast

✳

Sharon Risher, the oldest of Ethel Lance's five children, was the only one who didn't live in Charleston. While the victims' family members gathered at the bond hearing, Sharon slogged around her apartment in Dallas trying to focus on what to pack. She knew her middle sister, Esther, was overwhelmed with grief. So was her deaf brother, who had depended on their mother for help. Sharon hadn't spoken much to her youngest sister, Nadine, given the tension between them.

She and her siblings were still reeling from the loss of their second-oldest sister, Terrie Washington, who had died just two years earlier. Terrie was only fifty-three, and her fatal battle with cervical cancer had jarred them all. Then, right after Terrie's burial, the devil had gotten busy in her family. When Ethel and her children gathered with their families afterward, the combustible wells of grief had spouted into what should have been a small, stupid argument. Instead, a screaming match exploded. A shove. A swipe. Now, resentments lingered.

Back in Dallas, Sharon could barely figure out what to do next. A fifty-seven-year-old trauma chaplain, she never imagined that she would be the one standing in the sudden shadow of violent death. Network news blared from the TV in her apartment as she paced and smoked cigarettes and tried to think of what else she needed to pack to catch a late flight out. Suddenly, from her living room, Nadine's quavering voice reached from the TV.

"I just want everybody to know, to you, I forgive you!" Nadine cried.

What?

Sharon aimed her black horn-rimmed glasses at the sound. Other victims' family members, including her cousin Felicia, echoed her sister's sentiment. Sharon listened in shock. Nadine hadn't told her about any bond hearing. Neither had the police. Why hadn't anyone told her about it?

When the piece ended, the network anchors and their guests marveled at the families' words of forgiveness. Several more times, Sharon heard her sister's voice: "I will never be able to hold her again. But I forgive you!"

Those words infuriated Sharon. Not even two days had passed. She hadn't yet buried her mother. She knew few details about the shooting. She couldn't even absorb what the young man had done. Of course, she hoped to forgive him one day. God commanded it. Her very salvation would depend on it. But before Sharon could think about forgiving in any honest way, she needed to know more. She needed to be angry and cry and know exactly what happened.

"How can you forgive this man who just killed Momma?" Sharon screamed at the TV.

Sharon wasn't alone. Other victims' loved ones listening to the bond hearing shared her anger. To Sharon, it felt like the same old Charleston, where black people were expected to stand there and take every insult—even murder—with a gracious word and an acquiescent smile. That was one big reason why she had moved away in 1976 and hadn't looked back. Otherwise, she would have been stuck in the same old "you stay in your corner, and I stay in mine."

Sharon didn't much care for staying in any corner. Like Nadine, she was scrappy, a fighter the way their father had raised them. And she certainly didn't say things just because they were easy or sounded nice, not even about forgiveness. However, she did believe deeply in God's handiwork in people's lives. So, as she thought more about the bond hearing, she figured that God hadn't allowed her to know about it. Maybe Charleston and the nation needed to hear all that stuff—to temper people's rightful rage and to prevent the violence that had so recently erupted in places like Ferguson and Baltimore.

Sharon soon headed for the Dallas airport to begin the long journey back to Charleston. She met her two grown children in Charlotte, where they lived, then finally reached Charleston, the Holy City, and checked into a hotel before heading to Nadine's house. When they arrived, Sharon walked over and reached up to hug her much taller little sister. She didn't feel a lot of warmth back.

Nadine hadn't intended any. Sharon had waited three days to return to Charleston. Who takes that long to return home after a parent has been murdered? She just knew Sharon would swoop in with her uppity children and expect to take over everything—and Nadine wasn't having any of it. Sharon hadn't even come back to visit since Terrie died. What did she know about burying their mother or handling her business?

Worse, Ethel Lance hadn't left a will, no directions to tell the sisters how to handle her estate.

Sharon demanded to know why Nadine wouldn't let her into their mother's apartment. She wondered if her sister was hiding something or just being overly controlling. Why couldn't Nadine give her a key to come and go from the apartment just as Nadine did? Right now, Nadine could go in and take whatever she wanted with nobody looking over her shoulder. As the nation marveled at the families' words of forgiveness, the sisters found it wasn't so easy to extend this graciousness to each other. For any group of loved ones, a tragedy of this magnitude only amplifies every pre-existing hurt and grievance a million times over. It didn't take long for the people left to mourn Ethel's death to say things to each other that none of them would soon forgive.

ten

A New Breed

✳

The Lone Wolf

N ow living in the jail's isolation unit for his own protection, Roof spent twenty-three of twenty-four hours locked in his cell. Every prisoner in this section of the jail, during his allotted one hour of "recreation" time, could leave his cell to shower and walk around the rectangular unit's common area, a barren open space encircled by other prisoners' locked metal doors, all painted stark white. In fact, the whole two-story unit was painted white, the fluorescent lights always left on, eliminating most sense of day or night or the passing of time at all.

While out of his cell, an inmate could talk to the others through a narrow window in the solid metal cell doors. Some took the opportunity to socialize. Others banged on their fellow prisoners' doors and turned their cell lights on and off—the switches were outside. A few preferred not to venture out unless forced.

About two-thirds of the men jailed on the unit were black. When Roof's hour of rec time arrived, and he stepped out of his cell, always alone, some of them yelled racial slurs at him. Others hurled threats at the scrawny man they could beat to a pulp. But to a lot of them, he was the highest-profile inmate in a place marked by the slow passage of endless time. He was a curiosity. Most also didn't yet know the depths of his racist views, and he didn't offer much about them.

Some inmates tried to lure him over to their doors when he was out of his cell. They wanted to engage him in conversations to find out what he was like, what drove him to do something so horrible. Surprisingly few threatened him.

Instead, many asked: "Why'd you do it?"

"I had to do it," he always responded. And that was pretty much all he'd say.

It was hard to tell if he simply had nothing else to add, or if he was just being cagey. Maybe his lawyers had warned him not to talk. Maybe he was in some sort of delusional world of monotony. They didn't know his history of social anxiety, that he'd been happiest when holed up in the isolation of his bedroom.

He did occasionally talk with Michael Slager, the white officer charged with murdering Walter Scott who was locked in the adjacent cell. Either man could climb on top of a contraption, mounted on their shared wall, that served as both toilet and sink and talk through a vent. They didn't talk about Roof's crimes or Slager's crime or white supremacy or police shootings, though.

Mostly, they just bitched about the jail and discussed what they'd bought from the commissary. Roof bought a radio, a junky little device with a clear case, and earphones to listen to music, NPR, and right-wing radio host Michael Savage. He also bought golf pencils and a notepad because he had more ideas to write down. He wished the last words he'd left behind on his website weren't so clumsy and filled with punctuation errors. That was embarrassing.

After all, he was a hero, to himself at least, the truest defender of his race. Some white nationalists had shown themselves to be cowards, as he'd expected, and had condemned his actions. Others had stayed quiet. And if they ever found the courage to rise up, perhaps they'd rescue him. He'd be pardoned and given a high position, maybe even governor, in the post-revolution government.

But most likely, he would remain stuck here like a political prisoner. He considered himself that—a jihadist of sorts, a warrior for his cause, like a Palestinian stuck in an Israeli jail for killing Jews. At least he had succeeded in his mission. Sacrificing his freedom on behalf of his race, he figured, was a small price indeed. And on his website, he'd left behind his manifesto, a direct appeal to his race. Surely, someone out there would discover it soon.

Before Roof had driven to Emanuel, he'd sat at his father's computer and typed up his racist ideology, which he had first written out in a brown leather-bound journal. He wanted to explain his awakening and alert other whites to the enormous threats to their race. Then he'd uploaded the text onto his website, lastrhodesian.com, so that everyone would know why he had to kill.

As he'd hoped, a blogger discovered the site shortly after Roof's bond hearing and introduced his ideology to the world. His homepage featured the gruesome image of a dead skinhead, blood dripping from his mouth, soaking his white T-shirt as he died on the wet sands of a rocky beach. It wasn't real though. The shot came from a Russell Crowe movie.

To the right of that picture, one button linked to "photos," another to "text." That's where he had uploaded his 2,444-word essay, a manifesto of sorts. As news of the site spread, people everywhere learned about what he considered his racial awakening, the dawn that transformed him from a painfully shy and anxious youth into a racist killer. This awakening had begun with the case of Trayvon Martin, a black teenager killed by a community watchman in Florida. Roof couldn't understand why the killing, which generated a national conversation about racial profiling, got so much attention. So, he had done some research, clicking onto a Wikipedia page about the killing, then typing into Google the search terms "black on white crime."

There, he stumbled through a gateway into the world of white supremacy. He clicked onto the website of the White Council of Conservative Citizens (CCC), an organization that sprang from the White Citizens' Councils of America, a 1950s-era organization that had once blanketed the South to oppose court-ordered school desegregation. Some folks had called them the "uptown Klan" because they presented notions of preserving the white race with a glaze of respectability and civic engagement.

The CCC's webmaster was Kyle Rogers, a thirty-eight-year-old computer engineer whom the Southern Poverty Law Center had recently placed among its "30 to watch." This was not an honor; it described him as one of a new crop of extremists "leading a powerful resurgence of the American radical right" by pushing conspiracy theories and racist propaganda into the mainstream. Sites like his increasingly nipped at the outer edges of conventional right-wing politics as a way to attract users who might warm to its message but remain wary of more overt white supremacy. Once lured in, readers encountered claims of massive white victimization left ignored by a mainstream media cover-up.

Rogers also was a South Carolinian. He operated from a nondescript brown brick-front ranch in Summerville, a suburb of Charleston about thirty minutes from Emanuel. Rogers would denounce Roof and deny knowing him, but Roof didn't need to know him personally to feel his influence. The old days of Klan rallies had faded, replaced by a new kind of meet-up. Instead of hiding behind white sheets, racists now hid behind user names on a host of flourishing websites that Roof soon discovered, including the Daily Stormer. Named for the Nazi Party's newspaper, its founder, Andrew Anglin, considered it part of the political "alt-right."

Sites like his had gotten a big boost the day before the Emanuel shooting when Donald Trump announced his candidacy for president. Anglin quickly endorsed Trump and re-cast the Daily Stormer as "America's #1 Most-Trusted Republican News Source," an opportunistic grab for new readers who supported the candidate's views on immigrants and the loss of American—namely *white* American—power. Once on the site, readers found news and commentaries that cast whites as victims of black violence, the very propaganda that soon would drive Roof to act. He wasn't alone.

A year before the shooting, the Southern Poverty Law Center published a report documenting almost one hundred murders committed by members of the largest hate site, one that Roof also visited, called Stormfront. The center described these killers' archetype: a frustrated, unemployed white man living with his mother. "Instead of building his resume, seeking employment or further education, he projects his grievances on society and searches the Internet for an excuse or an explanation unrelated to his behavior or the choices he has made in life," the report said.

When Roof, an unemployed white man living with his mother, sat down to write out his ideas, he tapped the language of the racist websites he'd been devouring:

> I think it is is fitting to start off with the group I have the most real
> life experience with, and the group that is the biggest problem for
> Americans.

Niggers are stupid and violent. At the same time they have the
capacity to be very slick. Black people view everything through a
racial lense. Thats what racial awareness is, its viewing everything
that happens through a racial lense. They are always thinking
about the fact that they are black.

This is part of the reason they get offended so easily, and think
that some thing are intended to be racist towards them, even when
a White person wouldnt be thinking about race. The other reason
is the Jewish agitation of the black race.

Black people are racially aware almost from birth, but White
people on average dont think about race in their daily lives. And
this is our problem. We need to and have to.

This, he explained, was "the truth."

Black people had lower IQs, less impulse control, higher testosterone—
the perfect cocktail for violence, he typed, as if unaware of the tragic irony
of the violence he was planning.

I have no choice. I am not in the position to, alone, go into the
ghetto and fight. I chose Charleston because it is most historic city
in my state, and at one time had the highest ratio of blacks to
Whites in the country. We have no skinheads, no real KKK, no one
doing anything but talking on the internet. Well someone has to
have the bravery to take it to the real world, and I guess that has to
be me.

He apologized for being in a hurry. His best thoughts might be lost forever. But he had to go.

Please forgive any typos, I didnt have time to check it.

He had taken time, however, to include a downloadable zip folder with sixty
favorite photographs of himself ensconced in the white supremacist identity he'd adopted. He sat on a beach at Sullivan's Island in one, crouching
where he'd carved the number 1488, a new favorite of his, into the sand.

The 14 stood for the number of words in a favored white nationalist slogan: "We must secure the existence of our people and a future for white children." The 88 stood for Heil Hitler, "h" being the eighth letter in the alphabet.

In another picture, he glared over the top of round sunglasses, shirtless with a farmer's tan, pointing a handgun at the camera. His rumpled bed in an otherwise seemingly normal bedroom at his mother's house sat in bizarre contrast behind him. In another, he posed alone in front of a row of slave cabins at a popular Charleston plantation.

In them, he always was alone—a "lone wolf" as authorities called his type of killer, a dangerous new form of homegrown terrorist. Led by no leader, beholden to no organized group, lone wolves' self-guided actions often slip beneath the radars of law enforcement, as had Roof's. Radicalized by writings on hate-filled websites, lone wolves have claimed an increasingly prominent role in anti-government and white supremacist propaganda and brutality. They are acutely tough to track and preempt.

In the dozens of photographs that Roof had posted, not a single other person appeared. He did, however, pose in several with a Confederate flag. And few images could inflame racial divisions in the Deep South quite like that symbol.

When he left his home near the state capital on June 17, the flag—specifically South Carolina's version of the Army of Northern Virginia Battle Flag—flew on a pole in front of the state's Capitol building. Until fifteen years earlier, an oblong version had flown with even more prominence atop the building's copper-covered dome. Lawmakers had raised it there as part of a Civil War centennial celebration in the early 1960s.

After years of bitter feuding over what it represented, over exactly what "heritage" meant and to whom, lawmakers in 2000 reached a compromise to lower the banner. They moved it from the dome to the flagpole, where it flew as part of a Confederate War Memorial directly in front of the State House, along one of the capital's busiest streets. Now Roof held it up like an emblem of his racist crimes.

eleven

The Power to Forgive

✳

Late Saturday afternoon, as the narrative of forgiveness spread from the bond hearing to households across the nation, Emanuel's secretary Althea Latham left a meeting at a high school downtown, where she had gathered with church members for the first time since the shooting to cry, pray, and lay out a basic plan to move forward. They needed some order amid the devastating loss and grief. It wouldn't be easy, given most of the church's ministers lay dead and the district's bishop had just received a kidney transplant. The Reverend Norvel Goff had only been a presiding elder, a middleman between the pastors and bishop, for seven months. Although he was a seasoned minister, only a few of those who gathered knew him much at all.

Goff had to lead them regardless and had laid out a much-needed plan: All media and other requests would go through him. He and the steward board members would go to the home of every victim's immediate family, if they lived in town, on Saturday. He would meet with the families as a group on Monday to discuss funeral plans. However, given that Emanuel remained a crime scene, he wasn't sure if they would be allowed back in time for Sunday services the following morning. If not, other AME churches had opened their doors.

Althea found Goff's style unpleasantly authoritarian. Given the overwhelming pain all of them suffered, she thought his message ought to have emphasized that the church was there for its congregants and ministry, available to anyone who needed it. At the same time, she was relieved to have someone taking control amid the chaos. The church's office phone was routed to her cell phone, and it had been ringing nonstop. As Althea left the meeting, it buzzed yet again. This time, a friendly police detective's voice greeted her on the line.

"Hey, Miss Althea. Y'all want to get into the building?"

After three days of intensive work, the police had finished their crime scene investigation. A cleaning company's crews had come in and done their best to erase every trace of the carnage, mopping the fellowship hall's floor and throwing away blood-soaked items. The congregation could come home.

Althea quickly dialed Goff. He'd meet her at Emanuel.

As she entered the church through the side door, the moist iron stench of blood lingered in the stuffy hallway where Reverend Simmons had collapsed outside of Althea's office door. Bullet divots pockmarked the floor. She walked into the office where she'd last seen Clementa Pinckney alive and paused at her desk. Jennifer Pinckney and her little girl had cowered beneath it. Above the desk and to one side, a bullet had pierced a wood-paneled wall near a light switch cover and struck a window in the office. In the adjoining pastor's office, police had kicked in the door.

Althea didn't linger long. The next stop was unavoidable.

As she entered the fellowship hall, once such a warm and homey place, a chill scuttled up her spine. She didn't want to picture what had happened in here, but as she stepped over a bullet hole in the floor, she couldn't help it. Tears burned her eyes when she saw more holes in two white fold-out chairs. She tucked them away where the members wouldn't see them and retrieved white tape to cover the bullet hole in the floor.

Soon a small group of church leaders joined her, including Goff, who led them in much-needed prayer. In a firm voice, he added that they would hold a normal Sunday worship service in their sanctuary tomorrow. Through its two-hundred-year history, this congregation had survived slavery, segregation, wars, a massive earthquake, hangings, and fires set by white racists. They would show the world that, while devastated, Emanuel wasn't destroyed now, either.

Evil had entered this sacred space, but Emanuel still meant "God with us."

As the sun rose on Sunday, people lined up outside of the stately white church, threading themselves around an enormous mass of colorful flowers, shiny balloons, and teddy bears covering the front sidewalk. Others stood praying and talking, taking pictures. Thousands of people descended, far too many to fit inside of its sanctuary for worship. This wasn't only a church's celebration of survival. It was a community's for worship.

Emanuel members were let in first, then visitors. Calhoun Street remained closed to traffic, and as the 9:30 a.m. service time arrived, the four-lane road transformed into a vast sacred space jammed full of people. Groups sang together and held hands to pray in the day's heat, brutal even by Charleston's standards.

> *I once was lost but now am found*
> *Was blind but now I see . . .*

Members arrived, as always, in their Sunday best. While Charleston still harbored great education and economic disparities between black and white residents, Emanuel's membership rolls were filled with attorneys, educators, public officials, nurses. Beneath their feet, at street level, sat the fellowship hall. A large framed poster of The Lord's Prayer hung in one corner near an arrow pointing to the ladies' restroom. Every Sunday, the congregation recited that prayer.

> *Give us this day our daily bread.*
> *And forgive us our trespasses,*
> *As we forgive them that trespass against us . . .*

Upstairs, more than one thousand people, white and black, jammed into the sanctuary built for about eight hundred. Police officers stood sentry. A bomb-sniffing dog scoured the perimeter. In the choir loft near a giant pipe organ, Susie Jackson's robe had been placed neatly in her seat. Up front on the altar, a black robe shrouded Reverend Pinckney's chair.

None of the survivors and few of the victims' family members came. To some of them, opening the church so soon slighted the sanctity of their loved ones' deaths. Others couldn't yet bear to step foot inside. The state's political class, on the other hand, came out in full force: The church's front pews filled with dignitaries, including Governor Haley and her family, U.S. senator Tim Scott, California congresswoman Maxine Waters, North Charleston's mayor, Charleston's mayor, and more.

Ethel Lance's daughter Nadine Collier, who had become famous for her words of forgiveness, couldn't fathom going back to Emanuel and not seeing her mother, an usher, greet her at the door. She couldn't imagine returning to the choir and not hearing Susie Jackson's soprano. Instead, she fumed. How could church leaders be so disrespectful and open the building so soon? Nobody from Emanuel had called to ask her opinion. She wondered whether all the TV cameras in town had something to do with it.

That Sunday would have been Cynthia Hurd's fifty-fifth birthday. It also was Father's Day. It would be Tyrone Sanders' loneliest in twenty-six years, his first without Tywanza, his twenty-six-year-old travel partner, his road dog, his baby boy. It was Dan Simmons Jr.'s first without his father. It was the first of many for Clementa Pinckney's two young daughters.

But for the thousands on hand and many more watching on TV, this Sunday offered an opportunity to witness the remarkable forgiveness narrative in action.

Reverend Goff stood in the pulpit wearing the AME Church's purple and black robe. A seasoned preacher in his sixties, he stepped to the microphone, leaned on the wooden lectern, and scanned his massive audience with droopy-lidded eyes and a grave cast.

Before his promotion seven months earlier, he'd spent a decade as pastor of a large church in the state capital. Though a South Carolina native, he'd spent much of his career up north in New York and Connecticut, where he made a name working with the NAACP promoting civil rights issues, notably achieving major concessions from Eastman Kodak over racial biases in promotions and pay.

Now the father of two faced a whole new challenge, one for which he couldn't possibly have prepared. With most of Emanuel's ordained and licensed ministers dead, the bishop had asked him to lead a traumatized congregation. He knew few of the members well, if at all, and the licensed ministers who remained alive either were newer than he or too ill to help much.

He faced the sea of Emanuel's faithful, the rows of dignitaries, and the overflowing crowd of visitors now looking up at him, hungry for spiritual comfort.

"It's been tough," he began. "It's been rough. Some of us have been downright angry. But through it all, God has sustained us and encouraged us." Wiping his brow against the building heat, he thanked the many people who had sent prayers and emails and cards of sorrow. National media outlets streamed his words across the world.

"Lot of folk expected us to do something strange and break out in a riot." He paused as if to ponder. "Well, they just don't know us!"

Cheers of agreement erupted.

"They don't know us, because we are a people of faith. We believe that when we put our forces and our heads together working for a common good, there is nothing we cannot accomplish together in the name of Jesus!"

The people sprang to their feet, cheering him on with gusto. Goff mopped his brow again. Emanuel's faltering air conditioner proved no match for the suffocating heat outside and the body heat of so many inside.

Don't forget, Goff warned, but remember. Remember God. Remember His promises.

Then, Goff embraced the tradition of Christian forgiveness that had so captivated the world. "I'm reminded by some news media persons who said, 'I wonder why the nine families all spoke of forgiveness and didn't have malice in their hearts.' Well, on this Father's Day, you ought to know the nine families' daddy!" he said. The crowd responded, and Goff bounced a bit in the pulpit, energized. "If you knew the nine families' daddy, you'll know how the children are behaving!"

The family members' words at the bond hearing may have surprised many in the outside world, but to those at Emanuel, and generations of black

Christians across America, they were an essential part of their religious tradition and spiritual survival. The late theologian James Cone, the father of
Black Liberation Theology, described forgiveness in the church as a form of
"deep spiritual resistance." It didn't only help ensure salvation after earthly
lives spent bearing the cruelties of slavery, segregation, and oppression. It
also provided power to the powerless. It freed the forgiver from hating the
oppressor. It kept hate from corroding the soul. It offered a higher Christian
ground, where those who uttered the words at Dylann Roof's bond hearing
now stood before an admiring world.

What this forgiveness meant for the rest of the city, and its troubled
racial history, proved more complicated.

The morning of the bond hearing, a Facebook post from several local
white mothers invited people to meet "in memory of those who lost
their lives at Emanuel AME" on the long white bridge that connected historic downtown with the city's affluent suburbs to the east. Normally filled
with cars and joggers, its eight lanes offered panoramic views of Charleston Harbor and the city's skyline of steeples. Dubbed the Arthur Ravenel Jr.
Bridge, it was named after a longtime political fixture from Charleston who
many people didn't realize, or remember, had defended the Confederate flag
as well as segregated schools. At a pro-flag rally in 2000, Ravenel had infa-
mously called the NAACP the "National Association for Retarded People,"
and then apologized to disabled people.

The evening after Emanuel reopened, as the setting sun caressed the
bridge's white cables, thousands of people responded to the mothers' invi-
tation by gathering on both ends of the nearly three-mile-long bridge. Choirs
sang. Musicians played. Chants of "Charleston Strong!" burst from the
crowd. The unusually racially diverse group, for Charleston, emphasized
the desire to join together after such an outrageous and violent racist act.
Many carried handmade posters: "Love Never Fails" and "Forgiveness is
Key to Unity," among them.

The groups on either side began to march toward each other, filling a
wide bike lane as cars honked in support, until they met in the middle with
a roar of cheers. White people hugged black people. Black people hugged

white people. They held hands and prayed and sang. A chain of an estimated 15,000 people, most of whom had never met any of the nine victims, united.

National news outlets praised the forgiving and unified community. In the wake of tragedy, this beautiful old city provided a new example to follow. The narrative solidified. It inspired. It reassured a weary nation, a world even, that the goodness in people had won.

But amid this hopeful atmosphere, some black leaders began to wonder if making such public pronouncements in fact quashed the momentum for addressing modern racism more deeply. Charleston, historic epicenter of the nation's slave trade, had never sought forgiveness for its original sin, not in any formalized manner. Instead, local plantations regaled millions of tourists with lush grounds, historic houses, and tales of "African American artisans"—among other euphemistic remembrances of the enslaved people whose blood and skill built them. Despite the city's history, white natives hardly plied their own genealogies for honest accountings of familial ties to slavery, even though as the Civil War approached almost three in four white families here had owned slaves. White and black residents still commonly shared the largest slave owners' surnames, testament to the historic bond between them, even if few whites cared to plumb the reality.

Two historians who had moved to Charleston not long before the shooting at Emanuel later recounted in their book, *Denmark Vesey's Garden*, the day they inquired about renting a bottom-floor apartment in one of downtown's beautiful antebellum homes. The landlord described how "servants" once lived in the space. When further questioned, she insisted the people she mentioned were not enslaved. However, the historians, Ethan Kytle and Blain Roberts, discovered that, in fact, the family had owned human beings. The authors soon discovered that many white Charlestonians they met resisted acknowledging slavery at all—and when they did, "they often mischaracterized it as benign, even beneficial."

So, granting forgiveness and claiming unity now felt to some like reviving the old plantation mindset in which black people were expected to endure the worst of grievances with graceful acquiescence. As the writer Ta-Nehisi Coates noted on Twitter: "Can't remember any campaign to 'love' and 'forgive' in the wake of ISIS beheadings."

twelve

You Have to Pick a Side

❋

I n Columbia, Governor Haley headed back to the governor's mansion for the night and texted her husband, who had just returned home after several weeks of National Guard training.

"I need to talk to you when we get home. I've got some things in my head, and I just need to know if I'm thinking right."

Haley had a plan, one that might cost her politically.

She already knew that she would attend each of the nine victims' funerals. She would comfort their families. She would promise to do her best to heal the state. Yet, she also had read Dylann Roof's manifesto. She'd seen the pictures he posted on his website of himself waving a Confederate flag in all their faces. The KKK and other white supremacists had hijacked the flag a long time ago. Dylann Roof didn't invent that. But he sure had magnified it with new and horrific intensity.

Haley knew very well the power of symbols and judgments of skin color. She didn't view the pictures of Roof through the same lens as other South Carolina Republicans, nearly all of whom were white. She'd grown up a brown girl in a state divided by black and white. A Republican senator once called her a "raghead." She'd become used to filling in the last bubble on questions about ethnic background: other.

Her parents hailed from Punjab, India, but had moved to a rural swath of southern South Carolina before Haley was born. They settled into a little town called Bamberg near the historically black college where her father taught biology. Like many small towns, Bamberg was bisected by train tracks that divided people by race. At first, no one would rent to her parents. Others stipulated that if they did, the Randhawas couldn't entertain African Americans in their home. And while many Bamberg residents welcomed the new family, one neighbor who babysat other people's children refused to watch the Randhawas' kids.

Her mother, Raj, still wore colorful saris as the family settled in. Her father, Ajit, wore the traditional turban of their Sikh faith. Wherever they went, they stood out, a curiosity. When her father entered a restaurant or store, people pointed and whispered. Kids teased Haley and her siblings. It saddened her that people saw the oddity of her father's turban over his gentleness and intellect.

In third grade, other kids bullied Haley badly enough that her father went to talk with the teacher. Her mother spoke to the class—about India, about their traditions, about why men wore turbans and women wore saris, about what it meant to come from another country to a little town like Bamberg. She also brought Indian snacks. With a better understanding of this new family, the kids began to treat them differently. Some who'd harassed Haley the worst became her good friends.

Over those years, Haley also had learned to fit into places where she stuck out, a skill that would prove useful in politics. As she weighed her next steps en route to the governor's mansion, she remembered being a little girl at recess years ago. When she reached her school's kickball field, she asked to play only to discover the girls in her class had divided up for teams by race.

"You have to pick a side. Are you white, or are you black?" a girl holding the ball asked.

The young Haley's stomach had clenched. She'd always managed to avoid picking sides in the distinct lines between races in rural South Carolina in the 1970s when school desegregation was a strange new thing. What should she say?

She decided to change the subject.

"I'm neither," she said. "I'm brown!" Haley grabbed the ball and ran for the field. Soon, the girls were all playing together. But questions about her identity, and her racial allegiance, would continue to surround her even after she became governor.

Mulling Roof's photographs as she headed home, Haley also remembered the day during her first gubernatorial race when she realized why her father often stood in the back at her campaign events. He did not want people's racist notions about his appearance to hurt her chances of success. Now, a white man had killed nine black people, all kind and faithful churchgoers, simply because of what he saw: darker skin.

Haley and her husband stayed up late talking through her idea. She hadn't taken a strong stand on the Confederate flag before, instead mostly deflecting questions back to the contentious 2000 compromise that had moved it from the State House dome to the flagpole out front. During an election debate the previous fall, she'd dismissed her Democratic rival's call to remove it.

"What I can tell you is over the last three and a half years, I spent a lot of my days on the phones with CEOs and recruiting jobs to this state," Haley said at the time. "I can honestly say I have not had one conversation with a single CEO about the Confederate flag."

Dylann Roof had just changed that. It suddenly became much harder to argue that the flag represented southern heritage when a white supremacist who killed nine black people clearly thought it represented something else. As she and her husband spoke, the governor's office inbox swelled with emails from around the country urging her to remove the "Southern Cross."

"The world is watching," one person wrote.

Could South Carolina, birthplace of the Civil War, once home to the nation's largest slave port, lead the nation in racial healing? As Haley's staff fielded endless calls and watched TV trucks encircle the Capitol, she felt certain that it could.

Her husband, Michael, agreed. But it would be risky.

As details of the massacre and Roof's racist beliefs spread, most South Carolinians unified behind a common revulsion at what he had done and the vitriol he'd spewed. The deluge of emails pouring into the governor's office came from as far away as Alaska and Hawaii, and the phones rang nonstop. Mail arrived by boxloads filled mostly with correspondence urging Haley to remove the flag. One Louisiana woman emailed, "I am a Caucasian daughter of a Klansman! I KNOW what that flag means to white supremacists and to be honest, so do you. Stop the charade. Take it down NOW."

Some writers who wanted the flag gone even accused Haley of being complicit in the killings given her lack of leadership in trying to move it before nine black people lay dead. "Perhaps you should reflect on the ugly implications of flying the Confederate flag in the state capital," a California woman wrote. "What a disgusting, nasty government you head up."

Of course, not everyone wanted the flag removed. Vocal groups still insisted that it represented their heritage and the 260,000 Confederates, or more, lost in the Civil War. Many invoked their own loved ones who died fighting what they considered northern invaders. The issue was deeply personal to them and their families. "Go ahead and take the Confederate Flag down . . . because that will make White people Hate Blacks that much more," a North Carolinian wrote to Haley.

But as Haley, the nation's youngest governor, pondered what to do, she knew that she could flex considerable political muscle in South Carolina. She'd won her second election by almost fifteen points. National news outlets had dubbed her the face of the "New South," a female minority who in her first inaugural address had recognized "the horrors of slavery and discrimination" while noting how much the state had changed for the better. She'd since successfully portrayed herself as an outsider even while voting along predictably conservative party lines.

Presidential candidate Mitt Romney had considered her as a running mate in the 2012 campaign, although she'd declined that in order to fill out her first term. Now six months into her second one, she'd gained political steam voting reliably pro-business, anti-regulation, and anti-tax, cementing her status as a dedicated Tea Party Republican. She rejected the Obamacare Medicaid expansion and supported increased enforcement of immigration laws. She also signed a bill that required voters at the polls to present a photo ID such as a driver's license, even though some argued it would disproportionately affect low-income and black voters. She might have felt like a brown girl growing up among black and white children, but as an adult she clearly identified more with white politics than black ones.

However, Haley also irritated her fellow Republican lawmakers, who didn't always see her as a team player. When she clashed with state House members over road funding reform, she called them out publicly on Facebook. "Your Republican House just voted to raise your taxes by $365 million next year," she posted—with a link to their individual votes.

However, Haley also possessed an uncanny knack for sensing political winds and knowing how to steer them. With nine emotional funerals ahead, she knew she needed to harness the goodwill flowing from every corner of the state. She also needed to defuse activists outside of South Carolina who were heading to Charleston to stir dissent. She couldn't wait to act on the flag until January, when the General Assembly met again.

She also couldn't remove it unilaterally.

When lawmakers lowered the flag from atop the State House dome to fly it in front of the building in 2000, they purposely made it very hard to move any farther. As part of that compromise, they passed legislation requiring a two-thirds vote of both legislative chambers to do so. That legislation, the Heritage Act, referred to the Civil War as the "War Between the States," and its provisions meant that Haley would have to rally those from rural districts where the flag flew as a sacred emblem of southern pride.

Six months earlier, in November 2014, the Winthrop Poll conducted one of its periodic surveys asking people if they favored flying the flag over the Confederate memorial on the State House grounds. In all, 65 percent did. Not surprisingly, that number diverged steeply by race. About 77 percent of whites supported it flying; 69 percent of African Americans opposed it.

But that was before the massacre. As Charlestonians held hands across the bridge on Sunday, Haley summoned her key staff.

By the next morning, they had organized four meetings at her office in the State House: one with Democrats, one with key Republican leaders, one with civic leaders, and one with South Carolina's federal delegation. None of those who arrived knew why she'd summoned them, although most could guess. It seemed everyone was talking about the flag, its meaning, and its future.

Her staff sent out a press alert. Haley would deliver remarks at 4 p.m. It did not specify the topic, so as she held the meetings, speculation built. At each, she followed a basic script seeking to rally support for her plan—and temper opposition certain to erupt against it. "If you would stand with me, I would be forever grateful. And if you choose not to stand with me, I hold no ill will, and I respect you, and I will never let anybody know that you were in this room."

She assured the public officials that her goal wasn't to erase history. In a state rife with Confederate monuments, she wouldn't try to remove every reference to the war in every corner of South Carolina. But the flag was different. It flew in the wind like a living thing, a breathing symbol of the worst of their shared history. And that wasn't right. All children, she insisted, should feel welcome on the State House grounds, no matter their skin color.

Her last meeting, with the federal delegation, ended barely an hour before her press conference would begin.

Many people assumed the Confederate flag had cast its shadow over the State House grounds since the Civil War era. In fact, it had flown there for just fifty-four years when Dylann Roof sat down to type up his manifesto: "Segregation was not a bad thing. It was a defensive measure."

Officials had raised the flag on the State House grounds in April of 1961, ostensibly as part of Civil War centennial celebrations. Yet, it also happened to be the year that the Freedom Riders, a band of civil rights activists, set out to challenge segregation in southern states, including South Carolina. In those days, Charleston's city directory still listed "colored" people in a separate index behind white residents, and its public schools remained segregated.

A state lawmaker named John Amasa May, a white World War II veteran, led the push to fly the flag, temporarily at first, then to raise it atop the dome for good the next year. Known as "Mr. Confederate," he sometimes wore a rebel uniform on the State House floor and headed a commission overseeing the Civil War's big one hundredth anniversary.

May initially asked that the flag fly to honor activities in Charleston, which was a host city of key celebration events given its significance in the war. The move didn't draw much attention at the time, at least not in the local newspapers, even though it came just months after an incident known as the "Friendship Nine," when a group of black students from a junior college in the upper part of South Carolina were jailed for sitting at a whites-only lunch counter.

Six months after the centennial, May insisted to the South Carolina Division of the United Daughters of the Confederacy in Charleston that slaveholders weren't cruel to the humans they held in bondage: "The people of the South took care of their negroes," he told the group. "The feeling was one of mutual respect of one race for another."

Over the ensuing decades, however, voices rose against the flag's presence on government grounds. It was deemed a racist symbol by many who paid the salaries of the people inside. The dispute culminated with the 2000 compromise. Even after that, however, many remained deeply offended by the flag's continued presence. The NAACP launched an economic boycott of South Carolina. The National Collegiate Athletic Association (NCAA) banned key sporting events.

Nonetheless, white Republicans melded into a political brick wall against any further effort to banish the flag. When Roof walked into Mother Emanuel, its presence in front of the State House still reminded black residents of who controlled the halls of power inside.

A s Haley's 4 p.m. press conference approached, reporters set up camp outside the State House building, a massive light gray stone structure with forty-three-foot Corinthian columns. The red flag with the big blue X filled with white stars stirred beyond them in the hot afternoon breeze.

Haley waited tensely in her office. Her husband joined her. So did her closest staff.

Voices of arrivals echoed over the marble-lined west wing hallway outside of her office. She emerged to greet the state's two Republican U.S. senators: Lindsey Graham, a white man, and Tim Scott, the first African American to win statewide elected office in South Carolina since Reconstruction (and whom Haley first appointed to the Senate seat). The governor knew both men well and felt confident they would show up They joined white Republican congressmen Tom Rice and Mark Sanford, a former governor and early mentor of Haley's, along with Congressman Jim Clyburn, a senior black Democrat whose policies she frequently opposed.

Dozens of state lawmakers showed up, too—a good sign, but not a sure one. Who else would be waiting when they moved upstairs to the press conference?

Normally, Haley held these events in the first-floor lobby outside of her office, but this one would be held on the floor above in a larger, grander space that connected the state House and Senate chambers. As the group gathered in the west wing headed upstairs, Haley lingered with her husband and a few aides, along with Graham, Scott, and Clyburn. They ventured to a private room to await the moment when they would make their entrance into the press conference. Haley, in a tweed pale peach suit, looked for a moment unto herself. Arms crossed tightly over her chest, she bowed her head, lips pressed into a firm line. The group stood stone-faced. Clyburn took a call. Scott and Graham exchanged a glance.

The clock ticked. Tension swelled. Just how would all of this be received?

As 4 o'clock approached, it became clear that most of South Carolina's Congressional delegation, an almost all-white and conservative Republican lot with whom she shared much political ideology, wouldn't come. No-shows included Trey Gowdy, Jeff Duncan, Joe Wilson, and Mick Mulvaney. The next day, Mulvaney would release a statement essentially calling his absence a mistake. Also noticeably absent was Henry McMaster, the state's Republican lieutenant governor and former party leader, an early Donald Trump supporter and longtime flag defender who would become the state's next governor.

Stained glass adorned the room between the two legislative bodies, a large open space with paintings of renowned war battles, busts of famous South Carolinians, and a marble representation of the Ordinance of Secession. As Haley followed the men with her into the lobby, she saw that it was filled and overflowing up twin staircases leading to the balconies.

She felt every eye in the room land on her as the crowd quieted to a murmur. Journalists—locals and national press alike—formed a thick U-shape around a wooden lectern front and center, behind which lawmakers stood two and three deep in a long row. Notable surprises in the crowd included a handful of Republicans from particularly conservative districts, and state senator Paul Thurmond, son of the late longtime U.S. senator Strom Thurmond. A one-time segregationist, the elder Thurmond had fathered a child with his family's teenaged black maid and kept it secret for seventy-eight years.

Haley stepped stern-faced to the microphone, eyes darting over the crowd. Two black men, Scott and Clyburn, stood on either side of her. Reince Priebus, Republican National Committee chairman, stood over her right shoulder. Charleston mayor Joseph Riley Jr. and black Democrats who had spent decades fighting for this moment joined them, facing the crowd, in this very unusual mix of support.

"Alright," Haley began crisply.

Reading from a prepared text, her voice emerged in its usual tone, practiced and businesslike.

"This has been a very difficult time for our state. We have stared evil in the eye and watched good, prayerful people killed in one of the most sacred of places. We were hurt and broken, and we needed to heal. We were able to start that process not by talking about issues that divide us but by holding vigils, by hugging our neighbors, by honoring those we lost, and by falling to our knees in prayer. Our state is grieving."

She described Emanuel's re-opening, which she had attended with her family, and the grieving families' words to Dylann Roof.

"Their expression of faith and forgiveness took our breath away."

She praised the people of South Carolina for their calm after Walter Scott's shooting death. People didn't riot or harm each other. Instead lawmakers, black and white, passed the country's first body camera bill for police officers. The state had changed considerably in recent years. Yet, bigotry remained. Nobody needed reminders of that. And those who honored the Confederate flag had every right to fly it on their private properties. It would always be part of South Carolina's air and soil.

"But the State House is different," she added. "And the events of this past week call upon us to look at this in a different way."

Then she said it:

"It is time to remove the flag from the Capitol grounds."

A burst of cheers interrupted her, and she halted, glancing around. For the first time in days, Haley let herself smile. The cheers continued until she held up a hand to quiet the crowd.

"My hope is that by removing a symbol that divides us, we can move our state forward as a state in harmony, and we can honor the nine blessed souls who are now in heaven."

The General Assembly, she noted, would wrap up its work that week. However, she had the power to call them back under extraordinary circumstances. If lawmakers didn't ensure a debate about the flag took place that summer, she would do so. Who would dispute these were extraordinary circumstances?

As she left the lectern, Haley first turned to her right to hug the seventy-five-year-old Jim Clyburn, who had been the first black man elected to represent South Carolina in Congress since 1897. Next, she hugged Tim Scott, a black Republican and a fellow rising star, who grinned widely.

thirteen

A Restless Peace

✵

After Haley's press conference, as the victims' families prepared for funerals, pro-flag voices assailed the governor in response to her call. Emails—thousands of them—flooded her inbox. Many offered respectfully worded defenses of the flag's role in battlefield history. But others accused Haley of betrayal. They linked her actions to her Indian heritage and her purported exotic faith, though Haley was a Christian and her parents were Sikh, and not Hindu, as many seemed to think.

Regardless, their message was clear: Nikki Haley wasn't white enough, southern enough, or Christian enough to understand the flag's proper place in South Carolina.

"The fact that someone like you can be born to 1st generation immigrants who came to this country from a 3rd World hell hole, only to have their daughter take a steaming dump on the ancestors of the residents of her new host country is truly pathetic," someone from Georgia wrote to her.

Haley, a big Facebook user, until then often read the comments to her posts about family and positive happenings in the state—groundbreakings, sports team wins, upcoming events. The tone of her opponents now turned downright offensive.

"You suck!!!" one person posted on her page. "Go back to your home land and mess with their Heritage!!! You let the State Down just so you could gain popularity in the eyes of the country. Get on your magic carpet put on your turbin and fly the hell out of SC, because you will never get a vote for office from us!!!!"

And another:

YOU ARE THE BIGGEST DISCRACE TO THE SOUTHERN PEOPLE AND OUR HERITAGE!!!!! AS YOU SIGNED FOR THE CONFEDERATE BATTLE FLAG TO BE TAKEN DOWN YOU MAD ME SICK!!! YOU WILL NEVER UNDERSTAND YOU HAVE NO CONFEDERATE ROOTS!!!! YOU ARE A DISGRACE . . .

However, an even more powerful tide of public support had her back. Key business leaders, from Michelin to Boeing, also endorsed moving the flag to the nearby Confederate Relic Room and Military Museum. The chairman of a major utility sought support from other leaders and ran full-page newspaper ads. Advocacy groups delivered more than a half-million signatures calling for the flag's removal. Amazon, Walmart, eBay, and Etsy all announced they'd no longer sell Confederate flag items.

Amid a presidential primary, Haley's national star flared more brightly than ever. Reporters jostled to ask: Was she being vetted as a vice presidential candidate?

Despite the support, however, Haley harbored a nagging fear. South Carolina wasn't Seattle or California. She knew all too well that the state's last Republican governor who supported moving the flag had lost his job in the next election.

Exactly two weeks after Haley's press conference, after the nine funerals, the General Assembly got to work addressing the flag. State lawmakers in both chambers introduced bills to remove it from the flagpole in front of the building where they now arrived to face an emotional debate that would pin each one down to a yes-or-no vote.

On the floor above Haley's office, a black cloth draped over an empty desk in the elegant Senate. The chamber where Clementa Pinckney had served for fifteen years came to order. Beneath framed portraits of the state's most historic senators, the sitting members began to lay out familiar, long-held views of the symbol flying outside. Most agreed that the Confederate flag represented a critical piece of South Carolina's history.

But they disagreed over just what that history represented. Honor and bravery? Or slavery and oppression?

Vincent Sheheen, a white Democrat whose seat was right beside Clementa's empty desk, began the debate. He had pushed to lower the flag for years and had introduced the current bill to lower it. "This is not about heritage. It's not about hate. It's about healing wounds that go back many years," he implored. For him and others who had served alongside Clementa, lowering the flag offered a way to set legislative flowers onto the grave of their fallen colleague.

On the other side of the debate, the high-profile Senate majority leader Harvey Peeler disagreed: "To remove the flag from the State House grounds and thinking it would change history would be like removing a tattoo from the corpse of a loved one and thinking that would change a loved one's obituary."

Republican Lee Bright, who displayed the flag in his Senate office, likened its potential removal to a "Stalinist purge." After all, the flag in question wasn't *the* flag of the Confederate States of America's government. This flag was the popular military flag carried into battle. To many white South Carolinians, it represented the bravery of men who fought and died more than it made any political statement about slave ownership.

Nonetheless, nearly all of the senators gathered agreed that it needed to come down at long last, though not because they all suddenly viewed its history through a new lens. Instead, many recognized that the flag's symbolic meaning had been hijacked by racists like Dylann Roof—and that its presence was causing tremendous pain to people like Jennifer Pinckney, who listened to their debate in a room off to one side of the chamber.

Senator Larry Martin, a longtime flag supporter, said he'd changed his views since the shooting that left Clementa dead. People needed to be honest about history. Although the flag was hoisted for the Civil War's centennial, it had remained flying to oppose civil rights, including school integration. Martin, a white Republican, remembered how people he knew had lamented forced racial equality back then. "It wasn't pretty. You couldn't repeat it today, what was being said then about the fact that we were going to be going to school with black children." '

It was time, now, to recognize what the flag had come to represent. "It isn't part of our future," Martin added. "It's part of our past."

As Jennifer watched the proceedings on a large TV, nervous anxiety rattled her, though not due to the vote. She had faith that Clementa's colleagues ultimately would agree to lower it. Instead, she felt wholly out of place near the grand chamber now watched by thousands of people. For all their years together, Clementa had been the public one in their family. She preferred the background, raising their daughters and going about her life's work as a school librarian in quieter ways, as she fully intended to keep doing. To survive, Jennifer had to shut out the rest. She hadn't gone to Roof's bond hearing and had dodged most news coverage of the shooting to avoid hearing details about what happened to her husband. She had never wanted to be on display, and never less so than now. But she would step out of this room and stand before his Senate colleagues. She would remind them of what they had all just lost and thank them for their stand on the flag. She would do this for Clementa.

The vote was nearly unanimous; thirty-seven of the forty senators present voted to bring down the flag. Five were absent. The three who'd voted against it—Peeler, Bright, and Danny Verdin—were all Republicans from the upper part of the state, a particular stronghold of white tradition-minded voters.

Their vote meant Jennifer's time had come. She quietly left the side room and entered the chamber with her husband's close friend Kylon Middleton, the pastor she'd called the night Clementa died. The two-story room hushed as she entered. She hadn't appeared publicly since Clementa's funeral. Now, in a simple black dress, curly shoulder-length hair pulled back, she faced the senators who had just voted to do what she would have thought impossible just weeks ago. They all rose to their feet in a standing ovation. Jennifer stared at the carpet as they clapped.

Kylon placed his hand on her back, a note of reassurance.

Ahead, Senator Gerald Malloy, a black Democrat who was Clementa's friend and attorney, who would become Jennifer's attorney and front line of defense in the coming months, stepped to a lectern up front. He looked directly at Jennifer with the steel that would cocoon her and her daughters. She couldn't force her eyes to look up, not yet.

"This state loved Senator Pinckney," he said. She heard a rare crack in his strong voice. "And this state loves you and your girls. And they loved the entire Pinckney family. We will keep our arms around you and this family forever. It's the least that we can do for our brother, Clementa."

For Clementa. Those words sank in, and Jennifer looked up at him then. She nodded her thanks.

The senators, a group of nearly all middle-aged and older white men, soon formed a long line leading to her. One by one, Clementa's allies and political thorns alike approached.

As the Senate voted, furor over the flag boomeranged around the nation, and people debated whether to bring down other Confederate symbols. Five hundred miles up the coast in Washington, D.C., the Republican House Speaker prepared to call for a review of them, including those displayed in the Capitol. Lawmakers in Mississippi demanded changes to their flag, which incorporated a Confederate flag saltire in its design. Then came a fight to protect the sale and displays of Confederate flags at national parks and cemeteries.

Back in South Carolina, the flag debate moved from the Senate to the more raucous House chamber. Although a state journalists' survey of lawmakers showed enough votes to garner the two-thirds supermajority needed to lower the flag, its fate in the House of Representatives, a vastly white and male lot, loomed much more uncertain than in the Senate. Several House members and their constituents had been pushing back hard since Haley's press conference. The House, a GOP stronghold, marked their final stand.

At least twenty amendments to the flag bill already waited on the clerk's desk. One proposed placing the state flower, yellow jessamine, where the flag now flew outside. Another sought to move it to a bronze case beside the spot. Another proposed putting the entire issue to a public vote.

Inside the chamber, historic portraits ringed the walls, including the likenesses of John Calhoun and of Confederate general Robert E. Lee, widely

revered across the South as a gentleman warrior although he himself opposed war monuments so as to "not keep open the sores of war." Most people
didn't know that, however, nor had they read the stories of Lee's former
slave Wesley Norris, who'd once recounted an especially horrific whipping
he received under the general's watchful eye.

The chamber filled with nearly all of its 124 members. Charleston's
delegation came forward first, surrounding Wendell Gilliard, a black
Democrat who'd been friends with Clementa Pinckney and had gone to
the church the night of the shooting. Emanuel was in his district. He began
by reading the names of all nine victims and speaking of grace and forgiveness.

"So, what do we do now?" he asked. "The scales have been shed from
all of our eyes. The blindness that was our affliction that prevented us from
seeing that which divided us has been lifted, and we now see what needs to
be done. The right thing to do is what we call 'the healing thing,' the gentle laying down of the past and a hopeful road to the future."

Members stood to applaud, some out of respect for those killed, others
to show support for lowering the flag.

Representative Michael Pitts, the House's point man on flag defense,
stood next to speak. The retired police officer and ardent gun-rights defender had filed many of the amendments to derail the flag bill. Normally
an unabashedly outspoken member, he began in gentle tones.

"Folks from Charleston, I feel your grief," he began.

He remembered Clementa Pinckney's smile and described him as a gentleman. He thanked Emanuel members for showing the world Christian
love and forgiveness in the face of evil. He thanked the state's residents for
not rioting.

Pitts, a bald man in a taupe suit, then turned to history, or his view of
history. He recalled growing up playing with a Confederate ancestor's cav-
alry sword and waving the flag as a show of honor. His kin were proud,
self-sufficient Appalachian Mountain folk. To them, and to him, the flag
represented scrappy southern farmers who defended their property against
invading Yankees. His ancestors had grabbed their squirrel rifles and gone
to fight a war to protect their families. The flag didn't represent slavery or
anything negative about black residents, he argued. It conjured memories

of his grandmother reading him letters that his great uncles had sent home from the war.

"Some call it the War Between the States. Some call it the Civil War. Growing up in my family, it was called the 'War of Northern Aggression.' It's where the Yankees attacked the South, and that's what was ingrained in me growing up," he explained. Pitts conceded that slavery was a key reason for the Civil War—but so, he argued, was defending states' rights against an overreaching federal government.

After he sat down, black representatives took turns describing in emotional terms how even before the Emanuel massacre, the flag had long represented something very different to them: slavery and its legacy of ingrained racism. Yet, despite their pleas, a core group led by Pitts wouldn't budge. Dissent built. Momentum waned. Exhaustion crept in.

From the first floor of the State House, Haley watched it all on a TV at her desk. After three hours, the House took a break. Her fellow Republicans headed for another building nearby, to gather. She decided to join them— and share a story.

The House Republicans met where they often gathered during breaks and to eat meals. Inside the air conditioning, away from the press and public, they sat along rows of cafeteria-style tables beneath fluorescent lights. Out of seventy-seven Republican House members, just ten were women. Only one was African American.

Haley quickly stepped up front and began to talk. She wanted to tell them about a time when, as a little girl, she'd ridden with her father from their tiny hometown of Bamberg to the place where they now sat, the state capital. As always, her father wore the distinctive turban of his Sikh faith. As always, it drew stares. On the way home from Columbia that day, they'd stopped at a farmer's vegetable stand along a roadside.

As her dad began filling a basket with produce, Haley noticed a commotion at the cash register. The stand's owner and his wife gestured nervously at each other, and then the husband picked up the phone and placed a call. Minutes later, two police cars pulled in. The officers who emerged walked over to the owners and exchanged words, then looked at her father.

For his part, Ajit didn't acknowledge the commotion. Having finished his shopping, he strolled over, shook the owner's hand, said hello, and paid for his produce.

He then thanked them and quietly walked past the police. So did little Nikki Randhawa.

On the forty-five-minute ride home, her father didn't say a word. He'd later tell her he hoped she hadn't seen it. But she had. And she understood.

"I knew why they were there. My dad knew why they were there," Haley explained to the seventy or so Republican caucus members listening to her. She didn't use the words "racial profiling," but everyone knew what she meant.

As she spoke, a few grumbled. Pitts stood in back, arms crossed.

Haley knew that some of the House members didn't like her much to begin with. Before being elected governor, she was one of them—one who tended to buck the leadership until making a surprise bid for governor, to the dismay of members who'd given many more years of legislative sweat to the voters of South Carolina. Many supported her Tea Party views but found her self-serving. They didn't trust her to have their backs.

Nikki Haley was, to them, only out for Nikki Haley. And more than a few resented how in their view, as an attractive female minority, she could garner a whole lot more attention than the sea of white men who filled the seats.

Haley persisted to the point of her story. The produce stand, she explained, was still there. She saw it whenever she drove to the airport. "Every time I pass that produce stand, I think of that girl who loved her dad," she said. Her voice trembled. Tears stung her eyes.

South Carolina was better now. There was no more Miss Black Bamberg and Miss White Bamberg, and children no longer could be disqualified from the pageant for being brown, as happened to Haley and her sister when they were little. But every time she passed by the stand, even today, she still felt pain. Such are symbols and what they represent. She reminded those gathered that the State House belonged to everybody and that no child should ever drive by it and feel unwelcome.

Her voice rang firm again: "It should be one spot of unity."

She reminded them of the "Emanuel Nine," of their faith and grace. She

asked the caucus to honor those who died and to fly the Confederate flag
on their private properties, if they felt it represented the courage of their
ancestors.

"My prayer and hope is that when we all walk out of this building, we
walk out with a clean heart," she added.

Some felt moved by Haley's story. But not everyone. Pitts later told a reporter that he had taken out his hearing aids while she spoke. Others
thought her speech was unnecessary. Many already knew they would, eventually, vote to take the flag down. They didn't need her lecturing them or
claiming credit for it.

After the recess, they began to debate amendments again.

Pitts continued to file more and more of them in what the House minority leader soon dubbed a "filibuster by amendment."

As he did so, Representative Joe Neal rose to speak. A long-serving member and a black pastor, Neal was a close friend of Clementa Pinckney's and
had brought the senator's older daughter to the Embassy Suites the night of
the shooting. He called the flag "a thumb in the eye" of those in Charleston
who had lost loved ones. He also had a message for Pitts.

"I understand you loving and supporting your heritage. But grace means
that you ought to also love and support mine. It's not a one-way street. My
heritage is based on a group of people who were brought here in chains,
who were denigrated, demagogued, lynched and killed. Denied the right
to vote. Denied the right to even have a family," he implored.

Yet, the amendments kept coming. The sun set. Business hours ended.
Emotions boiled. And the chamber still lacked the votes to pass a clean bill.
Finally, after listening to sixty-seven amendments, a white Republican from
a town near Charleston got fed up. Really fed up.

Jenny Horne stepped forward. She'd had it. She stood before the microphone and unleashed a four-minute torrent of fury and tears over the
chamber's inability to act.

"I cannot believe that we do not have the heart in this body to do something meaningful, such as take a symbol of hate off these grounds on Friday!" she hollered at her colleagues. "If any of you vote to amend, you are
ensuring that this flag will fly beyond Friday. And for the widow of Senator

Pinckney and his two young daughters, that would be adding insult to injury. And I will not be a part of it! If we amend this bill, we are telling the people of Charleston, 'We don't care about you. We do not care that somebody used this symbol of hate to slay innocent people who were worshipping their God!'"

A blonde woman in a pink suit and pearls, she added: "I have heard enough about heritage."

To some lawmakers, Horne's tirade was too much, over-the-top grandstanding. However, news outlets and social media cast her words across the globe. Video of her speech went viral. People responded to her passion, and Horne became a key face of the debate to those watching across the nation.

Pitts, who had introduced most of the nearly seventy amendments at issue, felt the tide shift. As his amendments failed, he complained that he felt like Robert E. Lee at Appomattox, where the Confederate general surrendered his army.

Midnight approached. Yet, House members refused to adjourn without completing their task. Nearly thirteen hours had passed. Finally, just after 1 a.m., they cast three historic votes. The final tally: 94 to 20 ordering the permanent removal of the flag to the nearby Confederate Relic Room and Military Museum.

Haley had five days to sign it. She took fifteen hours.

Just after 4 p.m. the next day, a crowd gathered in the State House lobby again, this time to watch the signing ceremony. The two previous governors who had tried to remove the flag but failed stood behind her grinning. So did black lawmakers and loved ones of those killed in Emanuel. Outside, people crowded the steps of the State House where the rebel banner barely stirred in the relentless heat.

"She's signing the bill!" a woman screamed.

A black pastor took off from the steps, hollering: "Hallelujah! Hallelujah!"

The crowd clapped and cheered and sang, sweat dripping down their faces. They waved American flags. Car horns honked from the busy street beyond.

The Confederate flag came down at 10 a.m. the next morning.

Three weeks after a racist white gunman walked into Emanuel, a

Highway Patrol Honor Guard wearing crisp gray uniforms slipped the banner down from its pole and folded it twice, a book closing, its final chapter read. They then rolled it up like a scroll and tied a ribbon around it. An African American trooper wearing white gloves carried it away to be placed in the Confederate museum.

"Free at last, free at last," one woman bellowed. "Thank God almighty, we're free at last!"

Beyond notice of cameras, Felicia and Polly joined the crowd along with other families of the nine people whose deaths made this moment possible. In all, about 10,000 joyful people formed a thick ring around the State House to witness the moment. Thousands more watched on TVs across the nation. A few protesters came. Handfuls of Confederate flag supporters watched in solemn defeat, though the masses cheered the jubilee.

Yet, beneath the celebration, tension still simmered. The flag was an important symbol—but ultimately only a symbol. Wounds of racism remained. Resentments lingered. As the Reverend Joseph Darby, an AME presiding elder and NAACP leader from Charleston, noted dryly to himself: "All it took was the deaths of nine black people."

fourteen

The World Has Come

✳

As the people of South Carolina fought about the flag, and the nine families quietly planned funerals, their words of forgiveness continued to touch hearts across the nation, even reaching inside the White House. President Obama summoned his close aide, Valerie Jarrett. Would she reach out to Reverend Pinckney's widow? Obama had known the pastor, though not well, and wanted to eulogize the man. He also had a few things to say about racist gun violence in a black church.

Jarrett called Jennifer Pinckney.

Would she be interested in the president eulogizing her husband?

"I would be honored," Jennifer replied.

Over the next few days, President Obama talked with his wife and close staff about what he wanted to say. He'd given far too many eulogies already for victims of gun violence. Three months after he was sworn in, a man killed thirteen people at an immigration center in New York. Then an Army psychiatrist gunned down thirteen people at Fort Hood, Texas. A year later, a shooter opened fire at an Arizona supermarket, killing six. Then a man killed twelve in a Colorado movie theater. Another gunned down twenty first-graders and six adults in Connecticut.

A nonstop parade of death and grief.

Obama wanted to honor Clementa Pinckney and all that he stood for. He also wanted to applaud the family members' words of forgiveness and mercy. He wanted to honor Emanuel's open-door policy. Emanuel, like the country, couldn't wall itself off in the face of terror. He wanted to address gun violence. And he wanted to talk about race in America.

Could one eulogy do all of that?

Clementa Pinckney's funeral would take place in the College of Charleston's TD Arena, the college's basketball and volleyball venue, located just a few blocks away from Emanuel. The service would provide yet another large-scale opportunity for Charleston residents—black and white, churchgoing and not—to mourn together. Many of the 5,400 seats had been reserved for victims' families, VIPs, church members, and clergy and their spouses. The remainder would be first-come, first-served. So people lined up early. The smartest among them brought umbrellas to block the already scorching summer sun.

The first arrived at 3:30 a.m., and by sunrise, a thick line stretched from the front door of the arena, down Meeting Street, and past Marion Square—a full three blocks. Pastors in white collars and ladies in feathered hats stood among a decidedly more casual set, young and old, black and white, united in their desire to pay respects and to hear the nation's first black president.

Charlestonians, celebrated for their politeness, at first merely glanced askance when they noticed interlopers slipping in front of them in line. But as the clock ticked and the crowd bloomed, people began to worry that they might not get inside. Tempers rose with the heat index—which soon topped 100 degrees—as shuttle buses began to deposit people at the front of the line. An elderly black man, unable to tolerate the heat and the crowd, collapsed and was taken away on a stretcher.

A few doors down at Emanuel, members had gathered to prepare for the funeral beyond the glaring heat. Suddenly, a sea of them streamed out of their church home with hundreds of AME clergy following in support as they flowed down Calhoun Street, turned onto Meeting, and entered the arena.

At 10:40 a.m., word spread among those still waiting to get inside: The building's nearly 6,000 seats were full. Police tried to shut the front entrance gates. A frustrated mass pressed forward.

"Get back!" an officer hollered.

As they did, a black woman up front wearing her Sunday best collapsed onto the sidewalk, overcome by the heat, sobbing. A passerby poured cold water over her shoulders until paramedics gently whisked her away, too.

Arrivals received a funeral program that showed pictures of Clementa and his family, plus two short poems composed by his daughters that made many in the audience tear up even before the service began.

The older, Eliana, had written:

> When someone loves you they care
> Even if they are not there
> They motivate you to prosper and believe
> In any of your dreams.

Malana wrote:

> I know you were shot at the Church
> and you went to Heaven.
> I love you so much!
> I know you love me
> and I know that you know that I love you too.

She signed it with her nicknames, "Your baby girl and grasshopper."

Jennifer Pinckney added her own raw expression of grief. "You promised me you would never leave me! You promised me we would be together for years to come! You promised me we would watch our children grow, get married and have children of their own. You promised me that we would grow old together and spend our latter years without the demands of the Church or the State. I feel robbed, cheated, and cut short."

People arrived to see Clementa's coffin, covered in a heap of red roses, beneath a podium and atop a large, raised stage. Onstage, the Reverend

Norvel Goff and Bishop Richard Franklin Norris, whose district spanned
South Carolina, joined rows of other AME Church leaders, all bedecked in
the church's regal purple and black. A row of flags stood behind them, a
purple-draped lectern at the center. Clementa's favorite color.

Goff stepped to the microphone. "I want you to know the world has
come to you."

As Goff began to speak, Air Force One made its final descent toward Joint
Base Charleston, home to Air Force and Navy operations. President
Obama conferred with his wife, Michelle, about the eulogy he would de-
liver shortly. He had an idea and wondered what she thought.

"I bet if I sing, people will join in," he ventured.

Michelle encouraged him—but only if it felt right in the moment.

Once they landed, already two hours into the lengthy funeral, their car
rushed toward the TD Arena, about twenty minutes away. After arriving,
they emerged through a door to the right of the stage. The Obamas followed
Jennifer, grim-faced and flanked by her little girls. She wore all black with
a concise flowered hat tilted over her eyes.

The arena erupted in applause, drowning out the robust choir. President Obama stopped at his seat, clapping with the music despite a firm
downward turn of his lips. Across the aisle, Malana sat on the edge of her
seat wearing a white dress, a pink sweater, and a look of curiosity. To the
president's right sat the first lady, Vice President Joe Biden and his wife,
Mayor Riley, Hillary Clinton, Governor Haley, Senators Graham and Scott,
other dignitaries and spouses. Secret Service watched carefully from behind
them.

The funeral had been going on for hours by the time the president,
wearing a dark suit, stepped to the podium. From a young age, he began,
people knew Clementa Pinckney was special.

"He was in the pulpit by thirteen, pastor by eighteen, public servant by
twenty-three. He did not exhibit any of the cockiness of youth nor youth's
insecurities."

Instead, Clementa served his church, and died with his devoted members.

"Good people. Decent people. God-fearing people."

"*Yes!*"

"People who ran the race."

"*Yes!*"

Obama wondered aloud if the killer had known the special place of the black church in American history. Surely he knew his act drew on a long history of violence—fire bombs, lynching, arson—aimed at terrorizing a race of people. Surely he knew it would deepen divisions that traced back to slavery, "our nation's original sin."

Obama applauded Governor Haley's call to lower the Confederate flag. And he urged the grieving nation to plumb the causes of racism and hate. It wouldn't happen overnight.

"Every time something like this happens, somebody says we have to have a conversation about race. We talk a lot about race!"

"*Alright. Alright.*"

"There's no shortcut. We don't need more talk!"

The crowd leapt to their feet, answering him with cheers. Some of them, old enough to remember those fire bombs, closed their eyes to absorb the moment. Many waved their hands high as if to reach the face of God right there. All week, Obama added, he'd been reflecting on this idea of grace. God's grace. Grace of the families. Grace that Clementa preached about. Grace in a certain hymn.

"Amazing grace!"

Again, more softly, "Amazing grace."

He paused at the podium for eight distinct seconds, glancing down at his prepared remarks.

Should he do it?

His voice emerged, hugging the words slowly.

"*Amaaaaazinggg grace . . .*"

Behind him, Goff and the bishop smiled, and the crowd roared, some clearly overwhelmed by emotion, realizing what Obama was about to do.

The president glanced around and smiled.

How sweeeeeet the sound
Thaaaaat saved a wretch like meeeee.

The organist, caught by surprise, scrambled to find the right key.

> *I once was lost*
> *But now I'm found*
> *Was blind but now I see . . .*

Now this was church, the black church, the spontaneous and musical essence of its worship. And for at least that moment, it brought together everyone in that arena, and the entire city, and even more people watching live across the country. Obama closed by celebrating the lives of nine people killed.

"Clementa Pinckney found that grace.

"Cynthia Hurd found that grace.

"Susie Jackson found that grace.

"Ethel Lance found that grace.

"DePayne Middleton Doctor found that grace.

"Tywanza Sanders found that grace.

"Daniel L. Simmons Sr. found that grace.

"Sharonda Coleman-Singleton found that grace.

"Myra Thompson found that grace."

With a wall of church leaders standing behind him, Obama concluded. "May grace now lead them home."

After the funeral ended, the Obamas met with each of the families and survivors privately.

Nadine Collier, Ethel Lance's daughter, told him of her plan to start a camp for disadvantaged kids. Survivor Polly Sheppard offered a prayer for the victims but also for Roof. Melvin Graham hugged the president for his sister, Cynthia Hurd, now gone. He and his siblings took a picture with the president and first lady. In it, President Obama's hand rested on his shoulder. Mrs. Obama held hands with his other sister, who had just been diagnosed with cancer.

Pastor Simmons' family gave the Obamas each a T-shirt with the logo of the movement they soon would launch called Hate Won't Win. A few hours later, the first couple took a picture of themselves, still in their funeral attire, holding up one of those T-shirts. The president posted it on Twitter with the words: "So inspired by the grace shown by the Simmons family and all the victims' families in Charleston."

PART II

Looking to Man for Comfort

fifteen

The Loud Silence of Death

❃

The outpouring of grief and community solidarity that followed the killings provided comfort to the families. But as is often the case when tragedies become symbols of something larger, they soon found that the collective expressions of support did not always translate into actual support when they needed it most. Many struggled with the logistics of funerals and the inevitable weight of empty houses and survivor guilt.

Felicia Sanders had hoped to hold the joint funeral service for her son Tywanza and their Aunt Susie at her beloved Emanuel, but she didn't know who to turn to for help planning it. Reverend Pinckney was dead. So was Reverend Simmons. She barely knew the remaining licensed ministers, and they were overwhelmed with running the church, fielding calls, and welcoming concerned visitors. As for Reverend Goff, the presiding elder who had taken over as interim pastor of Emanuel—he hadn't returned her phone calls since stopping by to discuss the funeral right after the shooting.

As Emanuel came unmoored, Felicia struggled to dig from beneath her own grief and shock enough to plan. A year ago, she had held her mother-in-law's funeral at the church, and there wasn't enough seating even for that service. Now, Charleston filled with mourners from around the world who packed prayer vigils and gathered in thickets in front of Emanuel. Felicia knew she needed to find overflow space—somewhere with good air conditioning given the sweltering summer heat and the number of elderly mourners who would come to honor Susie, a matriarch of the church and her family.

She preferred to find extra space in a house of God and figured that plenty of church pews sat empty on a Saturday. Grand historic houses of worship dominated the skyline all around Charleston, defining it. Three fronted the streets around Marion Square alone. One of them, a big yellow Baptist church next door, offered its space. But it had a wedding scheduled at 2 p.m. on Saturday, precisely when Felicia would hold Tywanza and Susie's funeral.

She'd have to look elsewhere.

As she often did now, she called her friend Andy Savage for help.

Andy, a criminal defense attorney, had known Felicia and her family for decades, back to when a nephew of hers got into trouble. In fact, Andy had ties to many of those just killed at Emanuel. Despite its enormous recent growth, Charleston remained a small town at heart, where longtime residents shared multiple connections to one another. It often seemed Andy knew them all one way or another, even though he didn't hail from the city. A ruddy-faced Irish Catholic, he'd worked as a New York cab driver before moving south decades earlier and establishing himself as a force to be reckoned with. He once got a jury to acquit a police officer who beat a suspect to death with his bare hands. More recently, he defended Ali al-Marri, an accused Al Qaeda sleeper agent now enjoying his freedom back home in Qatar.

But Andy wasn't just a lawyer to his clients. People came to him for help during the worst moments of their lives, cast as villains by the criminal justice system. In fact, when Felicia picked up the phone to call for help right after the shooting, he was defending Michael Slager, the white cop charged with murdering Walter Scott. He'd taken on the unpopular case—for free—because he believed deeply in due process.

He also tended to become personally connected to his clients and their families, often going beyond his legal duties to help them, and now served as attorney for three of the survivors—Polly, Felicia, and her granddaughter—as well as several victims' families, including Ethel Lance's quarreling daughters.

After hearing Felicia's needs for overflow space, Andy called Charleston's longtime mayor, Joseph Riley Jr., for suggestions. Riley had been mayor since before most people in town were born, so he too had connections just about everywhere. One of his advisers suggested Second Presbyterian, which sat right behind Emanuel. Did Andy know the Reverend Cress Darwin there?

Andy drove Felicia to meet him.

The two grand churches had stood almost back to back for two centuries, although the space between might as well have been the Atlantic Ocean itself. As in other ways, Charleston remained a city mostly segregated when it came to worship, and these two churches were no different. Felicia had grown up just blocks away yet never gone inside. It was a white church, and she was a black woman. They had their house of worship; she had hers.

Cress Darwin greeted them warmly. A former actor with crisp features and the fondue voice of a radio announcer, he too had moved to Charleston from New York, although only a decade earlier. A white man, he had come hoping to create a vibrant interracial church—work that had proven much harder than he'd imagined. Although his church sat near tightly knit black neighborhoods, including the area where Felicia grew up, they were gentrifying rapidly, and his congregation still mostly looked like him.

When Andy and Felicia arrived, he led them through a massive set of dark wooden doors into an empty sanctuary. Almost immediately after stepping inside, Felicia paused. The sanctuary was painted bright white, even the balconies, with navy blue carpet that stretched toward the altar. Above it, a huge stained glass of Jesus, arms outstretched toward her, filled the wall.

She murmured to herself, "It feels right in here. Something just feels right."

Cress grinned. "Well, it *is* right."

"I'm supposed to be here. Something about this feels so right in here . . ." she repeated, her attention drifting as she absorbed the essence of the space.

Andy explained about Tywanza and Susie's funeral and how they'd like to livestream the service to overflow crowds. Cress made it clear that he'd do whatever was necessary. "There are 900 seats in the sanctuary, 100 seats in the chapel. The fellowship hall could be standing room only. And we'll do speakers outside."

Felicia tuned back in. "Do I need to send ushers over here?"

"No, I'll make one phone call, and we'll have ushers."

"Do you need me to send water and stuff?"

"No, we're going to take care of everything," Cress assured. "Every-thing."

Now that two funerals had passed and Obama had left town after eulo-gizing Reverend Pinckney, six more victims awaited their homegoing ceremonies. The next day, librarian Cynthia Hurd's family arrived at the church where she'd worshipped her entire life. The second funeral, for Tywanza and Susie, would follow immediately. Heavy stagnant air clung to a line of people five across eager to get inside, although most would not. The crowd grew thicker where Polly Sheppard approached the tall white structure. Behind her, several hundred people gave up and began to head for Second Presbyterian to watch the funeral from overflow space there.

Polly, however, was determined to enter her church of thirty-four years, where she was a trustee. And a survivor.

She hadn't stepped foot inside since the shooting. The first funerals had spared her the difficult task. Family members of both Ethel Lance, the church's custodian, and Sharonda Coleman-Singleton, a high school track coach and mother of three, had held their funerals at other churches. Clem-enta Pinckney's funeral was held at the arena.

Polly climbed Emanuel's front steps and arrived at the heavily guarded front door. Members were supposed to receive priority seating, but the people standing there stopped her. Inside, mourners crammed every pew and every inch along the walls. Cynthia's siblings sat up front. Her merchant mariner husband sat just feet away from giant posters of her on either side of the rose-draped coffin. Governor Haley, Mayor Riley, Congressman Jim Cly-burn, U.S. senator Tim Scott, and other dignitaries sat up front as well.

Nobody had thought to reserve a seat for Polly.

Fortunately, another longtime church member, Willi Glee, spotted her. A tall, older man who cut a Lincolnesque figure, he hurried over. Shaken, Polly explained that she couldn't get inside. Willi wanted to help, but the only place left to sit would be in the fellowship hall. Was she ready for that?

Polly nodded, thankful, and followed him to the side door. She forced herself to step back inside the large room, close to the spot where she had cowered beneath a plastic table for protection from the gunman. She expected to feel overwhelmed with something—sorrow, fear, anger. Yet, she felt only numbness.

As she headed for an office where she could sit and listen to a live feed from the sanctuary, she also noticed boxes of letters and donated items stacked around, addressed to the Emanuel Nine. Polly didn't like to think about herself. It felt selfish, especially now. But she also knew that twelve people had gathered in the room that night.

She forgot those thoughts, however, when the prayers and music began. She listened in silence as people remembered Cynthia's love of books, her passion for children, and how she would have turned fifty-five on the Sunday Emanuel had re-opened for services. People described her smile and her work on the local housing authority board helping low-income people find homes. Congressman Clyburn noted that Cynthia was his daughter's best friend. Mayor Riley remembered meeting Cynthia back when she worked at a local ice cream parlor. He said the massacre at Emanuel would go down in history alongside the 16th Street Baptist Church bombing in Alabama, which left four black girls dead in 1963.

From his seat at the end of a front pew, Steve Hurd also listened in silence, glowering through his glasses, broad shoulders squared, eyes fixed firmly ahead. He began to rock back and forth. His sister, Sheila Capers, held his hand, touched his knee, and patted his back as he struggled to contain his grief.

Cynthia's youngest brother, Malcolm, a former North Carolina state senator who lived in Charlotte, stepped to the microphone next. He remembered that every time he called Cynthia, she would give him the rundown of how people were doing. She always started with Steve. "He's working hard. He loves being on the sea . . ."

Malcolm looked at Steve then. Two strong personalities, the men often hadn't seen eye to eye, not even while planning this funeral. Steve and Cynthia's brothers had argued over what funeral home to use, what color casket she would want, who should eulogize her. Cynthia's brothers hadn't cared much for Steve, nor he for them, but they had all tried to keep the peace when Cynthia was alive. For her sake.

Looking at his brother-in-law now, Malcolm saw in Steve's scowl and fixed jaw the same anger and abyss that he felt inside.

"She loved you, Steve," he said.

As he prepared to finish, Malcolm paused to gather the last of his strength.

He understood why the shooting was part of a national conversation, as it should be. But he also asked those gathered to remember Cynthia's family.

"When the TV cameras are away, and the elected officials go away, it's just me and Steve and Jackie and Robert . . ."

His voice broke, and he was unable to go on.

From his pew, Steve had listened in hard silence. Resentment tinged his appreciation for the kind words about Cynthia because none of the people who had spoken or who filled the pews behind him had known her quite as he had, in that way a husband knows his wife. None of them could feel her touch and ache for it in the way he did now. None of them would leave this church and go home to a lifeless house where Cynthia's roses still bloomed out front and her books still lined the shelves. Nobody, Steve felt certain, understood the depths of his particular loss.

In many ways, however, another man did understand. The Reverend Anthony Thompson would bury his wife two days later. Both now faced empty homes and empty futures that had so recently held plans for retirements and new beginnings. Myra and Cynthia, both in their fifties, were widely known as hard workers and devoted Christians who'd dedicated their lives to helping professions. Cynthia was a librarian, Myra a teacher and guidance counselor. Yet, their husbands were as different as could be.

Anthony was a retired probation and parole agent turned minister from a deeply Christian family. Steve was a merchant mariner from a tough military one. If Anthony was sweet and stable, Steve was strong and restless. If Anthony loved to talk, Steve could be brusque.

Anthony forgave the killer. Steve did not.

Two days after Steve buried his wife, Anthony buried his.

Anthony had known Myra for almost forty years. They'd met as adult students at a historically black college two hours away. Anthony had spotted her on campus one day looking frantic. He'd stopped to ask: Did she need help? Myra, a single mom, had missed the bus home to her little boy, Kevin. Turned out, they both were headed back to Charleston.

He'd offered a ride. She'd given him the stink eye.

But Anthony had a certain innocence about him that won her over. He giggled. He spoke softly and smiled easily. He didn't curse. They also knew people in common. So, she accepted his offer—but no funny business. She was raising Kevin and getting her education. Nothing would stop her.

They had carpooled for a while after that but went separate ways, married and divorced, until years later when they reconnected. Things were different then. They fell in love. She supported his mid-career move to the ministry and began pursuing her own ordination. Just before this past Christmas, Myra had preached her first sermon. She had shared a story about the grounding that God had provided during the rockiest days of her life. "He was that seed of peace my momma planted in my heart when I was a little girl, and all my life he took care of me," she'd told the congregation.

Back when Myra was young, her father had fallen out of her life, and her mother struggled with alcohol badly enough that she couldn't care for her children. Myra moved in with close friends, the Coakleys, whom her obituary described as her "parents-in-love." However, she and her many biological siblings had gotten separated as the wider community reached out to help, so in the last years of her life, she'd embarked on a mission to find them all. Anthony helped her scour the area and comb the public library for clues to their whereabouts—no small feat given she had twelve brothers and three sisters. Before she died, Myra found them all.

Six months later, the day of Myra's funeral, it took two limousines and a bus to deliver the group.

Even now, Myra still took care of them. Unlike most of those who died, she had left a will and clear directions for her funeral. What mourners saw as they arrived at Emanuel, Myra had wanted. Her mahogany casket was crowned in red roses and white orchids. Anthony arrived wearing a necktie and pocket handkerchief covered in Christian crosses alongside their daughter, Denise Quarles, now in her early thirties, who had been just a toddler when he and Myra got together. People described how Myra was the person everyone called when the lightbulbs in the church's chandelier went out or the toilet needed fixing, because she was the one who got things done.

She and all nine who died were, as one man put it, Emanuel's "A-team." William Dudley Gregorie, a close friend and Charleston city councilman, explained: "God needed the ripest berries on the bush."

Anthony realized that his wife had finished her life's work. He felt comfort in knowing that God had a plan, and that Myra had served her role in it, ever a faithful soldier. But without her, he faced unimaginable loneliness.

How could he move forward alone?

After the funeral, people encouraged him to take some time off from his pastoral duties to grieve. But to him this seemed like exactly the wrong thing to do. He couldn't bear the idea of sitting around the empty house doing nothing. He needed to let his parishioners know he was okay, and that they would be okay, even after racial terrorism had caused them all such pain. God had given him words to speak at Roof's bond hearing, and nothing would stop him from continuing to speak those words.

Anthony would return to his pulpit on Sunday.

Mere days after burying Myra, he sat down with a notebook and a black pen to write his first sermon since her death. Across four pages, stopping and starting, scratching out words, then adding arrows, his thoughts jelled. Page after page addressed God's plan in times of tragedy, the importance of forgiveness and repentance, and the receiving of grace. He ended with, "That same plan God has for you and me is also for Dylann."

Then, in an afterthought, he jotted a note to himself: "talk about what I said at Bond Hearing."

Steve Hurd also returned from his wife's funeral to an empty house. He too faced an empty future. But unlike Anthony, he couldn't go back to work right away to find purpose and routine. The merchant mariner was scheduled to be home for a long stretch, time that he'd planned to spend with Cynthia—celebrating her birthday, fishing, arguing over what to watch on TV. Instead, the break from duties left him with vast empty hours to fill with memories of her and thoughts of what had happened in the fellowship hall the night she died.

One hot July day, he decided to stop by Emanuel. He wanted to be where his wife had died.

He sometimes attended the church, but given that his job kept him at sea eight months a year, he wasn't widely known there. He arrived at the side door, walked past the secretary's office, and stepped into the fellowship hall. A steady parade of church members and volunteers had milled through the space since Emanuel re-opened, and even now people wandered around. Steve stood silently, mostly wondering where Cynthia had sat that night and whether anyone had tried to protect her.

Many family members would imagine what they would have done had they been at the church that night, and Steve was no exception. A strong man—in persona and physique—he pictured tackling the scrawny white kid and beating him or taking the bullets instead of Cynthia and the others. His mind played through several scenarios as he stood there. They all ended with Cynthia alive and Dylann Roof dead.

When his thoughts returned to the present, Steve noticed three women sitting at a table near the pastor's office. Beside them, boxes overflowed with blankets, candles, crucifixes, all kinds of items people mourning with them had sent to Emanuel. The women, he realized, were sorting through bags filled with envelopes. Steve watched as they opened each of them. Some contained cash, which the women pulled out and stacked into a pile. Some envelopes contained checks, which went into another pile. Letters went into a third. If the women noticed Steve, or cared that he was there, they didn't say anything.

After watching briefly, he left the church, more concerned with the scenarios still playing out in his head than the donated mementos and money. The church staff would handle all that, he figured. He returned to the brick bungalow he and Cynthia had shared, now so suffocatingly quiet. Why hadn't he just come home when he was supposed to? He should have returned to Charleston in May, but there was still work to be done on the ship. He hadn't wanted to hand over the job to another engineer.

So, he hadn't been home. He hadn't protected Cynthia.

sixteen

Kindness of Strangers

✳

I n the Hollywood version of events, survivors of tragedy receive over-whelming support from the people who are supposed to help them. Ministers minister, sisters support sisters, and neighbors appear with trays of food and offers of companionship. Of course, in real life people are people: Sometimes they deliver, sometimes they disappoint.

As the national press and out-of-town mourners left Charleston, dona-tions continued to pour in from strangers who wanted to offer that support. Mail arrived at Emanuel in giant bags and boxloads, day after day, from around the country and the world. Soon, every room around the fellowship hall filled with packages and envelopes from well-wishers hoping their dona-tions might somehow soothe the pain and show solidarity. Most contained money of some amount: A box of cards from schoolchildren contained $47 in cash; a Boston hedge fund manager sent a $10,000 check.

Many of the envelopes were addressed to the church, but some contained letters inside indicating that the senders wanted their donations to help fam-ilies of the Emanuel Nine. Still other envelopes came addressed to Eman-uel AME but seemed specifically for the families, written in such terms as "Attention: the Family of Tywanza Sanders" or "In c/o Jennifer Pinckney."

The church leadership, already overwhelmed with funerals and the need to minister to their shaken flock, did not have the necessary bandwidth to handle this river of cash on top of everything else—and that worried the church's secretary, Althea Latham. If the money got separated from the letters, its intended recipients might never see it. Shouldn't they have some protocol, some oversight, someone from outside keeping an eye on such a fortune? And it wasn't just money coming in. People also sent gift cards and paintings and crosses and Bibles—you name it.

Who knew how much the stuff was worth?

One morning, Althea arrived at 8 o'clock to get an early start to what had become very long days. The box into which the church's mail slot led, which she'd emptied the night before, already had filled again. This had gotten so overwhelming that she'd taken her concerns to Emanuel's treasurer.

"This is just too much money coming in here," she'd said. "We need to bring somebody in to keep track of it." But her expressions of concern in the office went unheeded. Worse, every time she brought it up, it felt as if she were getting the cold shoulder. Or was she imagining it?

Althea watched with awe as people across Charleston held countless fundraisers for the Emanuel Nine. Poets wrote poems. Painters painted portraits. Quilters quilted. Chefs whetted palates. Musicians wrote songs and held tribute concerts. A pastor even wrote a hymn. Goff announced the church had created an account called the Moving Forward Fund to house the donations that continued to roll in. The focus, he said, was to ensure that the "monetary, spiritual, and emotional" needs of the victims' families were met. Althea hoped so, given how much money she had seen flow into the church.

Meanwhile, other entities in town also created funds—a half-dozen or more of them—including the city of Charleston, which opened one called the Hope Fund. Millions of dollars in donations arrived at the various funds, coming from individuals, wealthy and not-so-wealthy, and corporations like Boeing, Blackbaud, the Carolina Panthers football team, Starbucks, Google, Daimler, Volvo, and more. Anonymous donors from out of state donated $3 million for education scholarships in Reverend Pinckney's name to benefit victims' families and others affiliated with Emanuel.

One month after the shooting, Goff announced that well-wishers from around the world had sent more than $2 million directly to Emanuel. He maintained that nearly all that money was intended for the church itself, so it would use the infusion to repair termite damage in the 124-year-old sanctuary, complete the elevator, and maintain two church-owned houses. He did not mention how much of the money he thought was intended for the victims' families.

Two months after the shooting, the families still hadn't heard from him regarding how or when the church planned to divide up the funds. As families and survivors waited, bills piled up and tensions grew. So did suspicions. Why all the secrecy?

As journalists from the local newspaper pressed for details about the donations, the church's new attorney explained the crushing demands on Goff, who had stepped in to run Emanuel in the aftermath of such an enormous tragedy while also still presiding over almost three dozen other churches. The attorney, Wilbur Johnson, added that he understood why the length of time passed had raised concerns, but he urged patience and assured that answers would be forthcoming.

"When you have a pastor who already has obligations as presiding elder who has been asked to be interim pastor, and you have a congregation that has suffered collectively a huge traumatic event, there are so many things that have to be attended to," he said. "I don't think it's a surprise that it has taken a while for the church to get its arms around this."

Goff tried to set priorities amid the chaos of grief and trauma. He did so with no playbook, no seminary class for training, and no colleague to call who had been through all this before. How do you lead a church whose pastor and nearly all of its ministerial team have been killed?

First, he'd had to learn to handle the crush of attention from public officials, media, and the mourning public—on top of handling most of the nine funerals. But he also had decided to lead worship himself every Sunday. Members needed an experienced preacher in the pulpit who could provide consistency amid the chaos. Everything about Emanuel felt changed. Reverend Pinckney was gone. Reverend Simmons was gone. Myra, Susie, Ethel, Cynthia, Tywanza, DePayne, Sharonda, all were gone. But consistency wouldn't come easily—with such high-profile loss had come so many new people flocking to the pews. Visitors from all over the world packed the sanctuary on Sundays and Bible study on Wednesdays. So did TV crews and dignitaries from around Charleston, South Carolina, and the nation.

Goff told the Reverend Brenda Nelson, who had been licensed the night of the shooting, that they would split Bible study duties. It had become a huge event filled with even more visitors who presented an opportunity to spread the gospel. That's what Jesus commanded: Go forth and make disciples. God had provided them a tremendous opportunity to evangelize and spread the Christian faith, so they would do that.

Between preparing for Wednesdays and Sundays, Goff also tried to keep his office door open as a seemingly endless stream of people came to discuss events they wanted to hold for Emanuel—and at Emanuel. Memorials. Public health events. Gun violence events. Others wanted Emanuel's leaders involved in big discussions being held around Charleston about race relations and gun violence and civil rights. Plus, reporters wanted to interview him. Elected officials wanted to talk with him. The public wanted to meet him. And, as people began to notice, Norvel Goff wasn't averse to the spotlight.

He tried to handle it all, along with his regular presiding elder duties. Although Goff's schedule often became overloaded and he didn't return to the homes of the survivors, he also wouldn't miss a Sunday in the pulpit.

In August, Jennifer Pinckney returned to the long red-brick elementary school she had left for the summer just a few weeks before the shooting. The building stood as it had, still tucked back in a quiet neighborhood, as if nothing in the world had happened since school got out. A mural of swamp trees and birds still welcomed her when she slipped into the lobby. Down a long hallway of classrooms, the canary yellow and Lego blue colors of her library's walls beckoned her forward, back to the normalcy she desperately needed. The same words greeted her on a wall: "Today a reader, tomorrow a leader."

When other teachers spotted her, most of them approached with hugs and words of sorrow, including some who hardly paid her any attention before. One hurried over to her with a grin.

"I didn't know your husband was a senator!"

Jennifer smiled politely. But she wondered to herself: Why would it matter?

She ducked into her library, a cozy space lined with wooden bookshelves, and let the quiet surround her. It wouldn't last long. Once students returned to the school, their energy would bounce from the child-sized chairs. Jennifer opened the door to her glassed-in office and fired up her computer. She would return here every day to keep her life—and, more importantly, the lives of her two daughters—as routine as possible.

She was thankful that she lived two hours away from Charleston; it allowed her to find some sense of normalcy and avoid constant reminders of what had happened. So had the help of two key people. Since Clementa's funeral, Jennifer had relied on her attorney, Gerald Malloy, a Senate colleague of his, to deal with legal matters such as rigmarole over the donations. And she'd relied on the Reverend Kylon Middleton to deal with issues related to Emanuel. She especially appreciated that he periodically stopped by the church to pick up mail and anything else awaiting her there so that she didn't have to make the trip.

One day, he texted her to say that he was dropping off a bag of mail.

When she returned home, Jennifer opened it to find dozens of cards and letters sent from all over the country offering prayers and condolences. Their warm messages filled her with gratitude.

But something about several of the envelopes bothered her.

All were addressed to her but sent to Emanuel, or dropped off there, because people didn't know how to contact her. She'd guarded their private home address knowing that Dylann Roof's family and friends lived too close—and she couldn't have anyone associated with him aware of their proximity. Who knew how far his racist views reached among them? Jennifer also harbored a strong suspicion that Roof had targeted her husband for assassination. She wasn't convinced someone as young and seemingly naïve as him had acted alone.

She called Kylon: "Why is my mail opened?"

"I have no idea."

He hadn't looked in the bag before bringing it to her.

Jennifer wasn't the only one who received opened mail. Nearly all of the victims' families did. On a portion of those envelopes, someone had written: "empty." Suspicions that already percolated among the victims' relatives over the lack of transparency with the donations now began to boil. With August upon them, they still had no answers about how much money the church had received or when its leaders would distribute it.

A few days later, a member of Emanuel who kept Jennifer in the loop about church gossip called.

"You're not going to believe this!"

Goff had just fired Clementa's secretary.

Jennifer liked Althea Latham, and she knew that Clementa had too. Althea had agreed to have the church office phone transferred to her personal cell phone in the days after the shooting, when seemingly every police officer, news outlet, and mourner wanted to speak to someone at Emanuel. When Jennifer called, Althea always called her back.

Now, the church member explained that when Althea had arrived at Emanuel that morning, a woman had handed her a letter from Emanuel's personnel committee. It was signed by the chairwoman and CCed to Goff, the church's trustees, and its stewards. The message, simple and cold: effective immediately, Althea's employment contract wasn't being renewed. It gave no reason. Althea was sixty-three, jobless, with a child in college.

Jennifer couldn't believe what she was hearing. What on earth was going on at Emanuel?

seventeen

"I Want My Bible"

✻

As the heavy drape of shock lifted, Felicia Sanders began to analyze numbers, especially twelve. Jesus had twelve disciples. The Bible described twelve tribes of Israel. Felicia was twelve when her mother died. And twelve had gathered for Bible study that night. What if Tywanza had run late? Only eleven of God's faithful would have assembled, an imperfect number.

She pondered dates too, mostly June 17. It was the date nine people died at Bible study, of course. But June 17 also was the date a local chemical plant had exploded twenty-four years earlier. Her husband, Tyrone, had worked there, although he had taken that day off.

Nine people died then too.

And the day after the Bible study, June 18, was the anniversary of a massive furniture store blaze just a few miles away from Felicia and Tyrone's house. Nine firefighters died.

Then there was Denmark Vesey, whose life again touched hers. As white authorities had learned of Vesey's planned slave uprising, he'd quickly moved up the date of its launch to midnight of June 16, 1822, a Sunday, according to his official "trial" transcript. With a tick of the clock, the rebellion would have exploded into June 17.

What did all this mean? Was God trying to reveal something to her? Some days, she wasn't sure, nor did she have a minister to ask. Two months after the shooting, she still hadn't returned to Bible study. Even when she attended Sunday services now, she didn't eat or drink beforehand so that she would not need to use the ladies' room, which sat in a back corner of the fellowship hall.

Desperate for spiritual help, she called Goff. She wanted to return to Bible study. "But I don't want to come in the room where it happened. Would you move it up into the sanctuary?"

Goff said he would look into it. But he faced competing needs. Many members clung to the few aspects of normal church life that remained intact, traditions like holding Bible study in the fellowship hall. Since the first days after the shooting, they had used the space for regular events and meetings, as they always had. Reclaiming it helped many of them cope. It helped them know that evil hadn't won. And the hundreds of visitors each week provided important opportunities to spread God's word to potential new members.

Goff faced a tricky situation, which Felicia might have understood if he'd called her back and explained. Instead, she waited each week, hoping that he would send word that he had moved the Bible study upstairs to the sanctuary. Each week, that word did not come. To make matters worse, when Felicia came to church one Sunday afterward, Goff spoke enthusiastically of the Bible study's swelling ranks of newcomers.

"Bring a friend!" he invited.

It felt like the ultimate insult. Emanuel was becoming too much about the show, too much about the church, and not enough about ministering to people. At a recent memorial for the victims, an usher had sat Felicia and Tyrone in the very back of the church in their "reserved seats," where they barely could see a candle lit for their son. Despite lifetimes of faithful worship—of tithing and volunteering and worshipping—their needs seemed to mean nothing.

Anger crept into her heart. It terrified her more than anything. Because if she didn't forgive Roof and didn't forgive Goff and didn't provide that fertile soil for God's word, then she wouldn't go to heaven. And heaven was where she would find Tywanza.

After the shooting, the coroner's office staff had taken care to return salvageable items found on the victims' bodies and in the fellowship hall.

One woman had found and cleaned Felicia's purse. She was grateful for the woman's efforts, but what Felicia really wanted back was her Bible.

"You don't want it," the woman had cautioned.

"Yes, I do want it."

"We don't think you want it . . ."

"You can keep everything," Felicia said. "I want my Bible."

That Bible, however, had been tossed in the trash, thrown away with other things that seemed too damaged to return to victims' families.

When police lieutenant Jennie Antonio caught wind of that conversation, she didn't dismiss Felicia's request as impossible. A devoted Catholic, she understood what the Bible meant to the grieving mother. She also had been working with a national FBI rapid response team that flew in to help local police agencies and victim advocates handle mass casualty events. The team's members had dealt with tragedies at places like Sandy Hook Elementary and brought with them critical lessons learned—including that many of the devastated parents had wanted their children's personal effects, like backpacks and drawings, no matter how damaged. The FBI team also had discovered a Texas company that could salvage even the most blood-soaked items.

So, five days after the shooting, Antonio had called an FBI counterpart and soon drove to the first of two storage buildings that housed biohazards that cleaning crews at Emanuel had thrown away. There, they hauled out several big plastic bins that contained the life, and death, of nine people. In suffocating heat, with gloved hands, Antonio had rummaged through sticky papers that clung to what looked like a dark brownish-red bed sheet. She had peered beneath it. And there sat a dark leather-bound Bible soaked in blood. A bullet had pierced its pages.

She opened the cover, then plied apart pages. Stuck between two, a little torn-off piece of what might have been a receipt bore a name: Felicia Sanders.

Antonio had carefully wrapped it up and sent it to the company in Texas. Two months later, a box appeared in her mail.

Antonio soon drove down the winding road to Felicia's home and knocked on the Sanderses' front door. Felicia greeted her. Though her eyes were fogged with grief, Felicia managed to smile in welcome. Antonio sensed the tremendous effort it took for the survivor to greet the endless stream of people needing to talk with her for the investigation, random community members who suddenly wanted to know her, and the large circles of family and friends who stopped by to visit. She decided to make it quick.

As they walked inside, Antonio held out the box.

Felicia took it from her. She opened it, gently tugging aside tissue paper inside. There sat her black Bible, what she called her Basic Instructions Before Leaving Earth. She opened the front cover. A pinkish hue now tinted the gossamer paper inside. A tear, barely visible now, marked where a bullet had pierced the pages. Yet, despite a gunshot, the blood, and the cleansing, God's words still stared back at her in clear and bold black letters.

God was still with her.

Polly visited Felicia at her house one day. Friends for twenty years, they talked about God and the church, good and evil, and their many spiritual questions following the terrible ordeal. As they spoke about that Bible study and the great unlikelihood they would be alive after a man had fired more than seventy bullets all around them, Polly remembered an Old Testament story about a fire. It told of three Jewish men cast into a fiery furnace because they refused to worship a golden statue. The trio had held steadfastly to God in the face of death by burning, and sure enough, they walked unharmed through the flames.

From beneath a table, Polly had prayed out loud to the same God. She could still hear the blasts of endless gunshots around her and the sound of Roof reloading over and over. Yet, not a single bullet struck Polly, Felicia, or her granddaughter.

"We were in the fire," Polly said softly, glancing at the floor.

"And only thing I got was a sting on my legs," Felicia added. She still could feel the heat of bullets blasting so close to her. "Three of us came out without a scratch."

But what did it all mean? Felicia explained her questions to her therapist, seeking guidance.

"I can help you with the medical part of it," the woman cautioned. She could prescribe medication and guide Felicia through therapies. "But I cannot help you with the spiritual side. Do you know anybody who would help you with that part?"

Felicia didn't. She used to seek out Aunt Susie and several of the five ministers now dead. Who could she turn to now?

Goff had visited her before the funerals and not since. The bishop had never come. She desperately needed a person of the cloth to say, "God didn't leave you. He's still with you." That was all she wanted, an assurance that God would pull her through this, but she didn't know where to look. Goff was a stranger to her—and she to him. Felicia also didn't like to draw attention by demanding things for herself, not even a visit from her clergy.

So, one day she called Andy Savage, her attorney and increasingly close friend. Andy listened. Then he reminded her of how she had felt at Second Presbyterian Church when they visited seeking overflow space for Tywanza and Susie's funeral. She had said the place felt, somehow, right. He would call its pastor, Cress Darwin, for her.

Just as Felicia had walked past Second Presbyterian a thousand times or more but never gone inside, Cress Darwin had never been inside Emanuel. But when Andy called, he agreed immediately to help. Of course he remembered Felicia Sanders. He'd be delighted to meet with her again.

They did so, this time in his church office, this time alone. Cress stepped from behind a wide wooden desk and past a book-stuffed credenza to invite her into a sitting area where an overstuffed couch and chairs beckoned. There they sat and talked. They cried. They prayed.

Then they met again in that space. And again. Soon, Wednesday mornings became their time to explore her questions. Felicia felt different with Cress. Until then, she always had made sure she spoke properly to her ministers. The AME Church was a strictly hierarchical institution; its ministers were more deeply revered the higher they ascended the ranks, and Felicia deeply respected authority.

All that vanished now. Trauma left her too raw, too overwhelmed for show, and Cress wasn't her pastor anyway, not really.

Emanuel remained home.

Yet, he felt safe and knowledgeable. He called her. He kept appointments each week with her. He showed that he cared. So, she sobbed and raged and lost control in that office.

At one point she cried, "I don't know what my purpose is!" She expected him to say that she would figure it out eventually, with enough prayer and when God was ready to reveal it. Instead, he leaned over and asked: "Ever think you're doing exactly what you're supposed to be doing already?"

What happened at Emanuel called people to act, to ensure that something meaningful arose from something so senseless. Her words of forgiveness had helped to keep the peace after the shooting. They inspired the nation and set God's love above the gunman's evil. She could continue to speak them.

God had a purpose for her. She just needed to see it.

However, what Cress said, Felicia didn't want to hear. She didn't want to go out beating the drum of any big public message of forgiveness or racial equality. It wasn't that she disagreed with the message. She just wasn't one who liked center stage. That was Tywanza's place. His big grin, his giant heart and larger dreams suited that role. He loved to be heard. And people loved to hear him.

When Felicia got home, she looked at pictures of the nine who died, studying their smiles. She thought of their gifts and spiritual wisdom. They seemed so much better for this role, so much more prepared to go out there speaking publicly about God and forgiveness.

That wasn't her.

Felicia continued to yearn to hear from her church leaders, although none came to her home. While she waited, Governor Haley called instead with a surprising request.

"Can I come see you?"

Haley needed to meet Felicia. She needed to talk to her in person and let her know how sorry she was for all that she'd endured. So much well-placed attention had gone to those killed that she worried about those who had lived. It was selfish on some level, Haley knew. But she simply needed to know that Felicia was okay.

She also wanted to meet the woman who'd forgiven the racist killer. Haley, herself a Christian, wondered: *Could I do that?*

Felicia invited her over.

A few days later, Haley rode in a plain black SUV with two staffers and her security detail. They turned down a long, two-lane residential street, passing house after house, including one with a Confederate flag hanging on its porch. Then they turned down the Sanderses' long driveway, nestled by two big live oak trees.

Haley emerged from the SUV into the humid summer air, partly as the state's governor, partly as a mother herself, mostly as someone worried about the woman inside the house who had survived something so unimaginable. She walked to the front steps and climbed onto a long front porch with a white rail. Felicia and Tyrone emerged from the front door.

Haley had attended Tywanza's funeral. She had seen Felicia and Tyrone there and, later, at the ceremony to lower the flag. However, they hadn't really met, not in a quiet way like this one. Felicia led her into a living room just inside the front door, toward a couch, two chairs, and photos of Tywanza. She asked Haley to please choose a seat. The governor sat down facing Felicia. Tyrone joined them.

Yet, beyond their overt graciousness, Haley felt a wall of suspicion, as if the couple wondered: Why was the governor here? Was she hoping to gain something from them?

Haley presented Felicia with a crisply folded American flag that had flown in honor of Tywanza above the State House, along with one of the nine pens she used to sign the bill lowering the Confederate flag. They began to relax a little. Felicia described how she couldn't even hear gunshots on a TV show anymore, not without reliving those horrific moments.

Where Felicia seemed so sad and broken, Tyrone came across as edgy and hard. For a moment, the governor pondered two such different responses to grief.

Then she asked them to tell her more about Tywanza.

Felicia smiled widely. She described her son's poetry, his jokes, his dreams. Tyrone, a wiry bald man with a commanding voice, admitted that he couldn't stop listening to a *Lion King* song that reminded him of his baby boy. Tywanza was his Simba. They spoke about their granddaughter, the huggy little girl who survived the shooting, and how hard they were trying to keep her life as normal as possible. Theirs was a house that had welcomed so many children over the years—their own, family members', friends', others'. Felicia wanted to love and rescue them all. But she hadn't been able to save her own son.

When she cried, Haley handed her a tissue. When the governor cried, Felicia handed her one.

"Tell me how to help you," Haley finally said.

Felicia looked back with the saddest eyes Haley had ever seen. Felicia's answer had nothing to do with politics, not gun control or race relations or any of the things Haley typically heard. Instead, Felicia explained that they desperately needed spiritual guidance. They needed to know why their son had died in front of her, in a church, in *their* church, trying to protect them all. They needed to know God's intentions in this tragedy.

They spoke for more than an hour before Haley felt it was time to go. She didn't want to overstay her welcome. They said good-byes, and she stepped back onto the front porch. Haley had almost reached her SUV, her security detail still waiting in the driveway, when she heard Felicia's voice behind her from the porch.

"I got to tell him I loved him," she called. "And he told me he loved me, too."

In mid-August, two months after the shooting, just days after Emanuel had cut secretary Althea Latham loose, Felicia sat down at her computer to write a letter to Reverend Goff. She'd never liked to make a fuss and avoided conflict whenever possible. She respected the church's hierarchy. But Felicia desperately needed help. So, she began:

> Dear Rev. Goff,
> I am writing this letter to inform you of some things you may not have
> been aware of and to let you know my feelings about the AME Faith. First,
> I want to tell you how let down I feel. . . .

On June 17th's Bible study, I lost so much. I lost 9 members of my
church family, and 3 of them were my family members. In addition to
this loss, I was present and so was my granddaughter. As of August 15th,
no one from Mother Emanuel or the AME church clergy has called me.
Not one person has called to offer prayer, a word, or anything. I am
having such a difficult time.

She explained that she loved God. She had been a faithful member. Her
letter listed the many roles she had held at Emanuel: trustee, steward, usher
board. Even during her battle with breast cancer, she'd returned as soon as
she could walk up the stairs again. She had served her church, and now she
in turn needed its help. Goff oversaw many pastors, so why hadn't any of
them called or visited or anything?

"I have no disrespect for you, I just find it hard to believe that not any of
the Associate Pastors from any of the 31 churches has offered me any assistance. I am grieving my son's death, I am grieving the loss of the other 8
church members, and I am grieving the loss of the connection that I had with
my church," she wrote.

She also mentioned not being able to return to Bible study, although
she desperately needed to, because the group still met in the fellowship
hall. Nobody had contacted her about that either.

I really feel that my church that I love dearly and the AME denomination
has failed me and let me down considerably. I am not understanding the
lack of concern for the living, surviving members, particularly me,
Felicia Sanders, and my granddaughter, the lack of spiritual guidance and
well-being.

She ended it asking: "Who can I depend on, if I can't depend on my
church?" and signed it "Your Faithful Member, Felicia Sanders."

She sent a copy to Emanuel. She kept a copy. And she had Tyrone hand-
deliver one to the church office.

Goff called her the next morning and said he'd received the letter. Felicia again emphasized that she needed spiritual help. It didn't have to be him.
It could be a pastor from any church he supervised.

"No, I'll counsel you," he promised. They set a date, and he prayed with her over the phone.

Again, Felicia felt hope. Again, she waited at her home for the moment he would arrive and they could discuss her many questions about God and evil and death and suffering.

Once again, he didn't show up.

Through it all, Tywanza's bedroom sat locked. Then one day, their grand-daughter lost the key. About a week after Felicia waited in vain for Goff to visit, she and Tyrone decided to call a locksmith. They needed to feel their son's presence again. When the man popped the door open, a paper fluttered onto the floor.

It was a poem Tywanza had written, "Reasons Why I Lock People Out."

His writings hung everywhere, forever preserving his outlook on life after twenty-six years of it. He was the Sanderses' youngest child, a barber and poet of social consciousness, their "Wanza." When their grandchildren came to visit in the summers, Tywanza put on his own summer camp so the kids didn't sit in the house all day. He'd take them outside to play soccer, and when it got too hot, he'd teach them math and English.

At the end of last summer, he'd posted a picture of himself on Instagram towering over three grinning girls huddled up around him. "Camp @fresh-wanza coming to an end," he'd typed with three frowny face emoticons. He praised the girls, adding that he knew they'd do great in school during the upcoming year, and followed it all with a string of hashtags that pretty well summed up his outlook on life. #grindovermatter #ambition #de-termination #moneymotivatemoney #success #believe #giveGodcredit #thankyou.

A Jackie Robinson quote forever concluded that Instagram account: "A life is not important except in the impact it has on other lives."

After the locksmith left, Felicia and Tyrone sat in the bedroom amid their son's presence—his poetry, his writings, his old bicycle, his books, his instruments. Pieces of Tywanza hung everywhere, as if he'd left them there for his family. Eventually, Felicia and Tyrone walked out and locked the door behind them again, protecting his essence from the world beyond.

As August yielded to September, Polly and Felicia decided they were ready to share their story publicly for the first time. Denizens of the city and, indeed, the country hungered to know more about the adult survivors of that infamous Bible study and what exactly they'd endured. They spoke with a reporter from *The Post and Courier*, the local newspaper, and agreed to meet a photographer at Emanuel the next day around noon to take a portrait of them in their church home.

Felicia arrived at 11:57 a.m. in a classic black pantsuit and lilac shirt, despite the searing heat outside. Her hair hung in a smooth bob, her glasses shielding eyes clouded with pain. She walked through the side door that Dylann Roof had entered less than three months earlier and ventured into the side hallway she'd walked countless times before. The secretary's office door stood open just ahead.

Beyond loomed the fellowship hall. She walked no farther.

Polly already stood there in a brightly colored blouse and a turquoise necklace. Felicia's husband, Tyrone, rounded the corner, approaching from the fellowship hall. He too was a fixture at Emanuel. They explained to the office workers why they were there, that they were going upstairs to get a picture taken in the quiet sanctuary above.

The office ladies said no. They needed an appointment. Goff wasn't there, and they couldn't let anyone in without his permission.

Felicia and Polly stood shocked. The church always had an open-door policy for members in good standing, which they were—and had been for decades in Polly's case, lifetimes and even generations for Felicia and Tyrone. They had come and gone from this building hundreds, thousands of times without permission from anyone. This was their church, not Goff's. They survived a massacre in here, not Goff. Their loved ones and friends died here, not Goff's.

Felicia turned and walked back out the side door to wait for Tyrone and Polly to clear things up. Of course they could take a picture inside their church. How ridiculous. She stepped along the side parking lot where a killer once walked and ventured slowly toward Emanuel's front steps to wait. The church's bright white stucco front blasted the hot mid-day sunlight back at her. Noon traffic rumbled by on Calhoun Street.

The woman put in charge of public relations after the shooting called Felicia on her cell phone and reiterated that no, they couldn't go inside with a photographer—Goff hadn't approved this visit, and they didn't have an appointment. Felicia began to cry in front of tourists and others walking down the busy street behind her. "You're telling me I can't come in the church where I lost my loved ones? Y'all around here fixing up everything on the blood of our loved ones, and I can't come in?"

She reminded the woman just how long she had been a member of Emanuel, that her family went back six generations. She noted that her son had died here. Didn't Emanuel want to celebrate her and Miss Polly? Why did they need Reverend Goff's permission? This was a story about them, not him.

The woman explained again that they needed an appointment. Felicia hung up.

As tourists snapped pictures of the now-iconic church, Felicia repeated over and over to nobody, or maybe to God: "Why won't my church let me inside?"

She leaned against a rail, new wounds forming. One of the tourists, wearing a pretty summer dress and a smile, approached on the sidewalk.

"Are you a member?" she called to Felicia.

"Yes."

The woman wanted to take a picture to capture herself being there with an actual member. She had no idea who Felicia was.

Felicia didn't want to be rude. She stepped toward the church's front wall and stood awkwardly, her back stiff, in front of a small sign with the church's name. She tried to smile. The woman held up her cell phone and positioned Felicia in the center of her frame. She snapped a picture, hugged Felicia, and went on her way.

Polly came around the corner then from the church office and stood angrily beside her old friend. How she wished she had a key to let herself in. She was a trustee, a position that oversaw church properties. Her husband was a third-generation member. He'd taught Sunday school for decades.

Tyrone emerged from the church office, too, equally furious.

"Why do I need an appointment, with all of the money and worship I've done in the church?" Tyrone demanded when he reached Felicia and Polly. "I'll push the override button. It don't matter to me. My wife has been in this church just as long as I have, and nobody's going to stop me from coming into this church!"

"If they don't want us in there, we ain't going in there," Polly said.

They desperately needed air conditioning. They also needed privacy, a moment to calm, and a place to take the picture and move on. They didn't want to take it in front of Emanuel either. Why would they want to represent a church that had just rejected them? Instead, they walked across the back parking lot that connected Emanuel to Second Presbyterian.

Cress Darwin greeted them at the door in a light gray suit and a lilac tie. It matched Felicia's shirt, though they hadn't planned it. He wrapped her in a hug. She emerged from it smiling.

Quietly, he led the trio inside, ushering them up a side staircase and into an empty balcony. Below, several dozen clergy had gathered for a presbytery meeting. As the newspaper's photographer captured a portrait of two adult survivors of the Emanuel shooting, a pastor up front urged the Presbyterian ministers before him to reach out more, to embrace more diversity in their pews.

Founded in 1816 as a place of spiritual freedom for the enslaved and freed black residents of Charleston, Emanuel AME Church overcame a series of tragedies in its early days. After an 1822 slave rebellion, assumed to have been led by Denmark Vesey, whites burned the church, forcing congregants to worship underground. In 1872, members gathered to worship in a newly built wooden structure, only to see it destroyed again just 14 years later by an earthquake.

"Mother Emanuel," whose current building opened in 1891, features prominently in Charleston's civil rights history. Coretta Scott King spoke to a crowd of 3,000 at Emanuel on April 29, 1969, the night before she led striking black hospital workers on a march through downtown Charleston. Mary Moultrie (left) and Rosetta Simmons walked arm in arm with King. Her husband, the Reverend Dr. Martin Luther King Jr., had come to Emanuel seven years earlier in an effort to encourage voter registration. *Photo by Dewey Swain*

Charleston continues to grapple with its legacy as the epicenter of America's slave trade and birthplace of the Civil War. Some South Carolinians fiercely defend Confederate memorials like the 115-foot-tall monument to John C. Calhoun, former vice president and secretary of war who once called slavery "a positive good." Completed in 1896, the monument towers over Marion Square, a park in Charleston's historic downtown. *Photo by Grace Beahm*

In contrast, a more modest statue of Denmark Vesey stands only life-size, and was erected in 2014 after almost two decades of dispute. Unlike Calhoun's statue, it is located outside downtown Charleston, two miles away in Hampton Park, itself named after a Confederate officer who was one of the largest slave owners in the South. *Photo by Grace Beahm*

Charleston, known as the Holy City, is home to elegant historic churches that are central to the daily lives of black and white residents, although they typically remain separate. People still refer to Sunday mornings as the most segregated hours of the week. *Photo by Leroy Burnell*

TOP RIGHT: On June 17, 2015, Dylann Roof slipped into Emanuel's weekly Bible study. After sitting quietly with its twelve participants for an hour, he stood during closing prayer and shot nine of them, fleeing before police arrived.

MIDDLE RIGHT: Charleston police officer Andrew Delaney, among the very first responders to arrive on the scene, not yet aware how many shooters were involved or whether the attack was over. *Photo by Matthew Fortner*

s word of the shooting spread, terrified relatives rushed to the scene to learn the fate of their loved es. The Reverend Anthony Thompson was among the first to reach the church. His wife, Myra, as leading Bible study that night. When he realized she might be dead, he collapsed across the reet. *Photo by Wade Spees*

Before the shooting, Roof created a website that included a manifesto explaining his racist views. "Segregation did not exist to hold back negroes. It existed to protect us from them." Roof included photographs of himself with a Confederate battle flag, touching off a statewide firestorm over its symbolic meaning. Also shown is Roof's carving in the sand of the sequence "1488"—"14" being fourteen words significant to white nationalists, and "88" referring to the eighth letter in the alphabet, the "h," for "Heil Hitler."

Charleston is transformed into a city in mourning. Local residents and tourists from across the globe flock to Emanuel. *Photo by Paul Zoeller*

The church's welcome board still speaks of normal times in the days following the shooting. *Photo by Wade Spees*

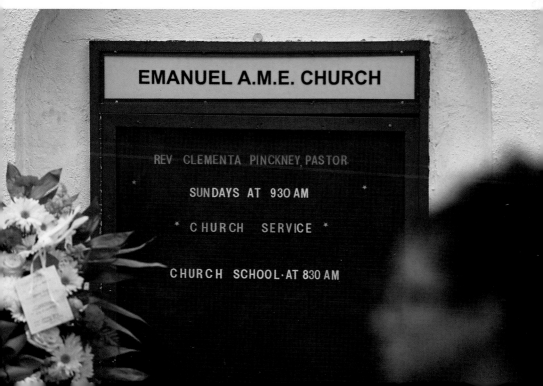

EMANUEL A.M.E. CHURCH

REV CLEMENTA PINCKNEY PASTOR

SUNDAYS AT 930 AM

* CHURCH SERVICE *

CHURCH SCHOOL·AT 830 AM

The morning after the shooting, a tip from a driver alerts police in rural North Carolina to Roof's presence; he is arrested without incident.

Less than forty-eight hours after the shooting, Roof's bond hearing offers the survivors, loved ones, and a horrified nation their first live glimpse of the killer. *Photo by Grace Beahm*

ABOVE: Nadine Collier (left) did not plan to speak at the bond hearing. As she describes it later, she felt the spirit of her deceased mother guide her toward the microphone. Nadine cries out, "I forgive you! You took something very precious away from me. I will never talk to her ever again. I will never be able to hold her again! But God forgive you, and I forgive you." *Photo by Leroy Burnell*

RIGHT: Survivor Felicia Sanders, shown here with her husband, Tyrone, hadn't planned to speak either, but worried that more violence would ensue. Her words of forgiveness and faith were heard around the world. "As we say in Bible study, we enjoyed you," she tells the killer. "But may God have mercy on you." *Photo by Leroy Burnell*

ABOVE: Just four days after the shooting, Emanuel reopens. With most of the leadership gone, the Reverend Dr. Norvel Goff Sr. is named interim pastor. Goff soon begins to receive accolades for his leadership. However, over the coming months, others would question his treatment of the survivors and his transparency regarding funds donated to Emanuel and the grieving families. *Photo by Paul Zoeller*

MIDDLE LEFT: The evening after the first service, thousands of people join in a grassroots unity march, gathering at each end of the Arthur Ravenel Jr. Bridge and marching toward each other. Some question whether such symbolic displays only serve to mask the city's systemic racism. *Photo by Grace Beahm*

BOTTOM LEFT: Outside Emanuel, a memorial of cards, flowers, teddy bears, and signs grows along Calhoun Street. Linda Blankenship and the Reverend Cornelius Brown, strangers until this moment, are among those who come to cry and pray together. *Photo by Wade Spees*

ABOVE: Emanuel would hold three funerals on one Saturday alone. Immediately after Cynthia Hurd's funeral, a joint service is set to begin for the oldest victim, Susie Jackson, and the youngest, Tywanza Sanders. As mourners transition between the two funerals, they are drenched by a sudden downpour. *Photo by Grace Beahm*

MIDDLE RIGHT: The Reverend Sharon Risher, the oldest of Ethel Lance's five children, is a trauma chaplain in Dallas at the time of her mother's burial in Emanuel's graveyard. Grief and anger divide her family in the aftermath of this sudden and violent loss. *Photo by Grace Beahm*

BOTTOM RIGHT: At Tywanza Sanders' burial, his father, Tyrone, grieves the death of his youngest child. *Photo by Grace Beahm*

Jennifer Pinckney stands with her daughters, Eliana and Malana, as a Highway Patrol Honor Guard carries Clementa into the State House in Columbia for a public viewing. This would be the first of many events that forced Jennifer, who preferred a private life, into the spotlight. *Photo by Lauren Prescott*

Two days later, on June 26, 2015, thousands of people lined up starting at sunrise with hopes of attending Reverend Clementa Pinckney's funeral, where President Barack Obama will eulogize the pastor. The funeral is held in the 5,100-seat TD Arena, which proves not nearly large enough to hold the mass of locals and those from around the country who came to attend. *Photo by Wade Spees*

TOP RIGHT: Jennifer Pinckney walks into her husband's funeral with their younger daughter, Malana, the child who hid with her under a desk while Roof killed nine people on the other side of a thin wall. *Photo by Grace Beahm*

MIDDLE RIGHT: President Obama hugs Clementa's older daughter, Eliana, as Jennifer looks on. This became an iconic photograph that many feel captured the president's deep personal connection to the tragedy. *Photo by Paul Zoeller*

BOTTOM: On the plane ride to Charleston, President Obama told his wife, Michelle, that he was considering singing at the funeral; she encouraged him to follow his instinct. After delivering a soaring eulogy for Clementa Pinckney that touched on forgiveness as well as racism, gun violence, and the historic role of the black church, the president sings "Amazing Grace." It became a defining moment of his presidency. *Photo by Grace Beahm*

ABOVE: Sympathizers of the Ku Klux Klan scream obscenities at counter-protesters during a rally on the steps of the State House. *Photo by Paul Zoeller*

MIDDLE LEFT: Flag opponents hold peaceful protests as well. *Photo by Grace Beahm*

BOTTOM LEFT: Civil rights activist Bree Newsome scales the 30-foot flagpole and removes the flag. She is arrested and later released, and the flag is replaced about an hour later. *Reuters*

FACING PAGE BOTTOM: The next day, thousands of people line the streets as members of the South Carolina Highway Patrol Honor Guard lower the flag. As they do, the crowd erupts into cheers. A woman hollers, "Free at last, free at last. Thank God almighty, we're free at last!" *Photo by Grace Beahm*

TOP LEFT: The Reverend Kylon Middleton, a boyhood friend of Clementa Pinckney's, accompanies the pastor's widow to the state Senate chambers where a black cloth covers Pinckney's empty seat. The vote to remove the Confederate flag passes easily. *Photo by Paul Zoeller*

MIDDLE LEFT: The battle is far more rancorous in the state House of Representatives where after several hours of debate, Governor Nikki Haley issues a personal appeal for the flag to be removed. Not everyone agrees. Representative Mike Pitts, who tells reporters that he took out his hearing aids during Haley's talk, takes to the House floor to argue a view common among flag supporters. He describes it as a symbol of southern heritage and the bravery of those who fought "northern aggression." *Photo by Paul Zoeller*

BOTTOM LEFT: After thirteen hours of debate, the representatives voted. The final tally: 94 to 20 ordering the permanent removal of the flag to the nearby Confederate Relic Room and Military Museum. On July 9, 2015, Governor Haley, who experienced racism as a child, holds a press conference to sign the bill into law. *Photo by Paul Zoeller*

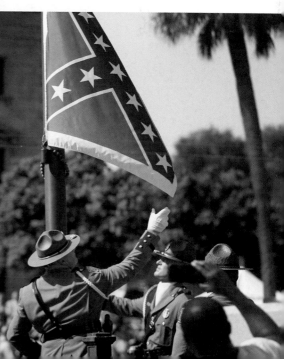

Survivors Polly Sheppard and Felicia Sanders decided to share their ordeal with *The Post and Courier*, Charleston's daily newspaper. Yet when they arrived at Emanuel to take a photograph for the story, church leaders wouldn't let them in, despite the decades both women spent supporting the church. Stunned, they stand outside. *Photo by Grace Beahm*

Arthur Stephen Hurd spends hours alone in the house he and his wife once shared, now quarreling with her siblings, struggling to sleep, and growing increasingly disillusioned with the church his wife loved. *Photo by Andrew Knapp*

As they grappled with the pain of their mother's death and disagreements over forgiving Dylann Roof, Ethel Lance's daughters could agree on little, including her tombstone. Two of them had their own made. *Photo by Grace Beahm*

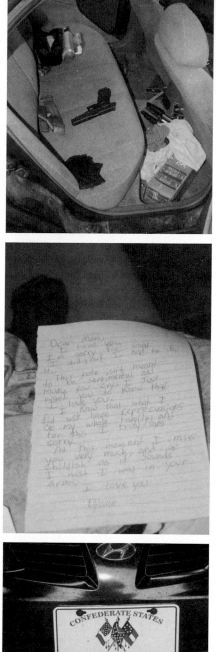

ABOVE: After eighteen months, the survivors and victims' loved ones faced the start of Dylann Roof's federal trial. Much of Charleston braced for possible violence as, right across the street, former police officer Michael Slager was standing trial for the fatal shooting of unarmed black man Walter Scott. Slager's attorney, Andy Savage, shown here, also represents Emanuel shooting survivors Felicia Sanders and Polly Sheppard. *Photo by Grace Beahm*

TOP RIGHT: Federal prosecutors introduced an array of evidence, including a photo of Dylann Roof's gun resting on the backseat of his car. MIDDLE RIGHT: Jurors saw this note Roof wrote to his mother after the shooting: "I know what I did will have reprecussions [sic] on my whole family," he wrote, "and for this I truly am sorry." He was arrested before he could send it. BOTTOM RIGHT: Roof's license plate.

BELOW: Months after convicting Roof and voting for the death penalty, jury foreman Gerald Truesdale and alternate juror Emily Barrett visit Emanuel to show their support. *Photo by Wade Spees*

Sunday, June 21, 2015

The Post and Courier

IN REMEMBRANCE

Cynthia Hurd
54, a library manager whose life was dedicated to books, children and church

Susie Jackson
87, a mother figure to generations in her family and a renowned cook of collard greens

Ethel Lance
70, a church custodian who found strength in a gospel song to overcome life's challenges

DePayne Middleton Doctor
49, a minister whose angelic voice could heal troubled hearts

Clementa Pinckney
41, a pastor and state senator who lent his booming voice to the voiceless

Tywanza Sanders
26, a barber, poet and aspiring entrepreneur ready to take the world by storm

Daniel L. Simmons Sr.
74, a minister who served as a model of endurance and service to God

Sharonda Singleton
45, a pastor and coach who became her runners' biggest cheerleader, on and off the track

Myra Thompson
59, a builder of faith who worked to restore her beloved church's properties to their full glory

TO HELP THE FAMILIES	TO COME TOGETHER	INSIDE
For details on how to contribute to funds to benefit those who lost loved ones at Emanuel AME Church, see Page A5.	There are a number of events in the Charleston area to help a city in mourning grieve and honor those who lost their lives. For a list of prayer services, vigils and more, see Page A5.	A look at the lives of the nine victims, and a poem by Marjory Wentworth, South Carolina's poet laureate.

The Post and Courier ran this memorial page the first Sunday following the shooting. *Designed by Chad Dunbar.*

eighteen

Money in the Temple

✳

A few weeks later, city officials called a meeting with the survivors and victims' families. A large group gathered at a fire station near Emanuel to hear how the city would distribute its Hope Fund, which city leaders had set up just days after the shooting for people to make donations. It was wholly separate from the fund Emanuel created.

Given the families were scattered around the country, those who couldn't attend the meeting in person chimed in over a speaker phone. Their attorneys joined them. Charleston mayor Joseph Riley began by expressing his deepest sorrow. He explained that people from around the world shared his concern, as demonstrated by how many had opened their wallets to make donations. People from all fifty states and four foreign countries had sent $2.8 million to express condolences to the people who had lost so much. Since then, pro bono lawyers and city staff had pored over laws and family trees to devise a strategy for divvying it up. Most of the victims had died without wills, so divisions of money within each family would rely on the state's law of "intestate succession," the method probate courts followed to divide estates when a deceased person left no will.

The attorneys explained the formula. The victims' family members asked questions. They received answers. Their attorneys issued praise.

But from Emanuel?

One month, two months, three months, four months passed. Still no word about how much money the church had received in donations or its plans for distributing it. The families' attorneys asked for an explanation, a timeline, anything. But none came.

Across the state, people followed the news. A group of members at Goff's previous church heard about the families' complaints about transparency— and thought they sounded awfully familiar.

For a decade, Goff had pastored a church called Reid Chapel in Columbia, the state capital. Toward the end of his tenure, one of its members had discovered that the church and its school had amassed more than $600,000 in mortgage debt, including one loan to buy Goff a house much larger than the church's parsonage.

The man realized something was wrong. To ensure accountability, AME Church bylaws require votes of two large church meetings to take out mortgages. Yet, the debt came as news to him even though he served on Reid Chapel's steward board. Given the congregation would have to repay the money, a group of members demanded to see the church's financial records. They didn't receive them.

Instead, shortly afterward, Bishop Norris promoted Goff to one of the state's presiding elder posts, this one over the district that included Mother Emanuel.

Now, as the Emanuel families also complained about Goff's lack of transparency, several Reid Chapel members still trying to get financial records from their own church spoke to *The Post and Courier* about what they'd discovered.

It turned out, the financial questions didn't start with them in Columbia or even in South Carolina. A judge in New York also had ordered Goff to pay $13,000 to refund a loan plus various other costs to a now-deceased member of another one of his former churches before she died. A decade later, Goff still hadn't repaid the woman's estate.

When the newspaper published a story about it all, Goff forcefully denied any wrongdoing. He insisted that people had made up lies for their own gain and to besmirch his reputation.

The day after the story ran, Steve Hurd, Cynthia's husband, filed a lawsuit demanding a full accounting of the donations sent to Emanuel. He wanted a

judge to put a freeze on the money until it received a thorough examination.
Steve's name appeared on the lawsuit, but it represented wide-ranging concerns from survivors and the victims' relatives, who felt increasingly frustrated that the church seemed to consider the donations—"love offerings,"
as Reverend Simmons' son called them—as belonging to Emanuel. Shortly
after Steve filed the lawsuit, a judge agreed to put a hold on the money.

The brewing controversy created rifts within Emanuel as well. Some
members questioned why Goff hadn't given them a monthly financial report since he arrived and wondered why exactly he'd let the church secretary go. Others figured he simply hadn't gotten to the financial reports, given
the massive disruption to the church. Others resented the tarnishing of their
church's name over money at a time like this. They dug in, determined
to support their church's leaders and stay focused on carrying Emanuel
through the tragedy.

The next day, Goff called a press conference to discuss the donations.
Tyrone Sanders arrived at his lifelong church without Felicia and
sat quietly off to one side of the press, AME clergy, and others gathering along the pews. He hadn't come to hear about money. He wanted to
ask Goff why he hadn't ministered to his grief-stricken family. Why had he
repeatedly stood up Felicia? And why hadn't he allowed Felicia and Polly to
get their photograph taken in the place where they had worshipped for so
many years?

Beneath a two-story stained-glass window of Jesus and flanked by a row
of supporters—most of them other AME clergy—Goff stepped to the front
of Emanuel's sanctuary wearing his pastor's collar. He had gathered his supporters to fill as much of the sanctuary as possible. But instead of discussing the donations, he launched into a diatribe against the newspaper for its
story about him, calling it among other things "satanic," going so far as to
compare its story to the shootings.

"Once again on Sunday, October 4, the worst kind of evil showed up to
rock Mother Emanuel and myself yet again. It was like pouring salt in an
open wound," he said. The words against him amounted to an "account of
twisted information from sad, disgruntled people." He blamed his former

parishioners at Reid Chapel and framed the story as an affront to the church body rather than an accounting of his own actions. Some of the clergy beside him nodded.

Reading from a prepared script, he also blasted Emanuel's former secretary, who had come forward with concerns about the church's opening of mail addressed to the families and handling of the donations. "I'm unaware if she assisted in opening private mail. There were only a few select people to do that," he said, apparently indicating that some people had indeed been opening it.

"If she saw mail addressed to victims' families, how did she know what was inside?" he continued. But then he himself explained what was inside— "cards offering a prayer and well-wishes"—which he said were boxed up and sent to the families.

Finally, after forty-five minutes of ranting, he turned to the donations. The church had hired an accounting firm to look at the Moving Forward Fund. Goff summoned a firm employee to join him at the microphone. Church officials, the uncomfortable-looking man said, had been cooperative so far. But he had no specifics on how much the church had received or how it would be distributed.

As he listened, Tyrone grew increasingly fed up with the pastors who gathered around Goff to support him but who never once had reached out a hand to help his devastated family. He was especially disappointed in the man up front.

When Goff opened the floor to questions, Tyrone stood.

Goff strolled over, hand on one hip, gesturing with the other while he spoke. Everything about him exuded confidence, smugness even. If he recognized Tyrone, he didn't indicate it as he passed off the microphone. Tyrone's deep voice filled the sanctuary.

"Within a hundred days, we sort of looked for somebody from the AME circuit to come and pray with us, and we hadn't seen one yet. And I'm hoping that all of these reverends and—"

"Well, let me—" Goff interrupted.

Tyrone persisted. "I don't know if the doctrine needs to be changed but—"

"No," Goff said, walking up the aisle toward Tyrone. "Let me speak to that."

"I'm just wondering why," Tyrone added.

Goff stood before him. "Let me see that." He pointed to the microphone and, making no eye contact with Tyrone, took it. Then he strolled away talking.

"I would suggest that even when we have, um, attempted to reach out to some, including that family, the coordination has not been there in terms of either coming to church or extending a welcome to come back and be a part of the activities of the church," Goff said.

"But if there is an ongoing and continuous need, we believe that we are more than open and we have been striving to do all we can do to address those kinds of concerns," Goff added, now back at the lectern up front.

In other words, if Tyrone and Felicia needed counseling or other help from Emanuel, they should come to the church to get it.

"Next question."

G off continued to hold Bible study in the fellowship hall. In church, even on Sundays, Felicia hardly could make herself sit in Emanuel's services and listen to him preach. Malice tinged her heart even more, which only made her feel worse. Much as she loved Emanuel, she would not lose her soul thinking bitter thoughts in a holy space.

One day, she felt the Holy Spirit speak to her: "You are looking to man for comfort."

A church was just a building. A pastor was just a flawed human being like herself. Felicia needed to look to God for direction. So, she began to look for God at other churches, often Second Presbyterian. Her granddaughter loved its Bible study for children. Felicia loved its adult study. And she continued to meet regularly with its pastor, Cress Darwin.

As Thanksgiving approached, she quietly attended an ecumenical gathering there. White and black pastors, along with many of the church's members, worshipped together in its elegant sanctuary. Then they all ventured to the fellowship hall to eat and mingle.

Felicia wound up talking to a local tour guide. The older black man specialized in African American history and Gullah culture, the surviving remnants of West and Central African heritage retained by the ancestors of enslaved people in the region. Many local African Americans, including Felicia, still spoke in distinctive clipped rhythms that echoed that connection.

She and the tour guide got onto the topic of Denmark Vesey, the freed slave who had organized the massive but tragically doomed rebellion in Charleston in 1822. He and many of those executed with him had attended Emanuel, where Vesey taught the Bible at a time when white slave owners and ministers used the sacred text to justify slavery. At a time when slave literacy was outlawed in South Carolina, Vesey, however, could read—and he taught a very different message, one of Israelite slaves freed from bondage.

"But do you know he started *here*?" the man asked Felicia.

"Well, no. I thought Denmark Vesey started at Emanuel."

"No," the man said, grinning. "Denmark Vesey started at Second Presbyterian!"

Vesey had worshipped there, in the predominantly white church where Felicia now sat, before he and others left for Emanuel. His elegantly handwritten name remained on Second Presbyterian's historic rolls of members in good standing, right next to a notation: "Black People."

Felicia went home, her thoughts filled with this man, once enslaved, then author of an insurgency. She prayed, asking God to reveal more about how their lives tied together.

nineteen

Prepare a Table for Me

✳

The mass shooting didn't only kill nine people. It devastated their families and, in far-reaching concentric circles, wounded people across the city. First responders, clergy, friends, colleagues, neighbors, attorneys, mental health workers, Embassy Suites workers, hospital trauma crews—nearly everyone in town it seemed. But within the nine families, the deaths particularly magnified every fissure that had existed before the shooting. The people affected were very human and deeply grieving. They didn't always respond like saints. They weren't saints. Divisions formed between many over everything from treasured possessions to gravestones to control over the victims' estates.

Cynthia Hurd's family was no different. The house she'd lived in almost her entire life would become the epicenter of divides that quickly formed after her death between her husband and siblings, even though—or perhaps because—it embodied the very essence of her: colorful, pragmatic, inviting.

Using a green thumb she inherited from her mother, she had tended flower boxes that still hung along the red-brick ranch's white picket fence and roses that smothered a trellis in the color of a fiery sunset. The property sat on a short lane in downtown Charleston next door to a Catholic church and its small school, not far from a library branch where Cynthia's smile once greeted all comers.

Not long after she died, her older brother Melvin Graham stopped by the house. He had grown up inside its walls with Cynthia and their four siblings. Tall and bespectacled at sixty-two, Melvin had been especially close to Cynthia over the years, and now he hoped to get a few sentimental mementos from inside to put away and save: childhood photo albums, a grandfather clock, a niece's wedding dress, a retirement plaque, some silver.

Much as he wanted the items, he dreaded the visit. Cynthia's husband, Steve, could be an overbearing hothead. The family had put up with him for Cynthia's sake, and besides, he normally was away at sea much of the year. Now her death had dissolved whatever thin bonds of family had tied them to him. Melvin hoped to get the items quickly and leave.

He walked past the roses and knocked on the front door.

Steve opened it. Inside with him was an attorney the family had been working with. Melvin walked inside and explained what items he would like to take.

"I don't think the things you're asking for are unreasonable," the attorney said.

But Steve said no.

Melvin turned to the attorney for help, but the man explained that Steve had the legal right to keep everything in the house. It was up to him what Melvin could take. If Steve didn't agree, Melvin could sue to try and get the items.

For his part, Steve resented that Cynthia's family acted like they were the only people for whom the house and the items within it had sentimental importance. He and Cynthia had shared it during their entire marriage. He too had created a life with her, memories of her, traditions and dreams with her inside its walls.

Melvin took the attorney's advice and waited several days before calling and asking again. This time, Steve seemed more open. He promised to gather a few of the things and call Melvin back in a couple more days. But he never called. Melvin finally snapped.

He drove to the house to demand that Steve give him his family's stuff. He parked out front and stepped through the white trellis of roses. In one hand, he carried a baseball bat. He knocked, then banged on the door. Steve refused to open it.

Melvin stood outside on the front porch screaming.

"You stole my family's house! You stole everything from my sister!"

Steve stayed behind the locked front door, although he didn't feel particularly threatened by the baseball bat. Cynthia had hated guns, but Steve loved to hunt—and had several firearms in the house if he needed them. Instead he fumed: Why did Cynthia's siblings act like they owned this place?

Neighbors, alarmed by the ruckus, called police, who arrived to find a tall, bespectacled man with a bat in hand. Through his fury and tears, Melvin explained about Cynthia, about the family items inside, about Steve, about the house. Melvin admitted that he shouldn't have come under such emotional duress.

"Go home," the officer said. "You guys have been through enough."

The officer didn't file charges.

Embarrassed, Melvin left.

Enraged, Steve locked himself inside the house.

E ach year, upon December's onset, the city of Charleston looks as if peace has indeed come to Earth. Snow remains a stranger most years, but red bows adorn wrought-iron gates outside of its historic mansions and single houses. Evergreen wreaths cling to streetlamps as white lights outline gnarled oak limbs and pointy palm fronds.

One night around 2 a.m. a couple of weeks before the first Christmas since the shooting, Steve woke with an urgent desire to get a tree. He and Cynthia usually bought two trees every year, one for their home, one for his mother's. This year, without his wife, Steve needed someone else's company. He called for a cab and told the dispatcher he'd be lying in his porch swing, in case the driver needed to rouse him. The tattooed seaman, his head shaved bald, yanked on a jacket and went outside to wait. In his porch swing, he listened to the night's silence and dozed. Cynthia's voice entered his dream.

"I got you. I'm your number one fan."

"I know, girl," he answered.

He awoke with a start; the cab driver stared down from the darkness.

Once he reached the car's warmth, Steve directed the man to drive to a nearby twenty-four-hour Walmart. They talked about fishing, about Emanuel, about the holidays. They talked about Cynthia and the shooting. It was nice to have company. When they arrived, Steve hustled inside and picked out a Christmas tree. The taxi driver helped him load it on top of the cab before they drove to Steve's mother's house. He woke the eighty-seven-year-old and said he'd be right back to set it up.

"Just wait for tomorrow," she suggested.

"It's already tomorrow!"

Steve asked the driver to return to Walmart, where he bought another tree. They loaded that one up, too, and drove to his house. After the cab driver left, Steve hauled the tree from his front porch to a corner of his living room. Then he walked the eight bone-cold blocks to his mother's house. He was the baby of his family, and her health was ailing. But before seeing her again, he needed the silence. He didn't want to drive and hear his favorite radio station, which paused several times a day to remember the Charleston Nine and recite each of their names. "Charleston doesn't forget," the announcer would say.

When he arrived, it was 3:30 a.m. He woke up his mom again, put up her tree, and headed out. She didn't like him walking alone under darkness, but her protectiveness only irritated him.

twenty

A View from the Front Row

✳

The East Room of the White House filled with the members of an ever-growing fraternity of sorrow, as survivors and loved ones of those killed in America's gun violence epidemic gathered to hear President Obama discuss his latest plans to tackle the problem.

Sharon Risher found her assigned seat on the aisle, five rows back from a lectern emblazoned with a bald eagle inside a golden circle that read: The President of the United States. She'd dreamed of becoming Charleston's first black woman mayor, but she'd never imagined she'd be in the White House, waiting for the president. In her lap, her fingers traced the edges of a picture of her mother. Despite her excitement at being in this place, her eyes welled with tears and her lips tugged persistently downward.

Former congresswoman Gabrielle Giffords of Arizona, shot in the head five years ago almost to this early January day, sat among them. So did parents who had lost children at Connecticut's Sandy Hook Elementary. And Columbine. And Umpqua Community College in Oregon.

Four rows up, in the front row, sat Clementa Pinckney's two little girls. Jennifer Pinckney stood facing them on a small stage wearing a light gray pantsuit, a photo of Clementa pinned to her right lapel, a photo of the nine on her left. Yet, the shooting at Emanuel, preceded by so many other incidents of mass killing, was no longer even the latest. A month earlier, a couple had gunned down fourteen people at a Christmas party in San Bernardino, California.

The crowd quieted as a middle-aged white man stepped to the lectern. With remarkable composure, he described losing his seven-year-old son at Sandy Hook three years earlier.

"We're better than this," he implored.

He then introduced President Obama and Vice President Biden, who arrived to a hail of applause. Reaching the podium, Obama described how Sandy Hook had changed him—and how he had so hoped it would change the country as well. He rattled off other mass shooting sites. Arizona. San Bernardino. Charleston.

"Too many."

"Too many!" the audience agreed.

"Too many," he repeated softly. Over his left shoulder, Jennifer nodded.

"In this room," he continued, "there are a lot of stories. There's a lot of heartache. There's a lot of resilience. There's a lot of strength. But there's also a lot of pain. And this is just a small sample."

Obama explained that he wanted to strengthen background checks, improve gun-safety technology, better enforce existing laws, and improve mental health care given that two in three gun deaths were suicides. Those "in the business of selling firearms"—including online or at gun shows— would have to get licensed and conduct background checks or face criminal prosecutions under new executive actions he outlined.

However, his term ended in less than a year. He couldn't change the laws alone.

Hearing his plea, Sharon made a promise. As a trauma chaplain who witnessed America's gun violence firsthand, she hadn't done enough to solve it before. That old life of complacency was gone now.

Obama paused at mention of Sandy Hook Elementary.

"First-graders."

A tear almost escaped his left eye before his fingertip thwarted it. Sharon's eyes filled, too. She wouldn't let the president down.

Neither would Jennifer, though she wasn't naturally drawn to public life in the way that Sharon was. Her return to work at the library had provided some sense of normalcy, and she'd busied herself with her daughters' homework, chores, and dance classes to create as much routine as possible for them all. A trio of men Clementa had known encircled them in a wall of protection from the tensions at Emanuel and the endless requests for interviews and speaking engagements. Mostly, Jennifer turned them away. But not now. Clementa would want her here, beside the president, trying to change the nation's gun laws.

Jennifer was a shortish woman, so when White House aides had positioned her on the stage slightly behind Obama, she felt relieved to be shielded by his tall form. She didn't realize that network TV cameras recording the moment were angled in a way that caught her every grimace and nod over his shoulder.

Jennifer did, however, know that back home in South Carolina, there was little popular support for curbing access to guns. Hers was a rural state, a place where folks living in the country needed to protect themselves—from wildlife and from thieves. If a person came onto a man's property without permission, he had every right to shoot him. And probably would.

People also duck hunted in the beautiful state's bountiful marshes and deer hunted in its thick forests. Men and boys in particular, but increasingly girls as well, rose before dawn to trek out for a day of hunting that involved hours immersed in woodland serenity, bonding and mastering the discipline of deer-stand patience. They learned the science of lures and tides and what fish bite when and the hard work of cleaning that night's dinner. In a state where nearly six in ten residents lived in a home with a firearm, guns simply were part of life.

A year before the Emanuel massacre, one state lawmaker even raffled off an AR-15 semi-automatic rifle at a campaign rally, and Governor Haley tweeted about the firearm her husband gave her for Christmas one year: "I must have been good Santa gave me a Beretta PX4 Storm." When people said guns were a part of life, that's what they meant. Owning guns wasn't considered dangerous or offensive to most of the state's residents. Gun ownership enjoyed massive support among the NRA-led Republicans who controlled the halls of power, allowing them to dismiss any efforts to limit their Second Amendment rights, including expanded background checks.

Jennifer knew the massacre in Charleston hadn't changed that, and neither would another speech by President Obama.

Charleston stayed constantly in the news in early 2016. Governor Haley delivered the Republican response to President Obama's State of the Union address. She spoke about growing up in the South and not looking like her neighbors. She mentioned Emanuel and the horrific shooting there. And she reminded people that the victims' families summoned grace and forgiveness, not hate or retaliation. The nation must follow suit.

"Today, we live in a time of threats like few others in recent memory. During anxious times, it can be tempting to follow the siren call of the angriest voices. We must resist that temptation," Haley warned. Most people considered it a jab at the Republican primary's rancorous tone, and it quickly provoked the ire of candidate Donald Trump's supporters—although praise from most everyone else. Then Republicans and Democrats brought almost back-to-back presidential debates to town.

Some of the victims' loved ones followed the news closely. Jennifer did not. She went to none of Roof's court hearings that Felicia and Polly so determinedly attended as their way to cope and ensure Roof's criminal accountability. In contrast, Jennifer's means of survival had been to withdraw into as much of her normal life with her daughters as remained. Jennifer had never seen Dylann Roof in person, and she didn't want to. Occasionally, she accepted one of the endless invitations to speak and receive honors on behalf of her husband. In death, it seemed everyone wanted a piece of Clementa, and of her, but too many of them just wanted to use his name for their own glory. It irritated Jennifer.

Every now and then, however, something beckoned her from that quiet, private life she had carved out. One had been Obama's speech about guns. Another was an event Clementa should have attended, but now would not. On Mother's Day, her first as a single parent, Jennifer arrived at a hotel in a swanky section of Washington, D.C. She wore jeans, a white T-shirt, and no makeup, as she preferred. If anyone recognized her, they didn't say so, and for that, she was grateful. Jennifer felt robbed now, of her life's companion and everything they had worked for together. She had traveled all the way from Columbia for what was supposed to be the capstone of Clementa's countless hours spent studying and doing homework while juggling so much else—including his family.

Instead, the next morning, she helped their daughters rise for the day when the Reverend Clementa Pinckney would posthumously become the Reverend Dr. Clementa Pinckney. Instead of cheering him on from the audience as he walked across a stage at the Washington National Cathedral to receive his Doctor of Ministry degree, Jennifer would receive it in his place.

Jennifer's taxi soon pulled up to the soaring neo-Gothic spires of Washington's National Cathedral. It was the Episcopal Church's cathedral, but many Americans considered it the nation's house of prayer, host of presidential memorials and state funerals. Martin Luther King Jr. had delivered his final Sunday sermon here, and the cathedral hosted a memorial service for him shortly after. Now, almost fifty years later, it would host a commencement honoring another black pastor killed by a white man.

Inside the cavernous cathedral, Jennifer sat in the front row with her mother. They sandwiched in the girls, who both wore pretty white dresses. Her mother's soft, steady presence reassured her. Cleo Benjamin lived with them, as she had before Clementa's death, and while Jennifer worked hard to remain composed in front of Eliana and Malana, she still cried on her mother's shoulder. But Cleo had cancer, and she wasn't doing well, something Jennifer couldn't bear to think about. She couldn't imagine losing Clementa and then losing her mother.

Malana's big white bow and Eliana's smaller peach bow faced back toward rows of their family gathered behind them, near where 142 graduates would soon arrive to sit. Onstage, diplomas waited on a purple cloth.

Jennifer clutched a pen from the hotel and a printout of the speech she'd soon deliver alone to the crowd filling the massive space, not to mention a live feed and cameras. She hated public speaking, and the huge cathedral seemed so very full of people, the stage so enormous. The seminary's president, David McAllister-Wilson, opened the ceremony and soon read a letter he had received, congratulating the graduates.

"You carry on the proud example set by one of your fellow graduates, a pastor and a public servant himself, Reverend Clementa Pinckney." The letter writer described Clementa's thesis and the need to turn service into action.

"Sincerely, Barack Obama."

A murmur, then applause, spread through the crowd.

It was all very nice, but as Jennifer listened, something didn't feel quite right, or not right enough, for Clementa's big moment. Discreetly in her lap, she texted her friend and attorney, state senator Gerald Malloy, who was sitting right behind her.

"Do u think I should take the girls up with me?"

He paused, thinking, then typed back.

"It's not in the plan but it's your time. Do it."

Jennifer whispered to Eliana and Malana as the graduates lined up. When the ceremony reached the Doctorate of Ministry candidates, a man arrived to escort Jennifer onstage. She left her mother in the front row and followed him. The girls followed her. A standing ovation greeted them all.

Then came the silence, the expectations. A dean handed her Clementa's diploma and his hood. Jennifer turned to the microphone and spoke words not on the printout of her speech.

"I was supposed to come and accept this award by myself," she began. "But Clementa was a family man."

The crowd murmured, "Amen."

"And so the Spirit hit me that our daughters, Eliana and Malana, need to be by their mother's side on this momentous occasion—and they be the ones to accept their daddy's diploma."

Even louder applause.

She turned to hand Eliana her father's hood and Malana her father's diploma. Then she paused to breathe. She felt her voice quiver.

"This is a bittersweet moment for my family and I. A few years ago, I remember Clementa telling us about this day—the day he would graduate—and that the whole family would be there. Eliana, the oldest, she doesn't like to miss school, and so she asked her father, 'I'm not going to have to miss school, am I?'"

The people laughed.

"Boy. How life can change in an instant."

Eyes welled as she remembered when he nearly took a semester off because life had become so hectic. Yet, he'd persevered.

"Clementa," she whispered, "you did it."

twenty-one

Depths of the Valley

✳

In normal life, wives usually outlive their spouses. Barely more than one in ten husbands get left behind to deal with the enormous loss, and grief hits them especially hard. They tend to lack social systems outside of their wives and are less likely to entrust their sorrow to confidants. Various researchers have speculated that the reason widowers die earlier than married men is that women tend to be the caregivers in marriages. So, when they die first, their husbands are left without someone to provide the very support they most need to cope.

This proved correct in the life of Steve Hurd, adrift since his wife Cynthia died at Bible study four days before her fifty-fifth birthday. She was a quintessential caregiver. At home, Cynthia had kept Steve grounded, even when he was at sea. She pushed him to take care of himself, to believe in himself, especially when he didn't. Without her now, he felt lost in time and space.

Steve turned forty-six on Super Bowl Sunday, almost two months after his Christmas tree run, and spent it alone. He and Cynthia weren't huge football fans, but they used to watch the game with a spread of buffalo wings, chips, sodas, and a meat-and-cheese tray spread across a blanket. He didn't watch the game now. Instead, he lay in bed except to get some Pop-Tarts and chips and didn't answer his phone, preferring to hear her voice which was still on the machine.

He still hadn't been able to return to his job as a merchant mariner and felt like the only shooting victims' relative left so alone. Without kids, their brick house sat unnervingly lifeless, although he could almost feel Cynthia's presence in the clothes that still hung in the closets and the books still packed onto shelves around him.

Like most nights now he couldn't sleep. He'd parked his car around the corner so that even his mom and sister wouldn't know he was home. He avoided calls from his brother, a Marine who was stationed elsewhere.

He again imagined what might have happened at Bible study if he'd been home that night. Then, he pictured slipping into Dylann Roof's cell at the jail. He'd tell him, in a syrupy voice of sarcasm, that he sure hoped the jail staff was treating him well. He would remind him that many people weren't enjoying a fraction of his comfort "because you took that away from those who were living."

Then he'd get real close to Roof and say: "What if black people who didn't like white people killed your mother or sister?"

Then Norvel Goff's face crept in, and the hamster wheel of angry thoughts spun faster, more frenzied. What if Goff had extended the hand of God's love to the families?

"That sorry excuse for a human being," Steve thought. "A spineless, weak, jellyfish of a man who, for lack of better phrasing, is an imposter. A shell of a minister who's no more than a storefront preacher! I have more respect for a lump of whale shit, which is the lowest form of shit on the planet because it's on the bottom of the ocean, did nothing to help us move along spiritually . . ."

Steve still wasn't forgiving anyone.

The researchers' speculations about men's difficulties after their wives' deaths proved less correct in the case of Anthony Thompson, the other man left widowed by the shooting. After Myra died, Anthony had stepped onto the treadmill of busyness to cope. He returned to his pulpit, to his community, working harder than ever to find meaning in her death and to fulfill God's plans for the life he was left to lead without her.

A trim man with salt-and-pepper hair, Anthony sprinted through each day's to-do list with a spry boyishness about him. But one day, he noticed a mild discomfort in his chest. By the time he ate dinner, a searing pain stretched from his jaw down one arm. Even his teeth hurt. The next morning, he went to his doctor, who in turn dispatched him straight to the hospital. Anthony didn't want to go, but the pain was unbearable.

He figured he'd get some medication and leave. As always, he was slammed with things to do.

At the hospital, they made him don a hospital gown and put him through a battery of tests. Anthony complied, anxious to be sent home.

"You need to stay," the doctor said. "We're going to keep you."

Anthony groaned, "Oh no."

He hadn't been admitted to a hospital since he was five years old. Luckily, the tests so far showed no problems with his heart. However, the doctor ordered him to take a stress test in the morning. And get some rest.

Anthony's sister, who worked at the hospital, came by to visit. He appreciated it. Then, in a hospital bed, with machines and hospital staff working around him, he tried to get some sleep. Away from his ringing home phone, he fell into a deep slumber.

The next morning, the stress test looked fine, too. Anthony's doctor released him, saying his heart was in great shape, although the rest of him could use a little more exercise and rest. In truth, Anthony used to be diligent about his physical health, but he admittedly had not gotten to it lately.

Mostly likely, the doctor said, the pain was caused by a little reflux and a heap of stress and anxiety. Anthony left thanking God his heart was okay and promising to do better.

A few days later, allergies stuffed his nose and fogged his head. He kept trying to exercise but was too busy. His bishop and everyone else had been contacting him about an important conference in Columbia on Saturday. Then he had his own church's service on Sunday. An endless list of things to do that kept him mercifully distracted.

twenty-two

Be Quick to Listen

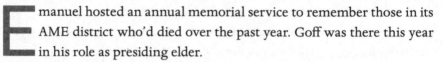

Emanuel hosted an annual memorial service to remember those in its AME district who'd died over the past year. Goff was there this year in his role as presiding elder.

Toward the end, he had an announcement.

He was running for bishop.

If many of the victims' families remained less than taken with his leadership and stewardship of funds sent by well-wishers, the outside world seemed to view Goff as a revered leader of those who'd spoken the now-famous words of forgiveness. He'd received a number of accolades for his leadership, including the Order of the Palmetto, the state's highest civilian honor. Governor Haley had presented it shortly after the shooting, along with a particularly stirring summation of his role: "He healed our state, and he will go down in history as being the person that really healed the country," she'd told an appreciative crowd in his hometown. The mayor gave him a key to the city.

Not long after, a more welcome rumor seeped out among the family members. Bishop Norris had replaced Goff as Emanuel's pastor so that Goff would be freed up more to campaign and raise money. Goff would remain presiding elder, meaning he still would supervise the new pastor. But the families and survivors would get a new, and perhaps more engaged, minister.

That replacement was Betty Deas Clark, a seasoned pastor who would arrive as the first female minister in Emanuel's two-hundred-year history. Clark, who hailed from a small town just up the coast from Charleston, didn't know about the divide between the church leadership and the survivors and victims' relatives. She knew little about their still-simmering suspicions about their opened mail, the unanswered requests for personal ministry, and the distrust over the handling of the donations, which remained on hold while Steve Hurd's attorneys sifted through the Moving Forward Fund's receipts.

Within a few days of arriving in Charleston, Clark did what Goff had not done in the seven months since the funerals. She began to call the victims' loved ones. She had known several of those who died, including Myra, and it felt like an obvious thing to do. Among them, she called Anthony Thompson to offer her sympathies. After they spoke, Anthony hung up and thought, "My gosh!" In seven months, he hadn't heard even that much from a pastor at Emanuel.

Clark also called Steve Hurd. "I just want you to know you have my condolences," she told him. She'd like to speak in person, if he agreed. She had known his wife, Cynthia, too. Steve told her that he'd think about it.

She also reached Sharon Risher and prayed with her fellow AME minister over the phone. Sharon was brought to tears and thanked the new pastor, noting that nobody else from Emanuel's staff had called her to pray in almost eight months.

"Hmmm," Clark said. "Well, I'm here now."

She also called Andy Savage, the attorney who represented Felicia and Polly, both of whom attended different churches now. Would he convey a message to them? Andy hung up, intrigued. Shortly after, Felicia and Polly attended a planning meeting to discuss the anniversary's long list of events. Clark was there, too.

She asked the two survivors: Would they consider coming back to Emanuel on Sunday?

For the first nine months after the shooting, Felicia almost always wore black. Recently, she'd begun to wear colors again. That Sunday, the Sunday of her return to Emanuel, she chose a hot pink sweater over a black dress. With worship time approaching, Felicia walked toward her lifelong sanctuary with Tyrone on one side, Andy Savage on the other. Her grand-daughter followed, accompanied by Andy's wife and office manager, Cheryl, and a contingent of family members. Felicia quickly marched down one aisle and led them to the second pew from the front. People turned to look.

Felicia had arrived home.

About a third of the people filling in the pews around her were white. A flock of visitors from some far-away college filled several in the middle. An armed, uniformed police officer watched as usual now from the balcony. Clark stepped up front, directly in front of Felicia.

"Well, amen!" Her rich voice filled the sanctuary. She wasn't a large woman. She didn't stand much above five-foot-three. With short curly hair, her round cheeks and smooth skin lent her a certain girlishness. But from the pulpit, her powerful voice flowed over the sanctuary in waves of vel-vet. "For truly there is a sweet, sweet spirit in this place!"

The people rose. The massive historic organ chimed. Voices rang from the pews.

"Praise God from whom all blessings flow . . ."

Felicia's granddaughter, a petite girl with her hair twisted into a bun, sat between Andy and Cheryl. As the people of Emanuel sang, the child whispered: "Granny's crying."

"Honey, that's because she's happy," Cheryl whispered back.

When the song faded, and a minister called to the altar those who needed prayer, Felicia joined people slipping from their pews to come kneel at a waist-high wooden rail that enclosed an area between the altar and the congrega-tion. Her fellow Emanuel members surrounded her. Many of them hadn't understood why she'd stopped coming to worship here in the first place. Many didn't know the details of why she felt so abandoned by church leaders.

As the congregation launched into a song, Clark approached, arms held wide. Felicia stood, and the women embraced for several seconds. Felicia headed back to her seat. En route, a man reached out and hugged her.

Clark began. "Our father, our God, our creator and our sustainer. We pause at this hour in the morning, God, to tell you thank you for allowing us to see a brand-new day!"

"Yes!"

"I pause at this moment to tell God thank you for the Sanders family being here," Clark said. "You do not have to stand. You are at home, and we just want to tell God thank you for your being here." Loud clapping answered her. "We just want to reiterate the fact that our love is overflowing for each of you and to remind you that your pain is our pain. And that better days will come—that is the crux of our faith. Amen."

Soon the choir kicked up, and the people sang in joyful rhythm.

Felicia's head bobbed. She rocked in her seat. She stood clapping. A palpable joy pounded on the walls and shook the pews of Mother Emanuel. People stomped and raised their hands high to a God that had awakened them for another day. This was Emanuel the church, not Emanuel the tourist stop or Emanuel the shrine. When the service ended, the choir joined to sing, *"The Lord is my shepherd. I shall not want . . ."*

Clark plucked the microphone off the lectern. Singing with them, she slowly descended several steps, walked through the wooden railing, and maneuvered down one aisle. She stopped at the first pews and made her way down to Felicia. She stopped and wrapped her in warmth. Applause filled the sanctuary.

Clark turned next to Tyrone, then to their granddaughter. She moved down the row, hugging the entire Sanders family.

"I shall dwell in the house of the Lord forever."

Felicia smiled. Clark's gesture before the congregation touched her deeply. As the service closed, others surrounded them, embracing them, smiling, crying. Tyrone kissed an older woman, his round hat in hand. An older girl in a choir robe approached their granddaughter with a hug.

As the people left, Clark stood at the back door saying good-byes and hugged each of Felicia's group as they left. Outside, visitors on the sidewalk took cell phone pictures of the front gates, colorful flowers woven into its bars. A white bus sat parked across the street.

Clark muttered to herself, "Oh God, there's a tour."

Felicia was grateful for the warm reception at Emanuel, but Second Presbyterian had nourished her faith and heart over this time of desperate need. She loved the people there, too. She loved its pastor, Cress Darwin, who still met with her one-on-one every week. And she especially loved the church's Bible study and the warm welcome she felt in its pews.

So, on Palm Sunday, Felicia stood in front of Second Presbyterian's sanctuary with a half-dozen other people formally joining the church.

The other new members joined the church in full. Felicia, however, became an affiliate member, which meant that she would hold joint memberships both there and at Emanuel.

Indeed, when the service began to wind down, Felicia slipped out the back door and walked across the wide parking lot between them. Deep in her heart, where her memories of Tywanza and Susie lived, where the essence of Felicia's life before the massacre lingered, Emanuel still remained home. She hurried toward it.

Outside, yellow cones blocked one lane of Calhoun Street in front of the church. White tour buses rumbled into the reserved space to deliver a group with the Faith & Politics Institute, which took a Congressional delegation on a civil rights pilgrimage each year, this year to visit Emanuel. Police and FBI agents stood as armed guards.

Members and visitors flowed inside to find a huge swath of the sanctuary taped off for the dignitaries. In that reserved section, Jenny Horne, the white state lawmaker whose impassioned speech had helped bring the Confederate flag down, greeted U.S. Rep. Jim Clyburn, the first black congressman from the state since Reconstruction. Tim Scott arrived. So did Congressman John Lewis, the civil rights icon.

Even the balconies filled. Ushers urged people to squeeze in. A camera crew filming a documentary moved up and down an aisle, holding out giant boom microphones. Visitors used cell phones to record.

Felicia joined Tyrone in a pew, and Polly slipped in quietly as well to sit unnoticed in back as Clark stepped up before a sanctuary full of motion. The camera crew crouched in front of the choir as the people waved green strips of palm fronds.

"Forget the cameras," Clark warned. "Forget the visitors. This is church."

She soon launched into a discussion about Jesus' strength of character, his refusal to let others define him or his critics to change him.

When Clark finished, Felicia stood up again. She slipped outside and headed back to Second Presbyterian. As the second morning service began, Cress welcomed the same half-dozen new members who'd stood up front earlier so the whole congregation could meet them. Felicia hadn't arrived yet, though. She was still greeting friends at Emanuel while trying to make her way back across the parking lot.

twenty-three

Competing Grief

✳

Ethel Lance's grave lay in eternal rest in Emanuel's graveyard ten minutes up the road from the church building in Charleston's "Neck" area, the upper peninsula that connected the gentrifying areas where Mother Emanuel stood to the persistent black poverty in North Charleston. A tapestry of two dozen other graveyards comprised what was the city's cemetery district, a patchwork of small cemeteries divided by race and ethnicity, in their own way monuments to their separate and unequal history.

The district's most famed inhabitant, Magnolia Cemetery, housed soaring monuments to the city's elite. On the other side of a brick wall, a small plaque read: EMANUEL AME CHURCH CEMETERY. No winding paths traversed the graves there, no gardens, no elaborate monuments, no waterfront beauty drew visitors to linger. Instead, simple headstones, many dating back well into the 1800s, marked most burial spots; mounds of rocks marked others. The surnames of wealthy plantation owners like Middleton and Drayton adorned many.

Ethel was buried in close proximity to fellow shooting victims Tywanza Sanders, his elderly Aunt Susie, and librarian Cynthia Hurd. It was a peaceful place, but eleven months after their deaths, Ethel's warring daughters hadn't been able to speak civilly enough to agree on a marker for her grave here. So, each had commissioned her own.

The Reverend Sharon Risher, in concert with their middle sister, purchased a headstone that was completed in April. Without her youngest sister Nadine's permission, she had it installed on their mother's grave.

A month later, on a warm spring day, Nadine stood watching proudly as a white pickup truck with a blue crane lowered the tombstone she'd commissioned down into the soft dirt—directly in front of the one that her sisters already had installed, creating the effect of one headstone having turned its back on the other.

But Nadine didn't just purchase Ethel a headstone. A large slab of smooth ebony stone soon covered the entire space of Ethel's grave and, beside her, their second-oldest sister's grave as well. White etching across it read:

> *From all your children*
> *grand children and*
> *great-grandchildren*

Beneath those words stretched a list of ten names, Nadine's first. Gary Washington, their only brother, was listed second. Then came most of Ethel's grandchildren and great-grandchildren in a long list.

Second to last came her middle daughter, Esther, who lived in North Charleston and had colluded with Sharon to support her tombstone. Sharon, the oldest, was listed last. Her children weren't listed at all. When the dirt was all moved into place and the workmen left, Nadine and several people close to her stood marveling at the eye-catching creation. Nadine, the first family member to speak of forgiveness at Roof's bond hearing, left the cemetery thrilled that at last her mother and sister now had a grave marker that did them justice.

The burial spot sat out in the center of a swatch of the graveyard, the sisters' dispute now a centerpiece of the dead.

Esther quickly got word about it. She hurried over and texted Sharon several pictures of this public display of the family's acrimony. Sharon was packing up her Dallas apartment to move to Charlotte, where her grown children lived. God, she felt certain, was calling her to leave her trauma chaplain post and take her ministry, speaking about racism and gun reforms, across the country. She also often spoke about forgiveness, given that she was among the victims' family members who publicly explained that she hadn't forgiven Roof yet.

When Esther's text came through, Sharon stopped packing. She held up her phone, flipping through the pictures several times. As her fury boiled, she stalked toward a giant framed picture of their mother she'd been preparing to pack and began to scream at it. If only Ethel had left a will or instructions for her grave or hadn't been so good at smoothing over her daughters' differences so that they could have learned how to do it themselves by now.

"It's making a mockery of you, Momma. I'm not gonna stand for it. No!" she raged.

How could Nadine get up and instantly forgive Dylann Roof, then turn around and treat her own family like this? Sharon might have wanted to forgive Roof one day. But right now, she felt certain that she would never forgive her sister for this.

PART III

✻

*What's Done in the Dark Comes
to the Light*

twenty-four

Appalling Silence of the Good People

❈

Shortly after turning twenty-one, just a few weeks before the shooting, Roof had spotted his old buddy Joey Meek's face on a website of police mug shots. He decided to reach out on Facebook, where he maintained eighty-eight friends, the same number of bullets he later would bring inside Mother Emanuel.

Roof sent Joey Meek a Facebook message. They hadn't hung out since middle school, but his friend still responded with the address of the mobile home where he lived with his mother and younger brothers. Soon they were smoking weed together again. They'd drink vodka, too, and sometimes use cocaine. Meek was happy to see his friend again, and besides, Roof had a car.

Though it had been several years, Roof initially seemed like the same shy, awkward kid Meek and his brothers remembered. But they soon realized that something was different. He was even quieter. He'd cut his hair into a bowl shape and tromped around in heavy boots. He talked about getting a tattoo of a dagger on his face. At one point, he asked Meek to take a picture of him burning the American flag, an odd request in this patriotic part of the country.

"Hell no," Meek had replied.

But mostly they were young twentysomethings with few if any real job prospects, meandering through life without much purpose other than to get wasted. A black neighbor of Meek's, Christon Scriven, sometimes joined them and later would insist that he never felt Roof's disdain, although a week before the shooting Roof told him he wanted to start a race war. Scriven didn't think he was serious. In fact, after the massacre, he defended Roof, even telling the BBC that Roof never treated him differently because of his race. "Everybody's making him out to be racist, but here I am in front of you today as a black man and telling you that I look at him no different today than what I looked at him last week, because he never said anything racist to me."

Caleb Brown, a biracial childhood friend who had since moved to Texas, echoed that. After the shooting, he told several news outlets that he too had never known Roof to be racist. "That was not inside of him the entire time I knew that kid, or his mom; they were not like that," he told CBS. He called Roof's mother one of the nicest people he'd ever met. Caleb's mom told investigators that her son had even invited Roof to their house. The young man struck her as skittish and shy. But not racist.

However, Meek caught glimpses of Roof's growing fascination with white supremacy. One day when just the two of them were driving around, Roof had started talking about Rhodesia, current-day Zimbabwe, where white rulers once had oppressed the black majority population. It had since become a favorite symbol among white supremacists. Roof attached its flag onto a black jacket he'd bought at Goodwill.

Then, Roof told Meek that he wished segregation was still enforced. Crazy at it sounded, Meek didn't argue the point, and it wasn't like he hadn't heard whiffs of the notion before in more backward company. Besides, Roof was hammered. He also had a dark sense of humor under any circumstances. He often said things that he meant as a joke but then didn't laugh. It was hard to tell when he was serious. Meek, dealing with his own mental health issues, didn't challenge his friend.

Then one night about a week before June 17, Roof came over with a jug of vodka. They drank about three-quarters of it, chasing it with some cocaine and weed while playing Xbox. Out of nowhere, Roof began talking crazy stuff about starting a race riot. There was too much black-on-white crime, he vented, and lots of white women were getting raped by black men.

Then Roof confessed that he had visited a historic AME church in Charleston where Martin Luther King Jr. once spoke. He wanted to kill some black people there. In fact, he wanted to attack on a Wednesday because fewer people would be at the church to potentially thwart his plans. He intended to spark a new level of racial tensions. He also planned to kill himself.

When Roof fell into a stupor, Meek remembered an old friend of theirs who had told his brother he was going to kill himself—and then did so. Roof had always been so odd and withdrawn that he couldn't even make eye contact with people. It seemed far more realistic that he would try to kill himself than hurt other people. Surely the rest was just drunken blabber.

Most concerned about what Roof would do to himself that night, Meek waited until his friend passed out, took the Glock from Roof's Hyundai, and stashed it under an air vent inside their trailer. However, by the time Roof woke up sober the next morning, Meek had returned the pistol to the car.

The very first line of Roof's manifesto read, "I was not raised in a racist home or environment," as if he'd known this would be the reflexive assumption given his crimes. He told the FBI agents who interviewed him that he hadn't alerted his parents to his beliefs and feared their reactions to the shooting.

His divorced parents both lived in Richland County, whose urban capital city, Columbia, formed a patch of blue in a staunchly red state. His father lived in Columbia, a city with a large public university and an African American mayor, where two in every five residents were black. His mother lived about thirty minutes away in Eastover, a mostly black area where the encroaching suburbs gave way to the country. Not that either represented diverse utopias.

Black residents, and not only elderly ones, still harbored memories of the state's bitter fight against integration and the hauntings of Klan justice. Even today, white and black residents live largely in racial silos, and a baseline of cultural racism has allowed severe disparities to fester untended. A short drive away from where Roof's father lived, one of the state's original "segregation academies"—private schools built for whites to avoid court-ordered desegregation in the 1960s and 1970s—still bustled with a robust, almost all-white student body.

However, Roof didn't go to school there. He attended the area's more diverse public schools where, once a good student, he had spiraled before the eyes of his family. As for parenting, while Amy and Benn Roof might not have fully realized their son's descent into racial hatred, they had noticed his continuous drift away from meaningful school, work, and social interactions—and an increasing amount of time spent online.

Yet, Amy still let him take meals in his bedroom because he preferred it. Throughout her son's life, she had tried to placate his anxieties and obsessive behaviors, seeking professional help when she was at her wit's end. For his part, Benn had focused on getting his son to man up and pull his own weight in the world, namely by getting a job.

Benn and Amy were as different as their approaches to parenting. Amy, a wispy figure, barely five feet tall with long blonde hair, could seem as emotionally frail as she was physically slight. She had married Benn in 1988 and, four months later, welcomed their first child, Amber, into their lives. The couple separated two years later, citing "marital difficulties," then divorced the following year. She became pregnant with Dylann and gave birth in 1994 after a brief reconciliation. They broke up again shortly after his birth.

Over the years, Dylann had lived primarily with her. When he was little, he'd kiss her three times and tell her that he loved her three times. She would say it back. She understood that it had to be three times, no more or less. She'd known that he liked to be washed head to toe, never with a washcloth that had touched his feet first. She used his favorite detergent so that his clothes smelled the way he wanted. Like any mother, she liked making her son happy.

Benn Roof, however, was the kind of anti-establishment conservative who soon would propel Donald Trump into the White House. He disdained "the swamp" in Washington, D.C., and despised Hillary Clinton. He planned to call her husband "the first bitch" if she got elected. A tattooed construction contractor with a proudly unfiltered persona, Benn disdained political correctness—and anything else elitist that tried to dictate he soften his edges. That included a penchant for jokes that offended, and he once remarked to Dylann that a classmate's penis must be small because he was Asian. Not long before the shooting, he had encouraged his son to sing a rap song with the n-word. On the other hand, nobody ever found a white hood in Benn's closet.

However, as the primary parent who witnessed Dylann's solitary behavior on a daily basis, Amy, like most parents in her situation, simply wanted her son to be normal, to fit in. She'd worried even back when he was a tow-headed little boy and noticeably shied away from other children. She'd comforted him when he complained that he looked weird and obsessed over his forehead being too big. In later elementary school, as he became afraid of leaving the house, she worried more.

By the time Dylann started middle school, she had grown concerned enough about his lack of friendships that, when a boy skateboarded by their house, she stopped him: Would he come meet her son? Dylann had no friends, she explained, and didn't come outside much to play.

Joey Meek had agreed. He came from a difficult, abusive background and understood what it meant to not fit in. One day, he'd gone to middle school with red marks on his neck where his stepfather had choked him. Somehow, he and Dylann hit it off, much to Amy's relief. They began skateboarding together, although Joey quickly realized that this new friend could be awkwardly quiet and had a thing about his forehead and acne. Dylann also hated dirt. He hated the outdoors. He did, however, like smoking weed. They began to smoke it together—a lot.

As Dylann's anxieties increasingly took hold of him in elementary and middle school, Benn Roof married again. He and his new wife Paige soon welcomed a daughter named Morgan. At the same time, Benn's construction business flourished. He and Paige moved to Key West, Florida, where their decade-long marriage ended. In contested divorce proceedings, Paige called Benn "irate and unstable" and alleged in court records that in 2008 he shoved her to the ground and hit her on the back of her head. He countered that she'd cheated on him and filed court documents from a private investigator alleging proof of it. Each denied wrongdoing.

After the divorce, Benn returned to Columbia. Dylann had remained there with his mother during that time, where he'd continued in school, went to a Lutheran church, even attended confirmation classes as a young teen. His pastor, the Reverend Tony Metze, had tried to reach out, but Dylann proved robotic, friendships seemingly beyond his social capacity. Metze couldn't think of a single friend Dylann had made at the church, despite attending for several years. When Metze spoke with Benn, he too confessed that he struggled to connect with his son.

By spring 2009, when Dylann was turning fifteen, Amy had become concerned enough about it all—her son's anxieties, marijuana use, plummeting grades—that she sought help from a local mental health center. A doctor described him as "very anxious." They all agreed he was addicted to marijuana and suffered from an anxiety disorder. Roof went to therapy for a few months and was prescribed medication for anxiety, but it wasn't clear he took it.

During freshman year, he dropped out of school, beginning a five-year descent into increasing isolation and anxiety fixated on his health. He sought medical care several times for a thyroid problem that he was convinced caused testosterone to pool on one side of his body. Indeed, he did suffer a thyroid disorder. But it was so minor that the endocrinologist who diagnosed it didn't think it required medication. Dylann, however, called the doctor's office back after his visit, anxious to start taking something immediately.

"He thinks his thyroid is getting bigger. It may be best if you call the pt [patient], he is extremely anxious," an office assistant noted to the doctor in 2014, the year before the shooting.

By then Dylann was spending nearly all his days parked in front of the computer in his bedroom. Benn focused on cajoling his son into getting a job. When Dylann turned twenty-one, in exchange for getting one, Benn even helped pay for a pistol—the one that Meek took away that drunken night. And then gave back.

It was impossible to conclude with certainty why Meek failed to call the police after Roof revealed his plan, although doing so could have prevented the deaths of nine people. What was certain: He would pay a severe price in terms of public scorn and legal consequences.

Ten months after the shooting, as the victims' families awaited Roof's trial, they also learned that Meek had agreed to plead guilty to "misprision of a felony," or deliberately concealing knowledge of the massacre. He also admitted that he had willfully made a false statement to an FBI agent the day after the shooting. He faced up to eight years in federal prison.

Now with a buzz cut, chipmunk cheeks, and a dark suit, Meek arrived in court bearing little resemblance to the young man who'd spoken to reporters about Roof after the shooting—a sunburned good old boy sporting a camouflage visor and a Carolina Gamecocks muscle shirt. It was his time to face a judge. In quiet and respectful tones, he admitted that Roof had told him he was planning to shoot multiple people at an AME church's Bible study. However, Meek's attorney also outlined his history of suffering physical abuse and mental health problems and how he'd thought his friend was just drunk and talking crazy. Not that any of it made his decisions right. Felicia and Polly listened grimly from the front row of the gallery. As they had promised themselves and those who died, they still attended every court hearing related to the massacre.

Meek's sentencing would come later, his plea subject to his cooperation in Roof's trial. After the plea ended, the survivors hurried away. Meek's attorney stepped outside and read a prepared statement to reporters.

"On behalf of Joey Meek, I want to first say that it is his sincere hope that his guilty plea is one step further in the healing process for the family and friends of the victims of the brutal murders at the AME Church," Deborah Barbier began. Then she said that Meek apologized to the victims' families. Unlike Roof, he asked for their forgiveness.

She didn't mention it, but Meek had also been writing letters of apology to each of the nine families. He hoped to send them later, once the court proceedings ended. Each one took him a while given his learning disabilities, but he wanted to mention all of the victims' loved ones by name and include details he'd learned about those who died.

His letter to Clementa's family included a note to the two little girls Roof left fatherless. He apologized for the pain they'd suffered. To Felicia, he wrote:

> Tywanza was a hero that day and should always be recognized for his brave act of shielding his aunt from any harm. I have learned while reflecting over the past that your son was a kind man, generous man, selfless man and not only loved his family, but showed a tremendous love for the Lord as well.

He added that he prayed for Felicia and her granddaughter. He wished they didn't have to go through this. He ended each letter with a request for forgiveness, adding: "I don't expect it."

twenty-five

One Year Later

✳

Three weeks before the one-year anniversary of the shooting, the family members and survivors dialed into a conference call with the U.S. Department of Justice to hear what punishment the federal government would pursue against Roof. He faced thirty-three charges—hate crimes, obstruction of religious practice, and gun violations—many of which carried a maximum sentence of death. In fact, Roof faced two trials, the federal one for hate crimes and a state case charging him with nine murders and three attempted murders. The local prosecutor, Scarlett Wilson, had long since announced that she would pursue the most severe punishment available to her and had set a trial for January, still seven months away. Now, the victims' families hoped to learn when the federal trial would take place—and when they would need to halt their lives for it.

Some of them, including Sharon Risher and Anthony Thompson, approached the call with trepidation. Both ministers, they opposed the death penalty. Jesus preached about love and forgiveness, not earthly vengeance. They saw life as a sacred gift from God, who wanted his creation to repent and be saved—and that was much more likely to happen during an extended stay in a prison cell.

As the phone call began, the survivors and families on the line chimed in and greeted each other with friendly hellos. Some were lifelong friends or relatives, others strangers until the shooting threw them all together for moments like this one.

A crisp, all-business voice arrived last.

"Good afternoon, everybody. This is Jay Richardson of the U.S. Attorney's Office here in South Carolina."

He thanked them for joining the call on short notice. Eleven months after President Obama held up the family members' forgiveness as an example, his attorney general, Loretta Lynch, had made her decision.

"We wanted a chance to speak with you before it became public. We have been directed by Attorney General Loretta Lynch to seek the maximum penalty of death for Dylann Roof."

Richardson was the federal case's lead prosecutor. His voice, firm and duty-bound, plowed through the silence that filled the phone line after his announcement.

"This is a decision that she has made following, obviously, a very extensive review process that you've heard quite a bit about, taking into account the varying views of all of you. But ultimately she determined that the nature of the crimes of hate that were committed and the harm that resulted compelled her to seek the death penalty."

The federal government had reinstated capital punishment nearly three decades earlier, but out of thousands of eligible cases, the U.S. Attorney's Office had authorized prosecutors to seek execution in only about five hundred. Of those, three men had been executed, the most recent thirteen years ago.

Richardson did not invite questions or opinions. A judge would set a trial date soon.

As news that Roof would face two death penalty trials spread around town, his lead federal defense attorney filed an interesting request. David Bruck wanted a speedy trial. If approved, Roof's federal trial would leapfrog over the state's case and potentially give him the best odds of avoiding death even if he received that sentence. The state of South Carolina had executed forty-three people over the past forty years; the federal government had put to death three in a half-century.

Bruck, a sixty-seven-year-old South Carolina native now working out of Virginia, was famously unafraid to represent clients despised by the public.

He'd taken on Susan Smith, a young mother who had drowned her two little boys in a rural South Carolina lake two decades earlier. Most recently, he had represented Dzhokhar Tsarnaev, sentenced to death for his role in the 2013 Boston Marathon bombing. Over a distinguished career, Bruck had devoted himself to saving hundreds of killers facing death, arguing seven cases to the U.S. Supreme Court.

The prosecutors had no objection, so a judge quickly approved Bruck's request for a speedy trial. Then he set a schedule. Roof's trial would begin the first week of November, two months before the state's trial was set to start.

That date created an interesting twist. Roof's federal trial now would overlap with the state's murder trial of Michael Slager, the North Charleston police officer accused of killing Walter Scott. The two most incendiary, high-profile, racially charged trials in modern Charleston history would take place almost simultaneously and at courthouses directly across the street from one another.

For locals, this would mean dodging an onslaught of doubled-up media coverage. For police, it would mean juggling two massive security challenges. However, for Felicia Sanders, the dueling trials dealt a personal blow. The scheduling meant that Andy Savage and his wife, Cheryl, her two trusted legal advisers and confidants, wouldn't be in court with her during Roof's trial. They'd be defending Slager across the street.

D ear Mr. and Mrs. Sanders," the letter from Emanuel began.
     "That's strange," Felicia thought. "How formal."
"As you know, in the wake of the tragic events of June 17, 2015, Mother Emanuel AME Church received an outpouring of cards, letters, notes, prayer cloths and many other expressions of sympathy and support." The letter, typed on church stationery, was from Reverend Clark. It had arrived by certified mail.

Two months had passed since Felicia's return to the church, and she had since been dividing her time between Emanuel and Second Presbyterian. She'd been feeling better about her relationship with her lifelong church, certain that the new pastor cared about reconciling with those who had left. So, it felt cold and abrupt to receive such formal correspondence from her.

The letter went on to say that members and volunteers had gone through the thousands of letters sent to Emanuel after the shooting. Many had included donations, so it had set up the Moving Forward Fund to house them. Church leaders had wanted to distribute those donations months ago, but they had been on hold while Steve Hurd's lawsuit moved forward.

Steve had recently dropped the case after church officials handed over receipts of money put into the fund. Pursuing a broader examination of the church's finances would have been expensive and uncertain given First Amendment protections afforded churches. Yet, it left unresolved the real crux of lingering suspicions: Had donations been funneled anywhere besides the Moving Forward Fund? That still wasn't known.

Clark's letter went on, its language less like pastor to parishioner than lawyer to client. The amount Felicia and Tyrone would receive from the Moving Forward Fund was based on the number of their immediate family members who were "victims and survivors" of the shooting, the letter said.

Their portion was $150,340.

Clark's leaders had announced several months ago that well-wishers sent roughly $3.4 million to the church. But Felicia had never thought in such concrete terms what her family's portion of that might look like. Placing a numerical value on her son's life felt so cold, so inadequate in light of the overwhelming sense of loss she felt. The sterile computer font only made it worse.

"I, as Pastor of Mother Emanuel AME, and the members of the Mother Emanuel AME Church family, know that a tangible offering of any kind is inadequate, considering the losses occurring on June 17, 2015. Please know that you always remain in our thoughts and prayers."

A form letter. Barely personalized. No phone call. No visit. Not to mention no explanation of the formula the church had used. Just a rote promise of "thoughts and prayers." Just as bad, the church had announced months ago that it would keep more than half of the donations—almost $2 million—for itself.

Then, as Felicia thought about the wording of the letter, and who was mentioned in it, she realized something even more hurtful: Given that Polly received the same amount of money as Felicia, Emanuel's leaders had shared not a single penny of the donations with her granddaughter, the child who had witnessed the slaughter and would live longer than any of them harboring memories of that night.

As the shooting's anniversary approached, gossip flowed along the phone lines that connected some of the most active of Emanuel's members: Reverend Clark seemed to be slowly falling into the same trap as her predecessor, becoming more focused on the personal glory attendant to guiding the famed church through difficult times than on actually guiding it. They heard she'd been invited to the White House to receive an award from First Lady Michelle Obama and then planned to attend an event at Martha's Vineyard—*during the shooting anniversary events.*

They also had gotten their hands on a press kit, perhaps created by her new chief of staff—and what pastor has a chief of staff, anyway? The kit appeared designed to market Clark's new image to the world. Following the tragic events at Emanuel, it claimed that she "has been hailed as 'America's Pastor.'"

America's pastor? She had been at Emanuel for all of five months.

"She is nothing but lights, camera, action," one lifelong member grumbled. And few things needled the congregation's closely held suffering quite like yet another person seeking the limelight on the back of their losses.

However, Anthony Thompson, who had befriended Reverend Clark, wanted to support her. The formal nature of the donations distribution hadn't bothered him. As a former probation and parole agent, he understood the need for lawyers and legalese when dealing with such large sums of money. He also lacked the others' deeply personal ties to Emanuel, which had been Myra's church home, not his. And as a pastor, he sympathized with the enormity of what Clark faced in her new ministerial job with no blueprint to follow. They also now shared a common goal of making the anniversary Bible study particularly special, given that she had asked him to run it with her as a way to bring together all of the people who loved Myra.

Anthony had agreed. They could offer the city an ecumenical show of love and joint worship between their churches. It would reflect the unity that Charleston had displayed after the shooting, a hope that soothed Anthony's gnawing dread of reliving the night of June 17.

Three days before the anniversary Bible study, another violent act of hatred struck the nation. A man walked into a gay nightclub in Orlando and killed forty-nine people, the deadliest mass shooting by a single person and the deadliest violence against the LGBT community in American history.

It all felt numbingly familiar to the victims' families.

Anthony soon heard that Reverend Clark had flown to Orlando to minister to the people there instead of going to the White House—and wouldn't be back in Charleston in time to help him with the Bible study. That shocked him. He considered stepping back from leading it. He wasn't an AME minister. It might seem odd for him to host the event at Emanuel without Clark beside him, and he didn't want to appear presumptuous in front of the church's own perfectly capable ministers.

But maybe she would show up at the last minute.

The night before the event, Anthony slogged home from his own church to prepare, exhausted and wracked with a cold. He hadn't slept for several nights. As June 17 drew closer, he felt more and more overwhelmed by the emotional enormity of the anniversary and pressure to lead a meaningful Bible study.

In the bedroom he had shared with Myra, he picked up his leather-bound Bible, easily finding the Parable of the Sower. Myra had chosen it to lead her first Bible study that night. Anthony chuckled to himself, remembering how she'd come to him so aggravated the first time she read the passage.

"I don't get this," she'd said.

"You'll get it," he had assured.

"I don't get it!"

"Well, read the whole thing."

"I did read the whole thing!"

"No, you didn't." He'd smiled at her.

Anthony knew very well that Myra would get it. A perfectionist, she was a tenacious studier of the Bible. She'd just stopped too soon this time.

"Read beyond where you are. Read the whole chapter."

He knew the answer waited at the end of the parable. Jesus didn't often explain outright what his stories meant. But he did in this one, telling his disciples privately, "The seed falling among the thorns refers to someone who hears the word, but the worries of this life and the deceitfulness of wealth choke the word, making it unfruitful. But the seed falling on good soil refers to someone who hears the word and understands it. This is the one who produces a crop, yielding a hundred, sixty or thirty times what was sown."

Myra had huffed away that day and climbed the wooden stairs to a second-floor bedroom that once was their daughter's bedroom and now served as Myra's sanctuary. She had spent hours in that room, studying and reading and praying. The house fell quiet as she continued reading.

Anthony waited, suppressing a smile until her voice cascaded down the staircase.

"Oh my gosh!" She rushed down. "Why didn't you tell me?"

Anthony met her with his boyish grin.

"I told you, read the whole thing."

Even now, worried over his own charge to teach the same parable, he chuckled remembering the moment. Myra had pored over the passage from there, pondering the notion of rocky soils and thorns that choked out seeds of faith. She mused about cultivating fertile soils of love where the seeds of God's word could sprout and flourish.

Anthony found peace in her realization. Myra had been that fertile soil.

Now, he would try to be as well. Anthony steeled himself to lead Bible study. He needed to reinforce the words of forgiveness he and others had spoken a year ago at Dylann Roof's bond hearing. And he needed to practice what he preached. He became determined to forgive Clark for leaving him to handle the study alone. She had gone to minister to other hurting people, and God had left him here to lead Bible study at Emanuel. So, he would cultivate that fertile soil in a church full of hurting people, no matter how tired and sick he felt. He stayed up until 3 a.m. writing the words he would speak the next day.

When the day of Bible study arrived, the city's newly elected mayor arrived at Emanuel and sat in the audience alongside many of Myra's large, extended family. Members of Anthony's church dotted the pews behind them, smiling in encouragement.

As the church filled, Anthony stepped to a wooden lecter up front.

"This week has been pretty tough."

He remembered the nine, the survivors, and the endless waves of people impacted by the shooting. Including himself. "I've had nothing but God's word to rely on," he said.

Anthony glanced down at his notes, which were derived from Myra's notes. He spoke about stony hearts closed off to God and thorns of materialism. Then he transitioned to thoughts of his own. He told the story of Dylann Roof's bond hearing two days after the massacre. He hadn't planned to speak that day. He'd even warned their children not to speak. But God had other ideas. So, when he heard his wife's name called, Anthony had risen and walked up front. He'd spoken words of forgiveness and warned Roof to repent.

"I immediately began to experience peace," he recalled.

Anthony reminded the crowd that, in the Parable of the Sower, one seed fell upon fertile ground and yielded a tremendous bounty of fruit. The seed could be any—or all—of those gathered now. The seed could even be Dylann Roof, if he chose to receive and nurture it.

"That's what hearing God can do!"

The audience nodded, and a few called out their agreement. Anthony ended with a prayer devoted to the same message.

"Begin to grow in love. We would pray for Dylann Roof and the Roof family!"

The people cheered, and he continued.

"Give somebody a hug and let them know that God loves them!"

A standing ovation from the church his wife had loved thanked him in return.

Once the crowd dwindled, Anthony filed downstairs with his family, and the group soon headed out for dinner. Myra's youngest brother, JA Moore, and his wife, Victoria, paused in the side parking lot, however, remembering the day last summer when President Obama had sung "Amazing Grace" at Clementa Pinckney's funeral. For the two, both young adults in their twenties, it had felt like their generation's "I Have a Dream" speech, an unforgettable message of hope amid devastation. JA had asked Victoria to marry him that night.

As they smiled at the memory and thought of Myra, the young wife pointed up at the late evening sky above Emanuel. A rainbow had formed, arching up from the trees across Calhoun Street, its colors growing more vibrant as they watched, cresting neatly over the church's brown spire.

"That's God," JA said.

"Look there!" Victoria pointed to just beyond the brilliant rainbow stretching, it appeared, across the entire Holy City. "It's a double one."

He watched a second rainbow brighten in the sky.

"That's faith."

twenty-six

Business as Usual

With the anniversary of June 17 almost upon them, Jennifer Pinckney sat her girls down for a talk. The city and church had planned twelve days of events to commemorate the tragedy. She told Eliana and Malana about all the events that people in Charleston were holding to honor their father and the eight people who died with him. A unity march. A service at the church. A big church event at the arena. A prayer vigil at Emanuel. Wasn't that nice?

And it was true that that she appreciated people's efforts. But she also dreaded the onslaught of attention, having to attend all those public events, and most of all, being forced to relive that night. Yet she also understood that their lives were so much more public now. People wanted to see them and hear from them.

Eliana, a slim twelve-year-old who bore her daddy's solemnity, spoke up first.

She didn't want to go.

"All they're going to be doing is crying. People gonna be all crying and saying, 'I'm sorry.'"

Jennifer listened. The little girl had a point. At so many events, that is what they heard from even the most well-meaning people.

Oh, you poor little girls.

Oh, you're gonna miss your daddy.

Oh, you sure must be sad.

Eliana and her little sister would smile and be gracious, of course. But those words, over and over, would mostly bring them down. They didn't need to be reminded of what they'd lost.

Just a few days ago, their grandmother, Cleo Benjamin, who had lived with them and provided the stability of routine after the shooting, had died after her long fight with cancer. The loss hit Jennifer especially hard. She and her mother had been very close, and Cleo's death meant creating yet another routine that might salvage some degree of normalcy amid so much sadness. Normalcy. Jennifer realized that Eliana had just given her the answer.

"We're not gonna go," Jennifer said.

They would visit Clementa's grave with his sister instead. The girls brought colorful pinwheels. Jennifer brought flowers. One by one, they walked to his grave and spoke to him. Jennifer set the flowers down. The girls poked their pinwheels into the soft earth and watched them spin in the hot breeze.

As part of the anniversary remembrance, hundreds of people gathered in Marion Square, from which they marched toward Emanuel and, beyond it, to a circle of trees planted at the Gaillard Center in memory of those who died. There, they gathered beneath a white tent to hear from Bernice King, the youngest daughter of Coretta Scott King and Martin Luther King Jr. In 1969, the year after a white racist shot and killed Rev. King, Bernice's mother had addressed 3,000 people at Emanuel, then led a mass march of the city's striking hospital workers the next day.

Bernice recalled how her father used to say that people feared each other because they didn't really know each other. Even now, during this march, people had gathered to show unity in this public space, for public consumption. But what about when they went home? When they decided whom to invite over for dinner or a beer?

"You have to find ways to come together in private spaces," King urged.

She paused then, letting the message sink in.

"That's your assignment."

Indeed, just a few days earlier, a new poll of South Carolinians had revealed that black and white residents held starkly different views about how the massacre had affected race relations. In the view of most white residents, those tensions had eased a great deal since the shooting—in fact, they were more than twice as likely as black residents to perceive race relations as improved as a result. Some spoke with pride about the shows of unity afterward.

More than one-third of black residents, though, held the opposite view. They saw white people willing to offer a hug or turn out for a unity march yet remain unwilling to address the huge disparities that persisted across the state, from education to income to treatment by the criminal justice system.

White people saw their gestures of unity as gracious and sincere, which they often were. But black people saw them as more akin to someone who writes a thank-you note after dinner when they really should have offered to pay.

The findings came from an institute at the University of South Carolina that had polled eight hundred adults to gauge race relations after the twin tragedies of the Emanuel and Walter Scott shootings. The portion of black respondents who deemed race relations as "poor," nearly 32 percent, was the highest since the institute had first asked the question almost three decades earlier.

It came down to how much each group saw racism as an ongoing problem. Far more whites perceived racial equality than did African Americans: 80 percent to 45 percent. The two groups even blamed different causes for racial tensions. Black residents often blamed the divisive presidential race and the Confederate flag's long tenure at the State House. Whites mostly blamed the media for focusing on the issue.

The disconnect remained despite countless conversations about race that had taken place in Charleston since June 17. Emmy Award–winning filmmakers Ken Burns and Henry Louis Gates Jr. had chosen Charleston to host the first in their series of national lectures on race. A&E Networks had hosted a three-hour forum on race in the city. And PBS journalist Gwen Ifill had held a televised town hall.

At Ifill's gathering, *New Yorker* writer and historian Jelani Cobb explained that it was difficult to have the same discussion of race—again.

"We've greatly overestimated two things," he said. "One, the power of conversation and, two, the extent of benevolence of white people in America." He noted surveys that showed more than half of whites considered themselves the primary victims of racism in America today. Despite that, these conversations often failed to plumb what Dylann Roof so readily and violently expressed: "the white belief that black people had something that they were not entitled to—that somehow or another, they were losing out. The currency of whiteness had been devalued," Cobb explained.

That was because these discussions tended to draw sympathetic whites, not those shielded from the firsthand hurts of black America. They rarely drew whites who resented efforts like affirmative action and who didn't understand African Americans' complaints about contemporary racism, which they just didn't see, or references to a racist history in which they didn't participate.

The USC survey results didn't surprise black Charlestonians like the Reverend Joseph Darby, an AME presiding elder and local NAACP leader who had no qualms deriding the "CHARLESTON STRONG" slogan people emblazoned on T-shirts and banners after the massacre.

"More like: Charleston Business as Usual," he said. "It's a niceness that comes with a caste system, and you're not supposed to buck the caste system."

He did, however, see subtle shifts. He had recently stopped at Emanuel's Bible study with a pastor friend. When it ended, a group of older white ladies were cleaning the kitchen as people left. To Darby, it was a small step in the right direction. Indeed, people of different races were making more intimate forays into the segregated silos of Charleston.

The largest and most organized of those efforts was the Illumination Project, the brainchild of Charleston police chief Greg Mullen, who had worried even before the church massacre that the rising tide of anger over police shootings sweeping the nation would arrive at his door. While the fatal shooting of Walter Scott had occurred outside of his jurisdiction, in North Charleston, he'd known that tensions could flare in his city as well. Even before Scott's death, Mullen had been working to shift the force's thinking from a "warrior" mindset to a "guardian" mindset, an approach of protection, not dominion.

Shortly after the Emanuel shooting, Mullen had woken up in the middle of the night with a new idea for bringing police and residents together, which he called the Illumination Project. A steering committee, a diverse lot of people, had started meeting that winter with very different perspectives about the relationships they were tasked with exploring.

Early on, a white cop had gotten up to introduce himself. "If I was to tell people about me I would say, 'I'm from Ohio. I have a wife and a daughter. I like to run,'" he said. "I'm a friendly guy." He emphasized that he wanted to be seen as more than a uniform and a badge.

But a black woman, a nurse administrator, had spoken next. She saw him as precisely that—a uniform and a badge, with the ability to kill. She had grown up watching her younger brothers get harassed by police for the mere crime of being young black men. "I'm sorry," she told him, "but I don't know you. I just see a man with a gun. And being a man with a gun, you can make a decision to shoot me."

The officer was stunned but tried to remain open to her perspective. He'd been a cop for more than a decade. He had a clean record and a reputation for helping others, so what could he and his fellow officers do to help change those perceptions? Over the coming months, he and the woman became friends, a small step in a larger effort, not unlike what was happening at Second Presbyterian when the first anniversary of the shooting finally arrived.

On the evening of June 17, at about the time Bible study had begun that night a year ago, Felicia walked toward the education building next to Second Presbyterian's sanctuary. She had found spiritual nourishment in this church, filled with white Charlestonians, although she hadn't intended to make a racial statement by coming here. God had led her to this place where she had realized, with new fervor, that the same red blood that flowed from Jesus on the cross and her loved ones at Bible study also flowed from all of the faithful, no matter their skin color.

It hadn't always been easy. When she walked into Second Presbyterian, people still sometimes asked, "Are you visiting?" And when she had volunteered recently at one of its big outreaches to low-income students, someone tried to usher her into the line of people receiving goods—not toward the volunteers. Felicia had just kept walking to her destination.

On the other hand, now that she and some of her sisters attended the church's Bible study, it had about twenty-five regulars, roughly half of them black and half white. After the weekly sessions ended every Wednesday, they lingered talking. Most of them wouldn't have known the personal details of each other's lives if not for those hours in this place.

Pastor Cress Darwin greeted her with a warm hug. They meandered, chatting, together into a quiet chapel inside the building where fellow survivor Polly Sheppard and other victims' loved ones gathered away from the masses arriving for the church's big anniversary service. Felicia hugged Polly, who also no longer attended Emanuel. Polly had switched to Mount Zion AME, the nearby daughter church of Emanuel, where she found her spiritual needs better met by Reverend Kylon Middleton.

Kylon also arrived now as they gathered for the service. Cress and Kylon had gotten to know each other since the shooting as well because both had joined citywide efforts to build ecumenical bridges across racial and denominational lines. Cress had invited Kylon to preach tonight in his Presbyterian church, where worship seldom involved acts more energetic than standing to sing. Tall and charismatic, Kylon preached in the AME tradition of call and response that required him to carry a handkerchief into the pulpit. He'd need one soon to mop sweat from his brow.

Andy and Cheryl Savage arrived as well, followed by Nadine Collier, who had uttered the first words of forgiveness that now defined the tragedy. They all gathered in the chapel, this new family of understanding.

As the service time approached, Cress ushered the larger crowd from the education building toward the sanctuary to finds seats before the service began. The survivors and victims' relatives stayed back until Cress summoned the small group to join him in the lobby. They formed a circle and held hands, black and white ones, the diverse lot that he'd imagined for a decade. He prayed that God would be with them and with all of those waiting in the sanctuary.

"Amen!"

"Here we go! Here we go!" he called.

Cress led the service until it was time for Kylon to preach. Kylon had grown up in this city, a divided one, and knew well the significance of a black pastor in a white pulpit. He approached with a ready step. When he got there, he beamed. "I never imagined in a million years coming to Second Presbyterian Church!" Sunday, he noted, remained the most segregated day of the week.

But why? They all served the same Christian God, the same one who'd brought them all together here tonight.

"Faith becomes the equalizer!"

In many ways, this was the most important change in race relations to come from the shooting.

"No one imagined our community would rally together based on our similarities," Kylon added more somberly. "This has become a beautiful opportunity for *all* of God's children."

The audience, a mix of black and white worshippers, stood to cheer as he stepped down toward them. But as the people recited The Lord's Prayer, Kylon didn't return to his pew. Instead, he roamed out into the audience, heading straight toward a white man with a long brown beard sitting toward the back. The man stood to hug him. Few noticed that Kylon hadn't gone back to his seat, given that most were too focused on the prayer to notice the brief exchange.

Forgive us our trespasses
As we forgive those who trespass against us.

The man Kylon embraced was Paul Roof, Dylann's uncle.

Kylon had invited Paul and his wife, and he wanted them to feel welcome. Paul was a professor at the College of Charleston, where he taught sociology. Most locals knew him for getting fired from a local Christian college after his face was printed on a beer can, giving him the moniker The Beer Can Professor. That had sent him forth to the College of Charleston, where Kylon had met him.

After the shooting, Paul had arrived at Kylon's office one day to apologize on behalf of his family for the grieving minister's loss, a gesture Kylon deeply appreciated. Kylon had accepted the apology and then asked Paul how he was doing, how his family was doing—even how his nephew was doing. Kylon did so in the Christian spirit of forgiveness and reconciliation that he held dear. He also wouldn't judge the family by the acts of one man. He and Paul had since become friends. As far as Kylon knew, this was the first time Paul had attended an event with the victims' families.

As they now hugged, the choir kicked in. For an entire year now, Dylann Roof never sought the forgiveness that many of those on hand had given him. But Paul Roof had come here tonight, and Kylon thanked him with this very public gesture.

twenty-seven

Saved Your Soul

❋

Three days later, in the thick of the anniversary events, Felicia received several calls from friends at Emanuel: *Did you hear about Reverend Clark?*

After just five months, Bishop Norris had reassigned her to a church in Georgetown, sixty miles up the coast. That church's pastor would, in turn, move to Emanuel. By Sunday, Emanuel's grieving congregation would have its third pastor in a year. The bishop gave no reason, and he didn't have to. It may have been discomfort with her increasingly public profile, or her absence during anniversary events, or something unconnected. But whatever it was, everyone knew that it was a demotion for Betty Deas Clark, who had just returned from Orlando.

Felicia didn't agree with everything that Clark had done. But she had at least reached out to offer ministry to the survivors and victims' families. She had invited Felicia back to Emanuel. She had encouraged its members to face the trauma they'd endured, to let themselves cry and seek professional help if they needed it. Few people realized how often Emanuel's grieving congregants had dried the tears of so many visitors over the past year, instead of the other way around.

So, the pastor's sudden reassignment made Felicia pause. No matter what, Reverend Clark was a human being who had dedicated her life to the church.

Felicia called her. The move might feel like a curse right now, she warned, but Clark should count it as a blessing.

"Probably saved your soul," Felicia said.

For Felicia, the bishop's action revealed three things with the clarity of a light flipped on in a room that had sat, for way too long now, darkened. First, the AME leadership didn't care about their pastors—or their people. They didn't care that they'd just thrown Emanuel into turmoil during the anniversary events. And they didn't care about the victims' families and the survivors trying to endure this agonizing time period either.

Felicia was finished.

After an entire year of waffling, of praying, of straddling two churches, and of hoping to reconnect to her lifelong church home, she would say good-bye. It seemed so obvious now. God had been telling her to move her permanent membership to Second Presbyterian. She would close the historical loop that Denmark Vesey had opened two centuries earlier when he walked out of Second Presbyterian in search of dignity and spiritual fuel at Emanuel.

She called Cress Darwin.

"Reverend Cress," she said. "I'm going to move my membership fully. I'm ready. This has been a year. I want to grow. I'm ready to move on. I'm ready."

Voting for new AME bishops took place the following month in Philadelphia during an international meeting of AMEs from across the globe. The church was celebrating its two hundredth birthday amid a terrible year of police shootings and gun violence, a painful reality for a denomination founded to provide refuge to its members in the face of violence, systemic inequality, and injustice. The church had since spread across the globe to thirty-nine countries across five continents.

At the meeting, the church would elect new bishops, and Reverend Norvel Goff was running for a post. A large group of survivors and families joined together to protest his candidacy. It looked like they would never get resolution to their concerns about the donations. But they could let the world know how they felt about Goff's lack of personal ministry and transparency.

One by one, they spoke with a reporter from the local newspaper, *The Post and Courier*. Nadine Collier summed up their complaints. "They say you're family, but they didn't treat us like family. 'What y'all need? What y'all want? What can we do to assist you?' I didn't get that."

Felicia agreed. She also wanted people to know that her feelings about Goff and Bishop Norris didn't extend to all of Emanuel. "It's not the people of the church. It's the two leaders. They put man ahead of what Christ said." She forgave them, yes, but the hurt lingered.

When the AME delegates submitted their first round of votes, Goff came in twenty-third out of thirty candidates. He withdrew his bid.

twenty-eight

A Tale of Two Trials

✳

The business suit crowd hurried toward law offices and banks. Delivery trucks rumbled outside of swanky restaurants. Leaf blowers drowned out rush hour traffic. Tourists strolled from their hotels. It felt like a normal early November Monday in downtown Charleston.

Normalcy, however, ended at the Four Corners of Law, a crossroads fronted by four historic buildings: city hall, the county courthouse, the federal courthouse, and St. Michael's Church, a grand symbol of ecclesiastical law in an old king's city. Heavily armed police and Homeland Security officers watched from every corner as the trial of a white police officer who'd shot an unarmed black motorist converged with the trial of a white supremacist who'd shot nine unarmed black church worshippers.

Inside the county courthouse, the trial of former officer Michael Slager had just begun. Already, there were murmurings about the fairness of the proceedings; of the twelve jurors who took their places in the jury box, just one was black. They soon would hear the story of how Slager had pulled over Walter Scott because his aging Mercedes had a brake light out, then shot and killed him after a physical altercation and a foot chase.

Across the street in the federal courthouse, U.S. district judge Richard Gergel prepared to preside over Dylann Roof's trial. It would be far and away the most high-profile case of his respected career. Many locals knew him as the judge who had just recently opened the door to same-sex marriage in South Carolina. What many didn't know was that he also had long studied

South Carolina's racial history. A silver-haired Jewish man in his early sixties, Gergel harbored a deep interest in the state's forgotten black residents and had written often about them and their accomplishments.

He would add to that history himself when he presided over Roof's trial in the same courthouse complex where his legal idol, the late federal judge J. Waties Waring, had written the dissenting opinion on school segregation in South Carolina. That dissent contributed hugely to the landmark *Brown v. Board of Education* decision in 1954. Judge Waring's views on what he deemed "the cancer of segregation" had earned him death threats, ridicule, and a cross burned in his yard. Six decades later, only a few months after the Emanuel shooting, the courthouse complex had been renamed for him.

Earlier in his career, Gergel had practiced law in his native city of Columbia, where he taught Sunday school at his synagogue and co-wrote a Jewish history book with his wife, Belinda, a history professor. The couple had refused to join the country club in their community because it didn't allow African Americans to become members. And as a founding president of the South Carolina Supreme Court Historical Society, Gergel had long trumpeted the achievements of Jonathan Jasper Wright, the nation's first black appellate justice. Gergel and his wife even tracked down the spot on Charleston's West Side where Wright, the son of escaped slaves, was laid to rest in 1885, and placed a headstone there.

The first two rows behind Dylann Roof's still-empty seat at the defense table, typically reserved for family, also remained empty as the press and the public crowded one half of the courtroom. The other half waited for the survivors and victims' families. Felicia Sanders entered first, followed by Polly Sheppard and her husband, who led a quiet procession of grief. Almost fifty people from the victims' families and members of Emanuel soon filled the entire right side of the courtroom behind the prosecutors' table.

Judge Gergel walked in and stepped to his large mahogany bench, raised three tiers above the courtroom. The crowd watched in tense silence as Roof slipped in through a side door wearing a worn striped jail jumpsuit, his sandy brown hair in the same bowl cut they'd seen in television footage. He sat down at the defense table between his two attorneys, bit his lower lip lightly, licked it, and glanced over at the prosecutors.

During jury selection the previous month, Roof had chatted with his lawyers animatedly. Now, he didn't even acknowledge them.

Gergel quickly began to read from what was clearly a prepared statement, his tone terse.

"I have received a motion in this case this morning requiring my immediate attention and the conducting of a hearing involving only the defendant and defense counsel. The hearing will be closed to the government and the public."

The survivors and family members glanced at each other, then rose slowly, engaging in speculation as they walked out. Why would the judge hold a private hearing with only Roof and his lawyers?

They didn't know it at the time, but Roof had just learned that his attorneys planned to paint him as mentally ill and autistic to try and avoid the death penalty—and he was furious about it. He absolutely would not let that happen. It would tarnish his legacy, undermine everything he'd done.

To derail his lawyers' plan, Roof had penned a letter, well crafted and with clear intent.

Then he'd sent it to the prosecutors.

Prosecution,
I am writing this letter to let you know that what my lawyers are planning to say in my defense is a lie and will be said without my consent or permission. Since they are my lawyers it might be assumed that we have worked on and decided my defense together. This is not the case and I do not endorse what they are planning to say.

My lawyers have purposely kept me in the dark about my defense until the last minute in order to prevent me from being able to do anything about it, which is why I have been forced to write to you.

Throughout my case they have used scare tactics, threats, manipulation, and outright lies in order to further their own, not my, agenda. For example, I was lied to repeatedly in order to get me to speak to mental health experts. I was told that I needed to talk to them in order to get medicine for a thyroid condition. Everything I was told about these experts and why I was being tested was an absolute lie, and I was never told what they actually specialize in.

Behind the courtroom's closed doors, Roof explained to Judge Gergel why he'd sent the letter. He would rather die than allow mental incompetence to be used in his defense.

His attorneys then did what he so vehemently objected to: They argued that he suffered mental and developmental disorders, the effects of which had rendered him incompetent to stand trial. The law said that Roof must be able to grasp the nature and consequences of the proceedings against him and properly assist in his defense—which, they argued, the letter demonstrated he clearly wasn't doing.

After they finished, Gergel delayed the start of the trial and ordered Roof to undergo a psychiatric evaluation. He needed to find out if this defendant was indeed competent to move forward.

Although they were long divorced, the two people arriving at the Charleston County jail as Roof's competency hung in question still shared a mutual bond over something nearly impossible for the rest of the world to fathom: an unabating love for Dylann Roof.

Amy and Benn Roof seemed eager to see their son despite his crimes and the damage he'd done to their family. If the tragedy had affected their relationship with Roof, it appeared to have only magnified the preexisting dynamics among them. Amy arrived worrying over her son's stress level and whether the jail was treating him well. Benn came hoping, as always, to push his son to engage with the world around him—currently with the attorneys trying to save Roof's life.

The jail's rules allowed them thirty minutes to visit over a closed-circuit video system, or maybe twice that amount if the place wasn't too busy and the guards were in a good mood. Amy and Benn had visited Dylann numerous times over the past year. By now, they knew the drill. They walked through the metal detectors, provided ID, and made their way toward a visitation area, where they spotted an empty set of folding chairs sitting next to each other. They scooted them closely together so a camera trained on the space would allow the son they hadn't been able to hug since the tragedy to see them both.

An old-fashioned telephone headset hung next to them on a long, thick, gray cord. A TV monitor ahead showed a tiny room, more of a booth really, back in the secure confines of the detention center where Roof had lived for almost eighteen months now.

Sometimes these visits went well enough. Benn would try to talk about normal things. Amy would check to see that the jail was meeting Dylann's needs. They'd make sure he had money for the canteen before they left.

On this day, as soon as Roof strolled through the door on the video screen, Amy grinned widely and leaned forward, pressing the headset to her ear.

"Hey, darlin'!" she called.

Roof picked up the headset at his end and wiped it off on his jumpsuit slowly, unhurried despite the ticking clock and his mother's obvious excitement to see him. He finally sat down before the camera. Amy's voice, high-pitched and eager, reached through the headset again as he lifted it to his right ear.

"Hey, sweetie. Hey, darlin'!" she called. Her tone was cheery. If he was in a bad mood, she'd try to perk him up.

For all of her son's life, this appeared to have been her role—to accommodate his fixations and soothe his anxieties. In return, he would look her in the eye and even hug her when few other people had been able to pierce the layers of his intractable social anxiety. The downside of this was that Roof had learned how to manipulate her. As Amy offered her most cheerful greeting now, he gave back no response.

"Can you hear me?" she asked.

A nod.

"Hey, how are you doing, honey?"

"Good," he mumbled.

To draw him out, she asked about his hair, which looked a bit rumpled. Had he gotten it cut? A trim around the ears? Again she smiled, a loving mom talking to her son whom she desperately worried about.

"No," he said, still without affect.

"So how are you doing?"

"Good."

"I miss you."

She received a blank stare in response. Maybe, she thought, Benn could engage him more.

"Want to talk to your daddy?"

Without waiting for an answer She passed the phone. For his part, Benn gripped the receiver and spoke into it with a more forceful tone that conveyed he expected to be answered.

"Dylann, how's it going, son?"

"Great."

"Doesn't sound like it. You been going to the courtroom and stuff?"

"What's a courtroom?" Roof smiled with the question.

"It's this place where people sit and have a judge and lawyer—"

Roof interrupted, "What's a judge do?"

He forced his eyes to widen with the inquiry, trying to look vapid. He was toying with his father, yet Benn kept trying to answer his questions about the most basic courtroom players as if his son were being sincerely curious. Roof clearly enjoyed feeling smarter than his parents.

He laughed out loud and interrupted: "Are you wearing a shirt?"

Again, Benn appeared to play along, trying to engage his son in a discussion about his shirt. Roof said he didn't like it. Benn shifted the conversation back toward the trial.

"Think you go back into the courtroom Monday for some stuff?" he asked.

"Yeah."

"What's going on Monday?"

"Nothing," Roof said.

"Wasting government money?" Benn asked. To that, his son laughed.

Benn smiled back and relaxed for a moment. This was safer ground, an almost normal moment of well-trodden conversation for them, the lamenting of corruption and cover-ups. They all thought that the federal government's pursuit of Roof's execution was a big waste. He had offered to plead guilty in exchange for life in prison—and that would have saved everyone a whole lot of time, money, and suffering. It was, to Benn, one more example of how screwed up the government had become and how much money self-serving politicians and bureaucrats wasted.

"Yeah, lots of it," Roof said.

"I already knew that!" Benn grinned widely. "Trump's draining the swamp now. I know you've been listening to NPR, haven't you?"

Roof laughed.

Benn paused. "What?"

"He's not draining the swamp."

"That's what he said," Benn added. "At least we don't have Crooked Hillary Clinton in there."

Roof dismissed him. "Don't believe that. He's not draining the swamp. It's all a lie."

To dodge an argument, Benn switched gears again, instead asking about his own parents' recent visit to the jail and bringing up how the family had just journeyed to see their older daughter's new baby. Yet, Roof asked nothing about this nephew. Instead, he made his dad guess how much money he had left in his canteen and brought up his attorneys, describing one as "evil."

"These people are not evil. They're trying to help you," Benn insisted. If only his son would realize that his defense team was actually trying to help him.

"Oh, no. They're evil," Roof said. "You just don't understand anything."

To this, Benn grimaced. "Buddy, you can say that again," he said, his voice weary. "You know, I haven't been able to understand since the beginning. So, yeah, I really don't understand anything. I'm just doing the best I can."

"It's not so hard to understand!" Roof laughed out loud. "Anybody could understand."

"Noooo," Benn insisted. "Not anybody."

He was getting fed up. He knew they were being recorded and that the recording might be shown at Roof's competency hearing, two days away on the Monday before Thanksgiving. He didn't want his son messing that up too. He didn't want Roof to do anything that, ultimately, might make the jury give him a death sentence.

He handed the phone back to Amy so he could calm himself down.

But when Amy grasped the receiver, Roof started in on her. She'd brought him the wrong crocodile shoes with buckles to wear to court. She hadn't brought him sweaters. The polo shirts were too big. As she became flustered, he stretched his arms out and smiled widely. He knew just how to make her feel stupid and incapable so she'd jump through hoops to try and please him. As she struggled to hold her tears in check, urging him to wear his clothes instead of his jail jumpsuit to court, he laughed and said he loved his jumpsuit.

Their thirty minutes to talk quickly wound down, so his parents requested another thirty to spend with him. Since the jail wasn't busy, they got it. A timer on the monitors that connected them updated.

Benn stretched his arm across the back of Amy's chair, lines of stress splaying out from his eyes. He looked exhausted. So did she.

Roof asked about his mother's cats then, knowing this would send her off on a tangent. Indeed, Amy smiled as she began talking about one's beautiful fur and love of treats and how one had pulled the screen off the back door. Yet, as she spoke, her right hand trembled clutching the headset.

Roof noticed it and declared that she had "tardive dyskinesia." He chuckled when she wasn't familiar with the term, which described involuntary movements that were side effects of antipsychotics. He'd seen it plenty here, he added.

Amy prepared to hand the headset back to Benn for their last five minutes.

"I'll be in the courtroom every day," she promised earnestly.

Suddenly Roof looked genuinely alarmed. "Don't come to the courtroom!" he barked. "You're just going to make it worse."

"Well, I'm coming."

Before he could protest any more, she handed the receiver back to Benn. Their son leaned forward anxiously and pleaded: "She's just going to make it worse! She's not going to like it. Trust me."

Benn leaned forward. "Oh, I already know. Oh, believe me. I know."

"Trust me, it's going to be worse than you think."

"Oh, I know it is. Oh, Dylann, Dylann, Dylann." He sounded weary. "I know what it's going to be like. Trust me!"

"Yeah, but I'm going to do something else that makes it even worse before I go to trial," Roof added.

Pause.

"What?" Benn asked, irritation visible.

Roof grinned, lips curling upward Joker style, and arched his eyebrows
at his father. "I'm telling you, don't come. You're not going to like it."

With that, Benn had had it. He held the headset away from his ear for
a moment.

Then brought it back.

"What's wrong with you, son?" he demanded. It was, in many ways, the
ultimate question, one that neither of Roof's parents could answer. They
still hadn't been able to discuss the crimes with him in private, away from
cameras and guards, and struggled to grasp how their once-docile and painfully withdrawn child had done something so incredibly destructive.

"Nothing, just tell—"

"What is wrong with you?" Benn demanded again. An angry edge
clipped his words. "You've got to be kidding me. Please don't do anything
stupid! I mean, you've already done enough."

Roof rubbed one eye, smiling gleefully.

"God dang, man!" Benn hollered. His upper lip curled with anger and
frustration. Tears welled in his eyes. Amy grabbed the headset.

"What did you say?" she demanded. "You brought your father to tears.
What did you say?"

"Nothing!" Roof smiled.

"You're making your father cry."

It wasn't a big deal, Roof insisted. He was just playing around.

He didn't seem to understand how painful this was for his parents or
how much his crimes had wreaked havoc in their lives. The possibility that
he might get sentenced to die was unbearable to them. Yet, he seemed to
treat it like a joke.

Benn rubbed his eyes. He rose and walked away as his son continued to
chuckle.

With his father gone, Roof suddenly turned on his mother again, this
time for making the moment worse. Why did she have to keep saying that
his dad was crying?

The timer on their visit ticked toward its end.

Amy ignored his attack. "Well, I love you," she said.

Roof stared back. "Alright."

"Well, um, I'd better go in case he's putting money in your account. We can do it at the same time."

"He might not put any money in my account now," Roof said, grinning again.

Benn suddenly returned, however, and sat back down. Amy handed him the headset silently, searching his face for clues to how he was faring.

"Hey."

"Hey."

Benn's steady voice quivered. "You know that everything you've done reflects on us as a family. Don't be a fucking dumbass." He paused. "Do you hear me? You've already been enough of one!" With that, he exhaled a quick burst of frustration and shook his head. "I mean . . . what? You're going to make it worse? Don't be an idiot, Dylann."

Roof muttered, "Joking."

"No, you weren't joking."

"I was!"

The timer threatened to end their visit on this note.

"Alright," Benn said. "Well, I love you, and I'll be back, and we'll see how things go. But if you weren't joking, I'll be pissed off. I'm already pissed off. Don't, don't . . . I don't know how you could possibly make anything worse, Dylann. But don't fucking do it."

Roof smiled back. Yet, his father was determined to end the visit on a nicer note.

"I love you. I'm gonna give you back to your mom. I'll talk to you soon. I love you, okay?"

"I love you too," Roof mumbled. Benn got up and strode away.

Amy clutched the headset. Roof started in on her again.

"You shouldn't have said anything about the money. He probably thought I asked you about that when he left. God! Don't you think about that stuff?"

The timer ticked to their last seconds.

Amy stared back with big, fragile eyes. "Sweetie, sweetie. I . . ."

Roof knew well that he could make her think the argument was all her fault. He lit into her again. "He walks back and you said, 'Well, did you put money in his account?' He probably thought I asked you."

"No, no, no!"

"Anyway, we've only got five seconds." He set his palm against the plastic window in front of him.

"I love you!" Amy called.

The timer ticked.

"Love you, bye!" she called one more time. Then the screen went dark.

twenty-nine

Before a Cloud of Witnesses

✳

After a three-week delay in the trial, everyone returned to Courtroom Six. Judge Gergel had heard from the defense team's psychiatric experts, who described Roof as an anxiety-riddled loner increasingly controlled by irrational fears of threats to his white race. After meeting with Roof for months and months, they had diagnosed him with various mental illnesses, including an anxiety disorder, as well as autism.

Surprisingly, however, the young killer also had an above-average IQ and had scored remarkably high on one expert's test of his verbal comprehension skills—in the 96th percentile. But that didn't offer a complete picture. The speed with which he processed information was low, in the 14th percentile, and his working memory also was weak. He probably suffered disruptions in decision-making and in modifying his thoughts and behavior, likely impacting how he interacted with the racist propaganda he discovered on hate websites. The defense experts had explained that they thought these impairments also now rendered him unable to assist rationally with his defense—and therefore left him incompetent to stand trial, at least for the moment.

However, Gergel also had heard from his own court-appointed expert. Dr. James Ballenger, who'd met with Roof three times, found that he understood the proceedings and was quite able to assist his attorneys. He'd simply chosen not to do so.

After a two-day hearing, Gergel had agreed—and found Roof competent to stand trial.

Now jury selection would resume. Roof sat at the defense table eagerly awaiting the moment, coming any second now, when he would drop the legal bombshell he had dangled before his parents during their recent visit.

"All rise!"

The judge took his seat. Rather than greet everyone with a smile as he normally did, he began abruptly. Late yesterday evening, he explained, he received a motion from the defendant:

Dylann Roof wanted to represent himself.

All movement in the gallery halted. The reporters assembled began to scribble furiously into their notebooks. Gergel told the killer to come forward.

Roof popped up from his defense table and strode toward the judge with an eager clip, although his shoulders still hunched. About ninety sets of eyes bored into his back when he stopped at a lectern silently facing the judge. Gergel began by advising in the strongest terms against the request, calling it "strategically unwise." Nonetheless, the judge had found Roof competent to move forward with this trial—and therefore would allow him to exercise this constitutional right.

Other mass killers had tried the same strategy before, and it had rarely worked in their favor, at least as far as avoiding a harsh judgment. Serial killer Ted Bundy, who confessed to murdering thirty women and girls in the 1970s, handled much of his own defense and ended up in the electric chair. More recently, Frazier Glenn Cross, who killed three people outside Jewish community centers in Kansas, received a death sentence after representing himself during a 2015 trial in which the self-proclaimed white supremacist goaded victims and unleashed anti-Semitic venom. Like Roof, Cross may have been less concerned with the trial's outcome than with gaining a bigger platform for his views.

Satisfied with Gergel's decision, Roof turned away from the judge. He stared down at the carpet, but his lips tugged upward into a smug smile above his dimpled chin as he shuffled back to the defense table. David Bruck reluctantly shifted down a seat, leaving the lead attorney's chair empty. Roof slipped into it.

E ver since it became clear that the Roof and Michael Slager trials would converge at the Four Corners of Law, locals had worried anew that protests and even riots might erupt. Perhaps emboldened white supremacists would turn out to support Roof, to be met by hordes of counter-protesters.

Those anxieties, however, proved unwarranted with testimony in Roof's trial about to begin and Slager's already underway.

Only three protesters stood outside the county courthouse. Two white men from New Jersey held framed posters that read WALTER SCOTT RIP in black and red letters. They had traveled to Charleston to demonstrate support for the man's family. As the day passed, a black man stopped to wrap his arms around the men. They all smiled for a picture.

Nearby, at a respectful distance, another man also held a sign, his defense of the police. It read, BLUE LIVES MATTER. The three protesters all held their signs up alongside the busy city street but exchanged no harsh words. People driving by barely reacted to them either.

Despite the importance of the two trials, most people simply weren't homed in on any single issue enough to prompt a huge organic coalescing of outrage that many had expected. Should they protest mass shootings? Racism? Police violence? To some, these felt like different problems with different causes and solutions, even though death had proved the common outcome. Just a few weeks earlier in Charlotte, riots had broken out after police there shot and killed a black man. And, in the upper part of South Carolina, a six-year-old white boy in tiny Townville had just died after a white teenager opened fire at his elementary school. Violence felt omnipresent in Charleston and elsewhere, but no single cause or solution seemed to jell the hurt and frustration enough to propel locals into the streets once the trials got underway.

Few people also seemed interested in bucking the respective families— those of Walter Scott and the Emanuel victims—who'd repeatedly asked the community to remain peaceful so that no one else suffered the pain they now endured. As importantly, Roof and Slager were both locked up and about to face justice. Charlestonians saw hope for righteous endings to their two history-making tragedies. Federal prosecutors were pursuing Roof's death, with state prosecutors snapping at their heels. And Scarlett Wilson, the smart and capable local prosecutor, had vowed to pursue Slager's murder charge vigorously—and appeared to be doing so.

Justin Bamberg, a prominent black state lawmaker and attorney for Walter Scott's family, had even described the Slager case so far as a "prototype" for how the aftermath of officer-involved killings should play out. He noted Slager's prompt arrest after the video became public, the community's peaceful response, and the city of North Charleston's quick $6.5 million payment of the family's liability claim. So, for the moment at least, residents were willing to let the system run its course. "What we are going to see now is a test of that system. We are going to see whether or not—even with a video capturing an unjustified shooting—a family, a community will be able to get justice," Bamberg added.

When Michael Slager, a youngish man of thirty-five with dark hair and brown eyes, prepared to take the stand in his own closely watched trial, the general vibe of the city was just that wait-and-see approach that Bamberg described.

Slager began his testimony by telling his version of what had happened on April 4, 2015. He had noticed Walter Scott's car that day because its middle brake light was out. He intended to give the motorist a warning, he said, but given Scott didn't have insurance documents, he'd had to call it in. When Slager returned to his police car to do that, Scott got out and bolted. The chase began.

"I don't know why he's running for a brake light," Slager told the jurors.

Slager fired his Taser at Scott's back, and the man went down. When Scott started to get up, the former officer said, he pulled his Taser's trigger again. Although Walter Scott was fifty years old, he was stocky, and Slager explained that he seemed even bigger and stronger as they wrestled. With his Taser in his right hand, Slager used his left to push a button on his radio to call for help. But then, Scott grabbed his Taser and ripped it away, he said.

"I see him with the Taser in his hand."

From the gallery, Slager's parents cried as his voice wavered as he described how Scott had leaned toward him then. "I was in total fear that

Mr. Scott didn't stop, continued to come towards me. I pulled my firearm, and I pulled the trigger."

Prosecutors played the now-infamous video on a TV screen above him. As the first sound of gunfire filled the courtroom, a prosecutor noted that Scott was about eighteen feet away from the officer—and running in the opposite direction. He stretched a measuring tape across the courtroom to show the distance that separated Slager and Scott when the officer first fired.

Slager said he perceived the space differently in those moments, that he'd made his lethal decision when he and Scott were still physically fighting, and he feared for his safety. "That decision was made when Mr. Scott was twenty-seven inches away, toe to toe. At that point, I made the decision to use lethal force. He was still dangerous." Slager wept when asked how many times he fired. "I don't know. I fired until the threat was stopped—like I'm trained to do."

The bystander who'd bravely recorded the video of those critical moments listened from the front row of the courtroom. Behind him, Walter Scott's mother pressed her hands together, as if in prayer. Slager, who'd become a parent himself shortly after the shooting, struggled to contain his emotions. As his testimony ended, his voice quivered.

"My family has been destroyed by this," he said. "The Scott family has been destroyed by this. It's horrible."

Three days before testimony would begin in his trial, Dylann Roof sat in jail scribbling a short note to the judge. It was a Sunday, so court was closed, but he still had a request.

Dear Judge Gergel,

I would like to ask if my lawyers can represent me for the guilt phase of the trial only.

Can you let me have them back for the guilt phase and then let me represent myself for the sentencing phase of the trial?

If you would allow that, then that is what I would like to do.

Dylann Roof
12/04/16

It was rare for defendants in federal death penalty cases to represent themselves as the judge already had let Roof do. But it was downright unheard of for one to act as his own attorney during part of the trial and let his defense attorneys take the reins for the rest. However, Roof didn't mind if his attorneys expended their own energies futilely trying to argue he wasn't guilty during that part of his trial. Everyone knew he was guilty. His goal was to stop them from presenting evidence that he suffered autism or any mental illness—evidence they would bring forth during the sentencing phase. He wanted to take back over his defense at that stage so they wouldn't undercut the message of his acts.

Gergel agreed to the change, adding a bizarre twist to an already deeply unsettling case.

The jury in Slager's trial deliberated for three days before reaching an impasse. Word seeped out of a lone holdout. The exhausted jurors had listened to weeks of testimony. So had the beleaguered public. When the jury foreman said that they wanted to continue deliberating despite their stalemate, whispered curses and shaking heads among Scott family supporters indicated a mix of astonishment and uncertainty.

The judge gave them all the weekend off.

Outside of the courthouse, James Johnson, state president of the National Action Network, said what many locals felt about Charleston's conspicuous place at center stage, with its communal patience being tested: "The world is watching what we're doing."

On Monday, they all returned and resumed their deliberations.

Attorney Andy Savage sat at a defense table with Slager, all too aware of the moment in which he found himself. For eighteen months, he'd assumed a front-row seat to the suffering Dylann Roof's crimes had caused people like Felicia, Polly, Sharon, and Nadine—all his clients and most also his good friends. They weren't thrilled he was defending Slager. However, despite many people's views otherwise, he didn't see Slager's case as one primarily about race. To him, that was an easy label affixed by a rush to judgment. He saw this as a case about police training, fair treatment of the accused, and the split-second decisions that cops had to make.

Andy's ears perked when the judge announced that Slager's jurors, after deliberating for several more hours, had sent him a note. The judge read it aloud.

"The majority of the jurors are still undecided, and we would like help."

Deliberate more, the judge responded.

Not long after, the jurors sent another note: "Despite the best efforts of all members, we are unable to come to a unanimous decision."

After four days of often-heated debate, most of the jurors thought Slager was guilty of the lesser crime of voluntary manslaughter—not murder, which required proof of premeditation. That included the lone black juror, who was serving as foreman. Nonetheless, all twelve people simply could not agree.

Reluctantly, the judge declared a mistrial. When he told jurors that this put the case back to square one, some bowed their heads. Others nodded. One woman cried. The prosecutor pledged to try Slager again.

"There will be another day," Scarlett Wilson promised.

Outside, Walter Scott's loved ones headed toward a bank of press microphones awaiting them. His mother, Judy, offered thanks to the people who'd supported her during the trial and pledged that she would never stop fighting until justice was served to the man who killed her son. "We are surrounded by a cloud of witnesses!" she shouted to the cameras and a small but supportive crowd before her. "He will get his just reward. I'm just waiting on the Lord."

It wasn't the verdict many black Charlestonians had hoped for, but it surprised no one. It also wasn't a disappointing end to the case. It was a pause. Walter Scott's family and various public officials, including Governor Nikki Haley, pleaded for calm. Reacting with violence wouldn't help anything, and many people didn't want to do anything to hurt the chances of convicting Slager when he was retried.

"We're not going to tear up this city," Anthony Scott, a brother of Walter's, said outside of the courthouse. "We're not happy, but we're not sad."

Some had seen a guilty verdict as a way to move on, to mend the wounds that Scott's death had opened among black communities who felt unfairly targeted by policing practices in North Charleston. They had long aired allegations of police abuse, but the video was the most significant evidence they'd ever had. While it wasn't enough to convince these twelve jurors about what crime Slager had perpetrated, the footage nonetheless provided clear-cut evidence of an act of police brutality, the type many black residents insisted had occurred regularly for decades. That proof wasn't going away with the mistrial.

"Oftentimes, what's done in the dark comes to the light," attorney Justin Bamberg said.

Then he added, "We've seen the light."

thirty

A Cold and Hateful Heart

❋

Anxiety overtook Jennifer Pinckney the moment she awoke. She had opted to stay at The Mills House, a historic hotel on Meeting Street that had served as a Confederate base during the Civil War. Guests who'd slept there before her reported seeing Confederate soldiers' ghosts roaming its hallways, but Jennifer didn't care about all that. The phantom she dreaded seeing during the trial would arrive in a couple of hours at the federal courthouse just four buildings away.

Eighteen months after he killed her husband, Dylann Roof still felt more like an apparition, an idea, a symbol of evil and hatred. He barely seemed real. Jennifer had yet to see him in person, and she dreaded it now more than ever.

It didn't help that she barely knew most of the family members with whom she'd forever be linked. She had never spoken to Felicia or Polly about the horrors they witnessed. Jennifer didn't know many of the details about what had happened that night and still hoped to avoid hearing them. This had given her the strength to survive the grief of losing her husband and then, a year later, her mother to cancer.

Barely a day ago, she had said good-bye to her girls, leaving them at home with a close friend, promising that she would call each night to let them know how the trial was going. Clementa's closest family would join her in court. Jennifer had become especially close to his sister, Johnette Pinckney

Martinez, her roommate for the trial. Johnette, too, had never seen Roof in person.

As the two women readied for the day, Jennifer thought of her young students and how, in her mind, everyone was born innocent, even Dylann Roof. Life experiences and influences framed people's views. He must have learned racism at a young age—maybe at home or in his community. Once, a white student of hers had called a black student a "nigger." When confronted about where he'd heard this term, he'd explained, "I got it from my daddy." The same white student later had met Clementa when he came to visit Jennifer at her school. Clementa had talked with him, laughed with him. Later, the white boy had told her, "I like your husband!" He hadn't connected the two things.

Was Dylann Roof anything like that boy?

Engrossed in thought, Jennifer stepped from their hotel wrapped in a gray jacket. Quiet clouds nestled Charleston beneath a soft dome as she hurried unnoticed past a side street where TV truck tires rumbled over cobblestones. Almost overwhelmed with anxiety, Jennifer made a plan: She would attend opening statements and then leave until she was called to testify later in the trial. Because if she stayed, she would hear *everything* about what happened to Clementa, and she didn't think she could handle that.

As she walked, dozens of the nine victims' loved ones boarded giant double-decker tour buses that picked them up from spots around downtown, including Emanuel, and carted them to the heavily guarded federal courthouse. When the buses arrived, a large metal gate opened to usher them inside.

Piling into elevators, they headed up to a place just for them beyond the public eye, the "family room" as people called it. They checked in at a small table leading into a space about the size of a preschool classroom. The smell of fresh coffee and breakfast wrapped them in a homelike embrace as they gathered at long rectangular white tables. Smiling faces of their deceased loved ones greeted them from photographs set out around the room.

Someone led Jennifer to a private room around the corner where the survivors would be able to find solitude during trial. Soft blue leather chairs filled the space. There she found Felicia already settled in and walked over to hug her. The two women didn't speak much; they didn't need to. They weren't close, but they understood the great internal conflict they shared. Soon, each woman would relive the worst moments of her life in front of a courtroom full of people, including Dylann Roof. Each dreaded it. Yet, each also desperately wanted to fulfill her important role in garnering justice for the precious people he killed.

A woman soon arrived to let them know they would get priority seating in the half of the courtroom reserved for them behind the prosecution table. Jennifer would sit in the second row, behind Felicia and Polly in the first, which suited her fine.

Then it was time to go.

As one big group, they headed toward elevators that would carry them all to center stage, Courtroom Six. It was the largest courtroom in the building, but it still wasn't built for the attention this trial would receive. On each side, each of the six rows of mahogany pews could fit about eight people. An extra chair set at the end of each row crowded the aisle. Closed-circuit cameras watched, sending a livestream into a courtroom downstairs, where more family and church members could watch, and to another one down the hall, where dozens more media from around the country gathered, ready to tweet and blog and post continually updated stories.

Polly and her husband led the group in. Reporters sitting in the rows behind the defense table turned to watch them as they slipped into the first row. Felicia's daughter arrived next with the Reverend Cress Darwin. Andy and Cheryl Savage strode in next. Yesterday, a quiet and rainy day between the Slager and Roof trials, they'd taken Felicia out to lunch and to a spa to relax and focus before this day she had been waiting eighteen months for. Felicia didn't especially like that Andy was representing Slager, but she also didn't consider it her place to hound him about it. He had a job to do. Mostly, she was grateful he was here, now, for her. He held her hand as they maneuvered down the crowded aisle. Andy looked ahead; Felicia watched the floor. Cress sat on one side of her, Andy on the other, her buffers in the storm for all eighteen months now. Tyrone slipped in behind them.

Lead prosecutor Jay Richardson, a thin man with a sharp mind, walked over to hug Felicia. He wore a lavender tie. Andy wore a striped purple tie. Tyrone wore a lavender shirt.

Purple, the color of royalty.

They wore it for Tywanza. They wore it for Felicia. Today, she would face a killer.

Kylon Middleton entered next, followed by Jennifer and Johnette. Without turning her head, Jennifer sneaked her eyes quickly over to the defense table. Roof wasn't there yet.

Behind her, every row filled with shared grief and dread as the family members filed in.

Then, so quickly and silently that Jennifer almost missed it, Roof slipped in from a door near the defense table. He was wearing a jail jumpsuit, which surprised her. He looked at nobody as he hurried in and sat down, then leaned back in his chair and stared straight ahead. His blank expression also surprised her. He didn't look cocky or angry as she'd assumed an evil man, a white supremacist who took pride in killing nine innocent black people, would look. Instead, she was forced to grapple with just how young and docile he appeared.

This was the man who hated so intensely that he'd robbed her of a lifetime with Clementa? It didn't seem real, as if she'd walked into the wrong person's trial.

Suddenly, someone ushered in a small birdlike woman with long blonde hair, clutching a purse, hunched over as if to hide her face. She scampered up the aisle, then turned at the second bench behind Roof, mostly empty still, and sat down.

It was his mother.

If Roof knew she'd arrived, he didn't acknowledge it. He sat statue-still in his chair, staring at the table in front of him.

Watching, Jennifer wondered if he could possibly grasp the magnitude of the pain he'd caused so many. His blank expression certainly didn't communicate it.

Once the judge assumed his seat up high, twelve jurors and six alternates filed in through a courtroom door up near his bench. The families strained to see the group—they were all too aware that Michael Slager's jury had only one black member and had worried they would get a panel of a similar makeup. At first, it appeared to be the case, as a group of mostly middle-aged white women arrived.

However, among the jury's eighteen members and alternates in fact were five African Americans, making it roughly reflective of Charleston County's overall demographics, to the relief of virtually everyone. Unlike most juries, however, these eighteen people didn't yet know who among them would comprise the actual jury and who would serve as alternates.

Richardson, the wiry forty-year-old lead prosecutor, soon stepped close to the dark wooden rail that enclosed the jury box to begin his opening remarks. His booming voice painted an image of that muggy night when the twelve gathered, old and young, to study the Bible. He looked hard at the jurors before him.

"They welcomed the defendant, Dylann Storm Roof."

The church's pastor had handed the young man a Bible when he arrived, even pulled out a chair right beside him.

"Little did they know what a cold and hateful heart he had," Richardson added, his tone grim, his manner calm and methodical.

During this trial, they would hear how Roof had cultivated a violent ideology filled with racial hatred, then chose Mother Emanuel and methodically planned his attack. They would hear how he came to Bible study to execute the most innocent group of African Americans he could think of.

"He hoped, he imagined, this would agitate others, would cause unrest, deepen longstanding divisions, and serve in the minds of the others as a catalyst of hate!"

In the gallery, Sharon Risher began to sob. Her sister, Esther, stood and rushed from the courtroom. Tears flowed down the cheeks of others. Richardson's opening statement, as powerful and jarring as he'd planned, shook them all.

Acknowledging what was to come, he concluded, simply: "This is going to be a long and difficult trial."

Lead defense attorney David Bruck, a perpetually serious man with thick white hair and a weary demeanor, now rose from the defense table. Like Andy Savage in the Slager case, he often took heat for the defendants he represented. But he, like Andy, firmly believed every person, no matter how heinous the charges against him, deserved a capable attorney. He also staunchly opposed the death penalty.

Standing before the jury, his voice emerged soft and reticent, as if to suggest he didn't really want to give this opening statement, or defend what Roof had done. He exuded sorrow for the families, appreciation for the jurors.

"You're probably wondering what we're doing. You're probably wondering, why does there have to be a trial?"

Several jurors leaned forward.

The trial, he continued, would have two phases. Prosecutors must go through this phase first to prove Roof's guilt. He noted the obvious: Roof had long ago offered to plead guilty in exchange for a life sentence, an offer prosecutors had rejected. Because the federal government was pursuing Roof's execution, the law required prosecutors to prove his guilt in court even if he was willing to admit it. The defense, Bruck noted, probably wouldn't call any witnesses or cross-examine anyone very much.

Then would come the penalty phase. The jury would decide between two options: death or life in prison without parole. That, he argued, wouldn't be so obvious.

"The question isn't just, did Dylann Roof commit these crimes, but who is he? Why did he commit the crimes? Where did he come from? What can we understand about him?" Bruck asked just above a whisper, pleading for the jurors to think more deeply, beyond the obvious horrors they were soon to hear about in great detail.

The jurors appeared to listen closely. As he spoke, a few jotted notes in their court-issued legal pads.

"You're going to want to understand who this person was."

Bruck didn't tell the jury this yet, but as it looked now, he wouldn't be able to pose these ideas later during the trial's penalty phase, the time when defense attorneys could present evidence of mitigating factors such as mental illness. Roof would represent himself then precisely to prevent any of Bruck's narrative from reaching the jurors. So, Bruck pushed the bounds of what he could suggest to them himself right now by hinting at the version of Roof he wanted to present, that of a sick young man pulled adrift by his own psyche. He hoped to get at least one juror to ponder: What drove a man barely twenty-one years old, mentally less mature than that, a loner and high school dropout living partly out of his car, to kill nine innocent people he'd never met?

"On what planet would someone have to be to think you could advance a political agenda by attacking and murdering these nine people who are the most kind, upstanding—I'll use the world 'noble'—people you could possibly find in this community or any other? Does it make any sense at all and, if not, what does that tell you?" he asked the jurors.

Richardson repeatedly stood to object to these efforts to slip in hints about Roof's mental state, and Gergel sustained his objections, admonishing Bruck to stick with matters related to the defendant's guilt or innocence.

Bruck, however, persisted. "Given the fury of this attack, you'd expect to see seething rage. But watch carefully." Notice what the defendant was wearing. Notice his demeanor.

"You're going to look at Dylann Roof and try to figure out who he is," Bruck added, peering at the jurors, and then wrapped it up. Judge Gergel called for a lunch break.

The jury left first. Then, the entire gallery waited quietly as the six rows of family members filed out. However, the reverence was interrupted by a sob across the gallery as Amy Roof began to quiver, then tipped over onto the bench like a seedling toppled by heavy rain. People rushed over to help, crowding around her.

From the defense table ahead, Roof glanced behind him to see what the commotion was about, but he did not move toward his mother. His face remained impassive; there was no indication that he cared about her suffering as she sat back up, still crying.

"I'm sorry. I'm sorry," she said softly.

Her boyfriend put his arm around her and asked someone to call for medical help. Soon, paramedics arrived with a gurney to take her to a nearby hospital, and the two rows behind Roof sat empty.

After the lunch break, Jennifer joined the other family members returning to Courtroom Six. She assumed the attorneys would handle a bunch of procedural matters during the afternoon hours, and then call it a day, leaving the testimony about the crime, which she planned to avoid, for tomorrow. Instead, while the attorneys did briefly discuss evidentiary issues, the day did not end there.

Instead, Judge Gergel said, "Government calls its first witness."

"Your honor, the government calls Miss Felicia Sanders," Richardson replied.

Jennifer panicked. She knew very well Felicia's role in the trial: to describe in detail what happened in the fellowship hall. She wanted desperately to leave. But that would require climbing over several people to get to the aisle, while the entire courtroom looked on, including Felicia. The weight of the moment trapped her on the bench. Jennifer found herself unable to move.

She glanced over at Johnette, who wasn't moving either.

Instead, they both watched Felicia step through a waist-high swinging door that separated the audience from the attorneys and court personnel. Felicia didn't look at Roof as she walked by him. Her dark hair, smooth and curled at her shoulders, bounced with her lilting gait as she stopped at a deputy clerk and placed her hand on a Bible, then stepped into the witness stand. She appeared resolute.

When she sat down to face the gallery, she angled her body ever so slightly toward the jury to her left—and away from Dylann Roof to her right, as if to signal that she would speak to them, and not to him. Tyrone, her daughter, Andy Savage, and Reverend Darwin all smiled reassuringly from the front row. She pulled gently on both sides of a purple open-front sweater jacket so that it wrapped more snugly around her body, a thin wall of protection.

Richardson, whom the survivors had come to trust and respect deeply, stepped closer to her. First, he led her through some basic biographical questions to put her at ease and introduce her to the jury. A spry man with a rolling southern accent, he was the grandson of a late South Carolina Supreme Court justice and had clerked for U.S. Supreme Court Chief Justice William H. Rehnquist. His fellow attorneys knew him as a tough legal mind, although now he came across as genial and caring as he teased Felicia about how she had her hands full being married to Tyrone.

From the front row of the audience, Tyrone grinned back mischievously as Felicia described happier days, when some of those who died in the shooting and others who gathered in the courtroom now had grown up together at Emanuel and in the neighborhoods around it. Felicia had gone on to cosmetology school, left Charleston twice, but found no place like home.

So, she'd returned, opened a beauty shop, and settled down to raise her children.

Richardson then led her through a remembrance of each of the other eleven people who'd gathered for Bible study that night. She described how Reverend Dan Simmons, the crusty retired pastor she loved who normally led the session, always arrived carrying five or six books and would beat on the table to make a biblical point, calling her "Felita" by mistake. Normally, Simmons led the Bible study. But that night was her friend Myra's night. She described how due to the late hour the group debated whether to cancel it until DePayne Middleton Doctor had suggested, "Let's just have it at least thirty minutes."

But with Myra, everyone knew that there was no thirty minutes. She loved the Bible, and she loved to talk. Felicia chuckled, remembering how people called Myra the "bugaboo" because she seemed to be involved with everything—and everyone—at Emanuel.

Several jurors smiled back at her. Myra's picture on the courtroom screens beamed, too.

As Felicia shared fond memories of each of the victims, a new support group was forming among the people who filled an entire half of the courtroom before her. They laughed and cried with the bittersweet remembrances that many of them shared. However, when librarian Cynthia Hurd's smile appeared on the screen, the tears Felicia had kept in check so far filled her eyes. Cynthia, she explained, hadn't planned to stay for Bible study that night.

"I kind of feel bad when I talk about Cynthia Hurd, because I asked her to stay," Felicia told the room.

Then Tywanza's picture popped up on the courtroom screens. Felicia looked at him with a mother's pride, smiling at the image with tears in her eyes.

There was no more avoiding the reason that Felicia was sharing these stories.

"After the conference was over, the twelve of you gathered together. Tell me how you started," Richardson said.

That night, she explained, they had welcomed a visitor. He had sat right beside Reverend Pinckney, his head hanging as he stared at their table all through the study. When the twelve stood for closing prayer, Roof shot the pastor first.

From the audience, Jennifer flinched. She hadn't known that Roof sat next to Clementa.

She hadn't known that Roof shot him first.

Listening to Felicia, picturing it all in her mind, Jennifer realized that the uh! sound she'd heard after the first gunshot was her husband. She'd never known whose voice that was.

Jennifer desperately tried to push away images her brain conjured of Clementa in those moments as Felicia described screaming, "He has a gun!" before grabbing her granddaughter and yanking her beneath a table.

Felicia described how her elderly Aunt Susie lay shot on one side of her and Tywanza fell on the other. She had begged him to play dead. Instead, wounded and bleeding, Tywanza had struggled to prop himself up and reason with the gunman.

As sobs emerged from the gallery behind Jennifer, tears streamed from Felicia's dark eyes, and she at last turned to the man who'd committed these acts, fixing her stare onto him. Felicia had hoped he would acknowledge her, do something, anything to recognize the pain he had caused. Instead, his head hung, eyes staring at the table in front of him.

Her voice rose with anger. "The defendant over there, with his head hanging down, refusing to look at me right now, told my son, 'I have to do this because you raping our women and y'all taking over the world!'"

Then, Felicia seized the moment she had dreamed of, the fuel that had carried her through the past eighteen months: Tywanza's words.

"My son said, 'You don't have to do this. You don't have to do this. We mean you no harm. We don't mean you no harm.'"

Felicia kept her eyes pinned on the small man trying to ignore her.

"And that's when he put about five bullets in my son. And the whole time I'm laying there, I felt the sting up and down my leg. Nothing but sting. I couldn't move. I was just waiting on my turn. Even if I got shot, I didn't want my granddaughter to be shot. I was just waiting on my turn. It was a lot of shots. Seventy-seven shots in that room, from someone who we thought was looking for the Lord. But the whole time, he just sat there the whole time—evil. Evil. Evil as can be!"

Her voice boomed over the courtroom. Roof still looked down. He tapped the table with a single, slender finger.

Felicia described the scene after Roof fled, when Tywanza writhed toward his Aunt Susie, his fingers finally touching her curly hair. "Then we watched him take his last breath. I watched my son come into this world, and I watched my son leave this world!"

With that, sobs wracked her body.

Everyone in the court save the killer—family members, jurors, reporters—cried with her.

Gergel called for a brief recess.

When the families returned from the break, Jennifer was with them. She sat firmly in her seat, determined now that she would stay for the rest of the testimony along with these other grieving people to offer whatever support she could. Felicia continued.

She finished by recalling her last exchange of words with her son.

"I love you, Tywanza."

"I love you too, Momma."

The words hung in the courtroom air until Richardson thanked Felicia. He had no further questions.

Defense attorney Bruck now rose from the defense table. From his waist, he bowed over reverentially, his voice soft, almost reluctant, addressing Felicia, as if they were two friends forced to discuss something they'd both prefer to avoid.

"Do you remember the man who did this saying something about that he was only twenty-one, and then talking about what he was going to do afterwards?"

"Yes."

"Could you tell us what he said?"

"He say he was going to kill himself." Felicia's normally warm tone took on an air of derision. "And I was counting on that. He's evil. There's no place on Earth for him except the pit of hell."

Murmurs of agreement rose from the gallery.

Bruck tried again to insert his own portrayal of Roof. "He said that he was twenty-one? And then that he was going to kill himself when he was finished?"

"Send himself back to the pit of hell, I say," Felicia added, ignoring the question.

"He didn't say that though. About hell. He just said he was going to kill himself?"

"That's where he would go, to hell."

Bruck had intended to show that Roof was suicidal after the shooting to insert a little bit more doubt about his client's mental state, but Felicia wouldn't just come out and say it. He couldn't risk turning off the jury by pressing her too much. And Roof's lips curled upward in the faintest of smirks.

"Yes, ma'am. I'm so sorry. Thank you," Bruck said, quickly turning away.

Felicia stepped down from the witness stand, her back straight, head high, dark eyes fixed on the swinging door ahead, and strode purposely from the courtroom.

After Gergel adjourned court for the day, Jennifer headed back to her hotel with Johnette. Seeing Roof for the first time, then hearing Felicia's testimony and witnessing her incredible pain, had left her overwhelmed. She couldn't get over how young and passive Roof looked. It seemed impossible to reconcile the person at the defense table with the terror in the fellowship hall. Her mind replayed Felicia's description of what happened against the clock of her own memories of hiding beneath the secretary's desk and the sounds she'd heard.

She realized the groans she'd heard in the hallway came from Reverend Simmons as he lay dying. The stranger's voice insisting he wasn't crazy was Roof. And she replayed over and over the *uh!* sound she'd heard when Roof had fired the first bullet. It was Clementa.

Jennifer wondered what else she didn't know. In their hotel room, Johnette looked as grim as Jennifer felt.

"I can't leave now," Jennifer said.

"I gotta be here," Johnette agreed.

With that understanding, Jennifer called her daughters, as she'd promised. Malana and Eliana listened quietly as she offered some basics about the first day's court proceedings, noting that the man who killed their daddy had been there and that the jury had listened attentively all day.

"Miss Felicia testified," she added, offering only generalizations about her bravery and what the testimony revealed.

Finally, Jennifer spoke the hardest words, the ones about Roof.

"He sat beside Daddy," she said. "And Daddy was first."

She paused then, to keep her own composure, and in case the girls wanted to ask her any questions. She wasn't sure how much detail they would want to know. When neither chimed in, Jennifer went on to explain that she would stay in Charleston and go back to court to hear testimony tomorrow.

Still, the girls remained quiet. She sensed that what she'd offered was plenty. They didn't need details. They needed normalcy.

"So how was your day?" she asked.

When court resumed the next day, Roof's mother didn't return, nor did her boyfriend. Benn Roof never came at all. His parents, Joseph and Lucy Roof, arrived instead, slipping in as unobtrusively as possible to sit a row back from the defense table. As they always had, they would try to provide some stability and love for their son's family. Joe, a retired and widely respected real estate attorney from Columbia, looked like an English professor with his thinning silver hair and glasses, a gauze bandage on one cheek, worry weighing down his features. His wife, petite and thin like her grandson, sat with her hands clasped politely on one knee. They slid close to one another, shoulders touching, silent and alone on their bench in an otherwise jam-packed courtroom.

They had struggled to understand how their grandson developed such horrible racist ideas, which they did not share. Several months before the trial began, the victims' family members had received letters from Joe expressing remorse on behalf of his family: "I have racked my brain for whether there is anything I could do to alleviate your suffering, for I would try if

I knew it would help," he'd written. Along with his endless regret, he'd expressed hope that one day he might be able to pray with them. He ended with, "I am sorry from the depths of my heart."

For some, it offered a bit of comfort. But many questioned the timing, given the letters arrived shortly before the trial began. Were they a ploy for sympathy so they would pressure the prosecutors to drop the death penalty? Jennifer refused to read her letter at all.

Dylann, for his part, never acknowledged his grandparents' presence.

Now, the family members focused on Judge Gergel's warning to them: The hours to come would be especially grim. Prosecutors planned to show images of the crime scene—and there was no shame in stepping out for that.

Nonetheless, the courtroom remained packed. Jennifer was among those who remained. So were Felicia and Polly and Sharon and Anthony. In fact, if anyone didn't return, it wasn't obvious from the crowded benches.

The investigator who'd taken the photographs of the crime scene stepped into the witness stand and looked at the images on a monitor in front of him. The rest of the room saw the same pictures projected onto two large screens facing the audience. At first, they saw the church façade at night with a few parked cars dotting the lot behind it. Nothing unusual. But as the camera entered Emanuel's side door, it revealed a pool of blood congealing on a green carpet runner along a slender hallway near the secretary's closed office door, where Dan Simmons had lain dying.

A few steps down, the short hallway opened into a foyer where trophies topped a wooden bookcase. A brown belt lay coiled there on the white floor. Bloody footprints led the camera forward.

The foyer opened into the rectangular fellowship hall strewn with blood, bullets, and brass shell casings. On the table where Clementa Pinckney had pulled out a chair for the visitor, a black ammunition magazine sat sentry beside a lone black Bible. Magazines and bullets littered all corners of the room, evidence of the killer's movements.

Four round tables sat in a row, each covered with cheerful lime green and yellow cloths.

On top of them sat remnants of normalcy: opened Bibles, drinks, papers. Beneath them: bodies.

The courtroom screens then filled with a picture of Clementa Pinckney lying on his side in his handsome dark suit out in an open area of the room. His head pointed toward the altar a few feet away. A stream of blood flowed toward it from his neck across the white linoleum floor. It headed toward the office door Jennifer had closed and locked before hiding with Malana. Jennifer realized that Clementa had died so close to the spot where they hid in his secretary's office.

Beneath the next table down, several women's bodies lay close together.

Then came perhaps the hardest image to see.

Susie Jackson, her blue floral shirt visible, lay curled on her side beneath the third table, her back facing the camera. Beside her, but out in the open, Tywanza lay sprawled on his back. His right hand rested on his chest; his long left arm reached to touch his elderly aunt's hair. Blood smeared everywhere, evidence of his fight to live despite grievous wounds.

One person in the gallery got up and left. Then another. But most remained, quietly resolved to accompany their deceased loved ones through this ordeal. Felicia and Tyrone watched stoically from the front row just a few feet away from a big screen. Felicia had promised herself that she would attend every court hearing and every moment of this trial to ensure justice for the nine who died. She would keep that promise.

Several jurors took notes. A few wiped tears.

Roof's grandparents glanced away occasionally as the pictures progressed. His grandmother rubbed her chin and pressed a thin finger to one eye. At the defense table, Roof continued to stare straight ahead, his face still devoid of expression, although now he rocked slightly in his chair.

thirty-one

The Confession of Sins

✳

Many in the public had read Roof's manifesto, or at least heard the worst of it, back when it was first discovered. But few knew much else about the person behind the vacant eyes and the statue-still body at the defense table. Now, on the third day of testimony, the courtroom TV screens flickered to life again, revealing an overhead image of three white men seated in leather office chairs around an oval conference table. The world would now see footage of Roof's initial interview with Shelby police on the day of his capture.

On one of the courtroom screens, the families saw FBI agent Michael Stansbury sitting at the head of the table, agent Craig Januchowski across from Roof.

Still dressed in the clothes he'd worn during the killings, Roof appeared calm and unfazed as the agents reviewed his Miranda rights. He showed no signs of being defensive or cagey, as they'd expected of someone just brought in on suspicion of murdering nine people. Once they got past the ice-breaker questions, Stansbury cut to the chase.

"Well, can you tell us about what happened last night?" he asked.

Roof glanced away from them. The agents leaned forward.

"Well, um, yeah, I mean, I just, I went to that church in Charleston and, uhhh, you know, I uh . . ." He paused for a second or two. "I did it."

"Did what?" Stansbury pressed.

Roof paused as if he didn't want to say it out loud. Yet, he released his breath and suddenly grinned at the agents, as if ready to accept credit for an accomplishment for which he'd tried to suppress great pride.

"Well," he said, "I did. I killed them. Well, I guess. I mean, I don't really know."

Stansbury pulled him on. "Do you know how many people you shot?"

"If I were to guess, five maybe. I'm really not sure exactly," Roof answered, his voice emerging in a thick monotone that seemed at odds with his barely pubescent appearance.

Before entering the church, he explained, he'd bought a tactical pouch, filled it with magazines, and hooked it onto the front of a belt like a fanny pack. "When I walked into the church, this thing was right on me, in front of me, you know. And I was like, oh my God they're going to see it, you know. And obviously they did because this thing, it's big. It's heavy!" He chuckled like a kid who'd done something naughty. "You know, 'cause it's got, what, seven magazines, and I put eleven bullets in each magazine."

He then described the shooting with all the gravity of having just egged someone's house.

"I just finally decided I had to do it. And that's pretty much it."

In court, several victims' loved ones exchanged looks of outraged disbelief and murmurs of disgust. One stood and walked out.

The FBI agents pressed Roof with the obvious question: Why? He leaned over the table, one hand on the arm of his chair, the other gesturing.

"I had to do it because . . ." He paused briefly, searching for the right words. "Somebody had to do something because, you know, black people are killing white people every day on the streets and they rape, they rape white women, a hundred white women a day. That's an FBI statistic from 2005."

What he did was so miniscule, he explained, compared to what black people were doing to whites. Their wrongs just didn't make the news.

Januchowski started to ask another question, but Roof interrupted: "I had to do it because nobody else is going to do it. Nobody else is brave enough to do anything about it."

Was he trying to make a statement on behalf of white people?

"Yeah, in a way, I guess," Roof said. It struck many listening that, along with sounding outrageously nonchalant, his tone sounded something like Droopy Dog, as if his words slogged through water before emerging from his mouth.

He recounted stopping a black woman getting into her car outside Emanuel one day and asking her when the church held its services. She'd mentioned the Bible study, and an idea had formed then. He knew that a Bible study meant fewer people. Fewer people meant less security. And a black church would draw only black people. "I wasn't going to go to another church because there could've been white people there."

"So you didn't want to kill any white people? Or shoot any white people?"

"Oh, no!" He laughed, as if to say, what a ridiculous question.

Some of the victims' loved ones had already seen the two-hour video, but many had not. Regardless, it drove home what they already knew: Dylann Roof had no remorse for what he'd done.

The agents asked Roof to sketch a basic layout of the fellowship hall. He did so, describing the scene with the indifference of a football announcer diagramming a play. He drew an imaginary line with his finger on the conference table.

"One woman was sitting over here." He pointed to one side of the line. "And I didn't even shoot her at all anyway because she was looking at me and stuff, and I didn't shoot her."

"So you didn't shoot that woman because she was lookin' at you?"

Roof snickered as if he found the agent unintelligent, the answer to his question so obvious.

Stansbury played along. "Well, it's hard to shoot somebody when they're looking at you, right?"

With that, Roof laughed knowingly. "It's hard to shoot somebody anyway."

Later, he explained how he'd saved his last loaded magazine, the eighth one, to kill himself if the police were outside.

"To be honest, I was in absolute awe that there was nobody out there after I had shot that many bullets! I was like, 'Oh my God. What are these cops doing? They're not even really doing their job!' If you heard how many shots—I don't even know how many shots that was," he said, doing the math aloud. "You know, what's, what is it—seven times eleven?"

"That's seventy-seven," Stansbury said.

"That's seventy-seven, you know, and there's not even a cop outside."

Tyrone Sanders arose and stalked out, muttering angrily to himself. If Roof noticed, he didn't turn around to look.

On the courtroom screens, Stansbury continued: "So it's safe to say, you know, you don't like black people?"

At that question, Roof paused to think. "Well, I don't like what black people do." He added that he wasn't in a position to go alone into a ghetto, where he figured the real criminals lived, and do something that would make a big splash.

"Obviously I realize that these people, you know, they're at a church, you know. They're not criminals or anything. But that's not the point. What is—that criminal black people kill innocent white people every day."

"So what's the point of targeting them?"

Roof exhaled and stared ahead, again searching for words.

"Because I just knew that would be a place where there would be, you know, the least, you know, a small amount of black people, you know, in one area." He'd thought about going to a black festival or something, but then security guards might be around, and he'd have to wait for a certain date and couldn't just do it whenever he wanted. So then he figured a church would be most defenseless, most accessible when it suited him.

He'd picked Charleston because he liked the city, its beauty and what it once represented in terms of slavery and segregation. During the peak years of slavery, Charleston had the highest ratio of black people to whites. He picked Mother Emanuel because it was a historic AME Church, a place where his assault would garner plenty of notice.

"Were you trying to start a revolution?" Stansbury asked.

"I'm not delusional. I don't think that, you know, that something like what I did could start a race war or anything like that," Roof said.

He paused for a moment, and his otherwise unconcerned tone warmed a bit.

"A race war would be pretty terrible, you know," he added.

"Yeah," Stansbury agreed.

"People dying all the time."

"Yeah, yeah it would."

"I'd rather just, you know . . ." Roof paused again, fingers fidgeting in his lap. "Just be able to, like, reinstate segregation or something like that, you know, without there having to be a race war."

So if I told you nine people died last night, how would that make you feel?"

"I wouldn't believe you."

"It was nine."

"There wasn't even nine people there!"

"There was just a little bit over nine."

Roof peered back at the two FBI agents sitting across the table from him. "Are you guys lying to me?"

Eight died at the scene, one at the hospital, they explained. Roof stared at them some more, sitting attentively, one hand on the table as silence filled the small room.

"Oh well," he finally muttered, rubbing the conference table with one finger.

"How do you feel? In all honesty," Stansbury asked.

"Well, it makes me feel bad!" Roof brushed the table with his palm.

Januchowski jumped in with a stern tone, reminding Roof of his stated goals, what he'd said about going to Emanuel, seeking out a Bible study, buying a gun, buying lots of ammo, targeting unarmed black people, shooting the people, then fleeing. And now, nine people were dead.

"What do you want people to remember Dylann Roof for?" he pressed.

The question made Roof groan softly. He rubbed his forehead for several seconds.

"Uhhh, I don't know."

Seconds passed with this, the pointlessness of so much death sitting on the empty table between the three men. Finally, Stansbury asked Roof what he'd say to the victims' families.

"Would you tell them that you shot their family member because of the reason you told us?" Januchowski added.

Roof perked up then and shifted in his chair. "No way!" he said. "I couldn't say that to them. I probably couldn't even look at them."

Indeed, as the two-hour taped confession played, he sat motionless, staring forward or at the ground, not looking at any of them.

When the video finally ended, Gergel called for a break. Roof slipped through the door beside him with his guards and disappeared.

Some in the crowded courtroom stood and stormed out just as quickly. However, many others remained seated, so stunned and beleaguered by the depths of Roof's cold indifference that they couldn't move. Jennifer, among them, wondered: Had they just heard a man confess to executing nine people, or one of her students scoffing about a dumb prank he'd pulled?

thirty-two

A Seed Cast onto Rocky Soil

✳

As prosecutors presented more and more evidence of Roof's guilt, they sought to answer a question that had obsessed everyone since June 17, 2015: Just who was Dylann Roof?

The picture they presented was that of a young man who, on his own, isolated in his bedroom, had stumbled into the dark alleys of white supremacist subculture, then eagerly embraced its ideas with such intensity that he planned the deaths of innocent people. Investigators described the clues they had discovered—notes in Roof's car, photographs he'd snapped of plantations and slave quarters, KKK history books he read, and skinhead movies he watched—that demonstrated how quickly he'd wrapped himself in this new racist persona. Given that there was little evidence in his real life to back up his racist views, not even a single bad experience he could recall with a person of color, it seemed his racism rose out of a hunger for something to define himself beyond the social anxiety, loneliness, and worries about his health that consumed an otherwise directionless life. Roof himself told a psychiatric expert that he hadn't given race much thought before his "epiphany."

It had begun one day when, out of curiosity about the Trayvon Martin case, he had Googled "black on white crime." The results led him to a website for the Council of Conservative Citizens, at that time the country's largest group of white nationalists by some counts. Its stated principle was to "oppose all efforts to mix the races of mankind." The website featured gruesome portrayals of African Americans committing atrocities against whites and claims of a vast media cover-up. For the preternaturally anxious Roof, the site provided an outlet, something to blame, for the anxieties that had long plagued him. Black people were destroying white culture and threatening the very future of his race. No wonder he was so anxious.

One can only wonder: What would have happened if on that day, in response to his Google query, he'd come across real FBI crime statistics instead of the Council of Conservative Citizens' site? The Southern Poverty Law Center had posed the question in a video it produced after the shooting called "The Miseducation of Dylann Roof." Google's algorithms, the piece argued, had introduced Roof to white supremacy. After all, his search didn't lead him to legitimate sites that would have explained that the vast majority of white people murdered are, in fact, killed by other white people.

But that question and its implications would have to wait. As it had happened, Roof started with the Council of Conservative Citizens and, later, discovered the neo-Nazi Daily Stormer and Stormfront, founded by a former grand wizard of the Ku Klux Klan. Stormfront's introduction greeted visitors with this welcome about the nation's first black president: "Many new White people who come here are understandably upset at how somebody like Obama (i.e., a left wing extremist with a mysterious and shadowy background who seemingly comes out of nowhere) could win the presidency. They also see how Blacks are gloating over Obama's victory. These Whites want a strong opposite reaction to counter it."

As Roof foraged around that and other sites, he fed on misinformation about race seemingly without confiding in anyone in his real life who might contradict it. He didn't tell his parents or his grandparents. They wouldn't grasp his beliefs, he'd told investigators. Instead, he worried about their reactions when they learned what he'd done.

Despite that, when the FBI agents who elicited his confession had asked Roof where he wanted to go after his arrest, he'd replied: "Home."

To his mother's house.

The prosecution next showed the pictures investigators had taken of Amy Roof's house. Dylann, they noted, had often taken target practice on a tree in their backyard. Planted pots, a picnic table, and a boat cluttered the yard, along with a littering of shell casings. On a brick-red shed nearby, vintage tin signs hung in rows, including one that read DON'T TREAD ON ME with two revolvers crisscrossed at their barrels, a pro–Second Amendment take on the old colonial-era Gadsden flag. The symbol of independence had more recently been embraced by Tea Party followers and others who liked its anti-establishment messaging. The vibe of the place wasn't uncommon in rural South Carolina. But in court, Roof's environment looked like a training ground for the gun violence he unleashed.

Police who had arrived at the house after Roof's family members had called in to identify him as the shooter took the stand to describe the moment they pulled in. Amy's boyfriend, Danny Beard, had come around a corner with his hands raised and insisted: "He's not here. He's not here!"

He and Amy had tried to answer their questions, but she soon collapsed, as she had in court. When she came to, she led a deputy through their neatly kept home to her son's bedroom. "There is something I think you need to see," she'd said.

They had entered a room with a queen-sized bed, crisply made with a grayish-blue plaid bedspread. An array of wooden furniture, a music keyboard, and a wood desk with a large flat-screen monitor perched on it encircled the room. A large painting of a small boat pulled up onto a beach hung on one wall. At first glance, the absolutely normal bedroom of a teenage boy.

Amy had picked up a neon blue Kodak camera sitting on the edge of the desk near boxes of ammunition and an Abraham Lincoln figurine, then scrolled through several dozen pictures on it while an investigator watched over her shoulder. The first showed their calico cat, whom Roof loved. But her son also had used the camera to take dozens of pictures of himself adorned in the symbols of his white supremacist identity—wearing the Rhodesian flag on his jacket, standing beside the number "1488"—and brandishing his gun. He took many of them in his bedroom, others in the yard, some with his Confederate flag on a stick. He also took some as he traveled, always alone, to Charleston.

As prosecutors called witnesses to paint a portrait of Roof's self-radicalization, they showed these photographs to the jurors, many of whom had visited the very sites where Roof posed for his selfies. He'd spent considerable time playing tourist at Charleston's plantations, once home to thousands of enslaved people, now popular tourist stops for visitors from across the world. He'd stopped on the beach of Sullivan's Island, where thousands upon thousands of those who'd survived the Middle Passage were quarantined before disembarking into this terrible new land. In some of the pictures, Roof looked menacing; in others, like a teenager trying to look tough.

Investigators explained to the jury how they also traced a bread crumb trail of Roof's travels using his GPS. It showed that he had driven to Charleston six times over the six months before June 17. During each journey, while playing tourist to the Confederacy, he also drove by Emanuel. He made the first of those trips during rush hour on December 22, 2014, three days before Christmas, around the time Myra Thompson gave her first sermon.

An FBI agent revealed other places where Roof had stopped as well—a local Starbucks, Chick-fil-A, a Shell station. As these details of Roof's forays around the Charleston area emerged in testimony, the city's denizens felt freshly unsettled, realizing just how often he'd slipped among them. It was hard not to wonder: Did I ever pass him on the street? Drink coffee beside him at Starbucks?

While he'd planned his attacks, Roof also sank further into his racist identity. From a computer in his mother's house, he joined Stormfront, the nation's largest white supremacist website, and created a username: Lil-Aryan.

Apparently Roof also began to seek connections in his new community. Prosecutors read jurors several private messages Roof sent to other members, most of which read roughly along the same lines: "Hi, I read on your posts that you live in the Columbia area, and I do too. Im interested in meeting someone in my state." There was no evidence, however, that he'd actually met up with anyone.

Eight days after joining Stormfront, Roof had stopped near Emanuel for several hours of reconnaissance. Three days later, he returned for more.

At the same time, he'd begun to get into trouble with his parents, who increasingly insisted that it was time to get a job. He also came to the attention of local police, getting arrested in February at a mall within a short drive of his father's house after employees became suspicious of a man asking weird questions about the number of employees in stores and when they closed. The police found Roof in possession of Suboxone, a painkiller used to treat opiate addiction, although he lacked a prescription. He was banned from the mall for a year.

A few weeks later, he turned twenty-one, old enough to legally purchase beer and a handgun, and his father gave him that birthday I.O.U. for money to buy a pistol.

Jurors watched surveillance footage from the gun store where Roof purchased his Glock. Then they saw a chilling video he'd taken of himself honing his shooting skills. Dressed in plaid pajama-style pants, a black Gold's Gym muscle shirt, round hipster glasses, and combat boots, Roof had set up a camera in the backyard of his mother's house to record his practice. The everyday surroundings—a purple plastic pool leaning against the back wall, birds chirping, traffic whizzing by—added to the surreal quality of the video as the families of the people he'd killed sat grimly watching.

Roof walked around his backyard a bit, then stood about fifteen feet from the camera, cocked the gun, and aimed. A red light from the laser sight beamed just above the camera as he fired four times, the sound blasting through the air. He wiped his brow with his left forearm, then aimed and fired again. To increase the challenge, he grabbed a thick phone book sitting nearby, and tossed it awkwardly up a few feet and fired again. It landed with a thud.

As the book lay on the ground, he pointed the Glock toward it and fired twice more, the gun thrusting his thin wrist backward.

To those in the court, it seemed all too similar to what they knew had happened to their loved ones.

thirty-three

Magic Decoder Ring

※

That morning, Sharon Risher had said good-bye to her blind old dog, Puff, and left him behind in her hotel room before heading downtown. As she waited for court to begin, she stood off to one side of the federal courthouse's entrance in a tailored red jacket, coffee in one hand, cigarette in the other. Neither would get past security. Alone, she watched passersby in the chill, wondering if her youngest sister, Nadine, from whom she was still estranged, would come strolling down Broad Street toward her among the myriad strangers heading about their normal lives.

Roof's defense team had announced yesterday that they would present no evidence in his defense. That meant today would bring closing arguments and, most likely, the start of the jury's deliberations. Would Nadine come to court for that?

Sharon hadn't seen her youngest sister in months and was surprised she hadn't shown up yet for the trial. If she did now, Sharon had promised herself that she would be civil, given that their last encounter, about a week ago on Facebook, had ended in the kind of sniping that had, unfortunately, characterized too many of their conversations since Roof killed their mother. Instead of coming to his trial, Nadine had visited Ethel's grave and posted a picture of herself there, in front of the grand marker she'd had made for it. In the photo, Sharon could see another tombstone, the one she'd had made, peeking from behind Nadine's. Her anger had swelled anew at the sight, and she'd tapped on the "comments" bar.

"Thanks for putting flowers on Momma and Terrie's grave," she had typed, referring to their middle sister who died two years before Ethel and lay in eternal rest beside her. "I know Momma missed you and Najee [their niece] in court with the rest of your family. Merry Christmas, Lil Sis!"

Nadine, who preferred to mourn their mother alone and avoid the media onslaught, retorted: "For the record my momma always get flowers every month, oh im sorry u just now seeing it and for court she's glad to see y'all and not on TV," a dig at Sharon's appearances in various news outlets.

To which Sharon responded with old-fashioned southern passive-aggressive kindness, "So u are alive. God Bless!"

"Thank u," Nadine added.

But as the start of court arrived, still no Nadine. Beneath the anger, where Sharon still loved Nadine deeply, she wondered if they would ever behave like normal sisters again, if they'd ever get together for holidays or call each other just to check in. The possibility seemed further away than ever. At times, forgiving Nadine, someone so close, felt even harder than forgiving Dylann Roof, so distant and evil.

Sharon squashed the tip of her cigarette and headed inside, pulling off her boots to go through security while trying not to think about the shattered state of her family. Instead, she focused on praying that Roof would be found guilty today so that he'd never know freedom again. Given that Sharon opposed the death penalty, this phase of the trial marked the mountaintop of earthly justice for her.

After she settled into her seat, Judge Gergel entered the courtroom and summoned prosecutor Nathan Williams to deliver his closing arguments. The blondish-gray-haired man, his face solemn, strolled toward the jurors, all watching intently.

"A church, a sanctuary, a place of safety, a place of fellowship, a place of welcome," he began.

As he spoke, Roof's grandmother slipped into the courtroom, dainty and elegant beside a man in a clergy collar. She arrived in time to hear Williams declare her grandson "a man of intense hatred" who paused in his carnage only long enough to load another and another magazine filled with bullets.

"He executed them because he believed they were nothing more than animals!"

Roof stared vacantly ahead, as usual. The gruesome crime scene photos appeared on the courtroom screens again as Williams spoke of racial
hatred, images of red blood horrific against white linoleum. This time, beside each body another pictured appeared—one showing the person still
very much alive. Their living selves smiled next to their dead bodies in
gut-wrenching juxtaposition.

Felicia put her arm around Tyrone. Jennifer's face fell ashen. A juror
wiped her eyes. Roof's grandmother dabbed a tear and rested her cheek on
one hand. When Williams finished, he returned to the prosecution table
and sat down.

Roof's attorney David Bruck proceeded with his thankless task. The ac-
complished death penalty opponent ambled toward the jury box, stopping
farther away than where Williams had just stood. He joked about being
soft-spoken before attempting, once again, to thrust a different portrait of
Roof through the narrow legal window open for him to press his client's
mental state.

"The issue in this case from the beginning has been—and continues to
be—*why?* Mr. Williams said, 'Well, it's really very simple. The answer is hatred.' That's true as far as it goes, but if you think about it, that's really just
another way of asking the same question. 'Why, why did Dylann Roof do
this? Why was he motivated? What is the reason for it? What is the explanation?' That's the question."

In the charges they would consider, jurors must consider intent. Yes,
Roof did this out of racist views. But those didn't illuminate the underlying
question, Bruck argued.

"You've got a twenty-one-year-old young man, really a boy, who gives
his whole life over to this idea that there is a fight raging between white
people and black people, that there is a vast conspiracy being covered up."

And the only one who grasped this was Roof. At age nineteen, he'd read
some racist vitriol online one day, and suddenly everything in the world
made sense.

"What had happened in that instant was that he'd acquired a magic de-
coder ring that explained, in his mind, everything wrong on this Earth—
that every bad feeling, that everything going on in his own head that he
didn't understand and couldn't tolerate, had an explanation, which was a

racial war that had been concealed by everybody, for everybody, except on the Internet and to him."

Bruck acknowledged that his client showed no remorse but, with Williams repeatedly interrupting to object, urged jurors to peer beneath the surface of Roof's obvious guilt. He described, again, Roof's descent into racism and the simplified way, perhaps the only way, that Roof always explained his actions, as if he too couldn't understand what had overtaken him: *I had to do it.*

thirty-four

Twelve Friends

✳

The eighteen jurors now found out which of them were on the jury and who would serve as alternates. The twelve who'd made the cut, including three African Americans, filed out of the courtroom and headed to a small room with a long conference table surrounded by twelve leather office chairs. They'd already spent a bunch of time in this room during breaks in the testimony and had begun to get to know each other. However, until now, they hadn't been able to talk about the case. For many, that had been the hardest part—weathering so much traumatic testimony with nobody to talk to about it.

Both the jurors and Judge Gergel unanimously chose Gerald Truesdale, a fifty-three-year-old white man with a fatherly countenance, to serve as foreman. A corporate executive who had spent much of his career traveling the globe teaching workers about diversity issues, he'd been the last juror selected and, by coincidence, had sat in the foreman's seat, the one closest to the witness stand, throughout the trial.

They settled in around the conference table, and Truesdale thanked them for their service. They had listened carefully, taken notes, and endured testimony most people couldn't even imagine. The oldest among them was a seventy-five-year-old black man who worked at an assisted living home. Several were nurses. A teacher. A social worker. A truck driver. Police office administrator. Dental hygienist.

Finally allowed to discuss the case, jurors let impressions bubble up from their previous restraint. One juror brought up a moment that had shocked those who noticed it. "Could you believe that SOB smirked at Felicia!"

Truesdale also had been struck by the moment. He was among those who had taken notes during the trial as a way to remember—and cope. In his notebook, he'd jotted down a few when that happened: "zero remorse—incapable of respect—mentally challenged."

Then he had written, "remind jury of this."

Clearly, he didn't need to remind anyone.

Before they dove into the evidence, Truesdale figured that they all first needed to release the pressure of emotions and observations that had built up during the trial. He suggested going around the table to give each person the floor for a few minutes to vent. Or pray. Or cry.

Their responses were as varied as the backgrounds they brought to the moment.

"I just don't understand how someone could do something so awful," one woman said.

"Why was I chosen for this?" another asked.

"I need a minute of absolute silence," yet another said. So, they paused to provide that.

One juror described feeling terribly helpless when listening to the witnesses' pain. "I don't know what I can do to make this easier for the families. But I've got to do something."

Then, someone had an idea. What if they went to Emanuel as a group after the trial to show support for the congregation and the families? "We've got to see the church and spend some time there."

They all agreed to do that later. But for now, Truesdale reminded them, they had a job to do.

Truesdale was thirty-one years older than Roof and the father of two grown daughters. He had noticed that the benches behind Roof sat mostly empty every day. What were his parents like? Did they care about what their son had done? Maybe Roof had been desperate for their attention. Then again, maybe Roof was just batshit crazy.

Truesdale mostly saw a young man who had willingly embraced white supremacist ideology to a violent extreme. Why Roof had done so—whether it was evil or hatred or mental illness—didn't really matter now. The law didn't allow them to consider any of that at this point. Their job was simply to decide if Roof was guilty.

It was time to take an initial vote to see where they stood. Truesdale read the verdict form aloud, listing the thirty-three federal charges against Roof.

Then they went around the table casting votes.

Guilty, guilty, guilty, guilty . . .

They had begun deliberating at 1:12 p.m. Two hours later, they had reached a verdict.

With word of a verdict due, loved ones of the dead hurried up from their private family room, where they had so often prayed and cried together. Many of them strangers before the trial, they now crowded into Courtroom Six as a community, wondering whether the criminal justice system would indeed provide them justice.

Felicia and Polly perched stoically in the front row with Andy and Cheryl Savage, as they had throughout the trial. Jennifer, Johnette, and Kylon sat behind them. Clementa's father, who used a wheelchair, sat farther back with more of their family.

While most of the survivors and family members didn't support the death penalty for religious reasons, Jennifer didn't have a strong opinion about it. The Lord would deal with Roof in his own way, in his own time, and it didn't concern her terribly what happened to him before that as long as he wasn't free to hurt anyone else.

She, like others gathering in funereal silence around her, primarily wanted Dylann Roof imprisoned for the rest of his earthly life. She couldn't imagine how the jury could have found him anything but guilty. The video of him laughing about his crimes surely must have sealed his fate, she told herself. Johnette clutched one of her hands. Kylon held the other.

Behind her, Sharon Risher rubbed her pants leg, trying to soothe her jangling nerves. She too couldn't imagine how the jury wouldn't convict Roof. But she also never imagined she'd be sitting here in the first place.

Back a row, Anthony Thompson and Myra's daughter, Denise Quarles, sat shoulder to shoulder, whispering solemnly to one another. Although

Denise was his stepdaughter, he'd raised her from a toddler, and when she called him "Father," as she always had, his heart swelled with love and pride. Her biological father, with whom she also shared a good relationship, had died just days earlier. Sorrow lurked everywhere. Denise mostly wanted to get this trial over with. So did Anthony. Mental health workers dotted the crowd around them, ready with tissues and calming words.

The jury filed back in.

Judge Gergel instructed Roof to stand. He did so as the deputy clerk, an African American woman, walked over to foreman Truesdale in the jury box, who handed her a stack of sky blue papers. The verdict form. She turned and handed it up to Gergel.

Roof stood expressionless, arms at his sides as Gergel began to read aloud.

"In regard to count one, involving the death of Reverend Sharonda Coleman-Singleton, we find the defendant, Dylann Storm Roof: *guilty.*"

Roof's blank mask never wavered. From the gallery arose only the silence of relief as the name of each life he stole rang out over the courtroom. Felicia nodded her head with the sound of each "guilty." DePayne Middleton Doctor's sister rocked in her seat. Sharon's knee began to jiggle as if champagne bubbles were about to burst from her body. Around her, people smiled. Some closed their eyes, rivers of relief cleansing any fears that Roof might go free.

After reading all thirty-three charges, each ending with the word "guilty," Judge Gergel set down the verdict form and peered at the jury. "Ladies and gentlemen, I want to thank you initially for your service here. But your service is not yet over." The next phase of this trial would begin in nineteen days, on January 3, after a break for the holidays.

Once he and the jury left, Felicia and Polly stood in the front row and hugged tightly. Jennifer slipped down the aisle, still clutching Johnette's hand. The families crammed onto the elevators to head back to the family room and wait for Richardson to come speak to them.

As they filed back into the room, their deceased loved ones smiled back from photographs. Colorful artwork—mostly intricate adult coloring book pages that many had created during stressful hours of waiting in this room—hung on the walls in splashes of color. Where tears and sorrow had defined the space until now, singing and laughter suddenly filled it. Many hugged anyone near them—friends, relatives, and once-strangers all thrown together by this trial. They were family now.

Richardson and his prosecution team appeared in the doorway. They too were part of this family.

As the celebration calmed, Richardson spoke up. Go spend time with your families, he urged. Relax. Enjoy the holidays. They all needed to be rested for the next phase of this trial, when many more of them would testify.

The families scattered back to their lives. A few days later, Anthony Thompson hurried to his church. Dylann Roof might be on trial for his life, but today was still Sunday, and this was still Advent. Christ's birthday approached, and after spending the past week sitting in the presence of living evil, Anthony planned to talk about love and wrestle with what seemed the ultimate form of it: forgiveness.

A rainy night had left the roads wet, the air thick and unseasonably warm as his car tires sizzled along the streets of downtown Charleston. A half-dozen city blocks down from Emanuel, Anthony turned onto Bull Street, a residential stretch where Denmark Vesey had once plotted to free the city's enslaved masses, and parked at Holy Trinity Reformed Episcopal Church.

Almost as soon as he stepped into the cozy white building, his nose tickled. The ceiling had a fresh coat of sky blue paint, and the place was still dusty from the painters' preparation. Irritation momentarily pierced his positive mood. The work was supposed to be done earlier, not in the middle of Advent. He wanted—*needed*—to speak about love today. Yet his nose stuffed up, and his voice felt gravelly.

He pulled on a white pulpit robe and strode out to watch his tiny congregation, a few dozen men and women, take their seats. Children settled among them. Unlike Emanuel, his church had no giant organ, no balconies, no majestic two-story stained glass, no trumpets or even a choir. Singing voices unfurled, a pure and unadorned sound of faith rising from the pews.

Anthony began by praying for President Obama, incoming President Trump, the Emanuel Nine, survivors of gun violence, and others. He recited The Lord's Prayer with the people.

Forgive us our trespasses
As we forgive those who trespass against us.

By the time his sermon came, Anthony's nose was clogged and his throat threatened to give out. He spoke of Jesus' birth and what it meant to Christians. "When he came to that manger, he was one big bundle of love. It's something we don't say a lot, something we don't show a lot," Anthony said.

Several parishioners smiled back.

God didn't request that people love one another. He commanded it. But loving people who had wronged you? Anthony had draped himself in that challenge. It meant he had to love Dylann Roof. He had to see the killer as a person created by God, a soul lost for now to the devil, much as Roof's words stung: *I do not regret what I did.*

Yet, Anthony explained, he felt certain that hope remained, even for Roof, and nothing would stop him from spreading this message. It was the one God had given him way back at Roof's bond hearing.

"God is what?" Anthony asked. His lips pulled up into a smile. His dark eyes twinkled.

"Love."

The clock ticked toward midnight on the eve of 2017 when a man's solitary voice rang out from Mother Emanuel's empty balcony, sweeping over the 150 or so congregants sitting below.

"Watchman. Watchman. Can you please tell me the hour of the night?"

Then the lights went out. Darkness fell over the sanctuary. Another man's solitary voice intoned from a different corner of the balcony.

"Watchman. Watchman. Please tell me the hour of the night."

Much of white Charleston knew nothing of what was happening at Emanuel or this long tradition of black churches across America. New Year's Eve "watch night" services stretched back at least to December 31, 1862, in the death-thick years of the Civil War, when African Americans awaited word that Abraham Lincoln had issued the Emancipation Proclamation, freeing enslaved people in the rebellious states. The faithful had gathered in churches across the North and around "praying trees" in clandestine spots in the South to watch, to wait, to hope for this sign that God and their earthly president had heard their prayers for freedom.

In those days, Emanuel's faithful had worshipped underground, their building having been torched by whites, their church outlawed. Three more years would pass before the war ended, and they were able to rebuild, adopting the name Emanuel, meaning "God with us."

Another man's voice leapt from the dark balcony.

"Watchman. Watchman. Please tell me the hour of the night."

Below, some people knelt at their pews. Others bowed in prayer, waiting. From the fourth corner of Emanuel:

"Watchman. Watchman. Please tell me the hour of the night."

Word of Lincoln's proclamation did come in time for those waiting. At the stroke of midnight, enslaved people in the Confederate States were declared legally free. Those living under Confederate control weren't really free yet, of course. The Civil War still barreled onward. But just the words, the possibility.

Reverend Eric S. C. Manning, draped in holy white, answered:

"The hour of the night is twelve o'clock."

With that, clapping burst out. The lights flashed on. People who had endured such hardship through history, and through the eighteen months since death slipped into their fellowship hall, stood to cheer and embrace one another. A new year began.

thirty-five

Nine Beautiful Lives

❋

Over the holidays, Roof was evaluated a second time to see if he remained competent to stand trial. Again Gergel ruled that, appalling as Roof's views and conduct were, the defendant understood what was happening. The defense team responded with a seven-page, single-spaced declaration of their frustration with Roof couched as their "collective observations" of his bizarre behaviors during the first phase of the trial.

He often obsessed over his forehead. He told one attorney that he wouldn't be executed because he was too special. He thought Felicia calling him evil would make jurors feel sorry for him. One day, he became fixated on how his sweater smelled and told another lawyer that she had washed it with too much detergent. It had a film on it. The texture was all wrong.

"You are trying to kill me," he'd accused her.

And just a few days ago, when Bruck visited the jail, he and Roof had argued. Roof retorted that he hated him. If he got out of prison, he would go to Bruck's house and kill him.

Disturbing as that was, Gergel still ruled that none of it rendered Roof incompetent. The penalty phase would begin, and Roof still would represent himself.

When court resumed, Jennifer Pinckney sat in the front row for the first time in the trial. She did so because she would testify first. The prospect of being cross-examined by Roof terrified her, and going first meant that she'd be the one to find out whether he planned to cross-examine any of them. She could hardly stand the creepiness of being in the same room even with him looking away from all of them. She couldn't imagine sitting in the witness stand facing him.

The day began with attorney Nathan Williams standing to deliver the prosecution's opening statement, touching on the sheer scope and premeditation of Roof's horrific acts, the vulnerability of the people killed, and Roof's galling lack of remorse. He noted that Roof had fired the most bullets—eleven rounds—into the oldest victim, eighty-seven-year-old Susie Jackson. His voice rose with outrage as the muffled sobs of Susie's elderly sister in the gallery accentuated his words.

Any one of the nine killings would warrant death, Williams argued. But all of them taken together clearly justified the jury imposing "the most significant penalty available to you."

He previewed evidence of Roof's continued racism and lack of remorse by reading snippets from a journal that officials had found in the killer's cell six weeks after the massacre. "I would like to make it crystal clear. I do not regret what I did. I am not sorry. I have not shed a tear for the innocent people I killed."

As the outrageousness of those words sank in, Williams thanked the jury and returned to his seat.

All eyes shifted to Roof, now dressed in a charcoal gray sweater and slacks. His grandparents sat somberly a row behind him as he rose from his chair, a gargoyle come to life. After slipping around the outer edge of the defense table, he stepped toward a wooden lectern set up about six feet in front of the jury box. Courtroom officials had placed it there. The judge wouldn't let him get any closer. The jurors and alternates stared at him warily. A white man on the jury crossed his arms tightly over his chest.

Shuffling forward, Roof held his hands together in front of him as if he wore permanent handcuffs.

Truesdale, the foreman, watched Roof stop at the lectern. He could see Roof's fingernails. Roof glanced first at the witness seat, then at Truesdale before the killer's expression glazed over, as if he was no longer focused on the people before him. For several interminable seconds, he just stood there looking around. It struck Truesdale as the moment beneath the spotlight that Roof had sought since the killings, the ultimate platform to state his views and rally his troops.

Roof began in a monotone voice that sounded a bit softer than it had earlier in the trial. "My opening statement is going to seem a little bit out of place after the prosecution's," he began, "but I'm going to give it anyway. First of all, I want to say that you may or may not have heard that the reason I chose to represent myself in this phase of the trial was to prevent my lawyers from, um, presenting mental health mitigation. And that's absolutely true."

His clothes hanging from a rail-thin frame, Roof looked so young and out of place holding court in the grand space, like a shy high-schooler forced to give a speech in front of a group of parents. His strangely flat, affectless voice only underscored his galling lack of emotion in an otherwise emotion-laden proceeding.

"But it isn't because I have a mental illness that I don't want you to know about. And it isn't because I'm trying to keep a secret from you. Because my lawyers forced me to go through two competency hearings, and in those hearings they outlined everything that they would have said had I let them represent me. And eventually those will become part of the public record. So in that respect, my self-representation accomplishes nothing. So you could say, 'What's the point?'"

The jurors stared intently, most of them looking incredulous. Several leaned back in their chairs, as if to get as far away from him as possible. One man cocked his head, scowling as Roof continued.

"And the point is that I'm not going to lie to you, either by myself or through anyone else," he added as DePayne Middleton Doctor's sister rose from her seat and stalked out of the courtroom, muttering angrily.

"Other than the fact that I trust people that I shouldn't, the fact that I'm probably better at constantly embarrassing myself than anyone that has ever existed, there is nothing wrong with me, except logic. And lastly, I would just ask if you happen to remember anything that my lawyer said in the last phase of the trial—and I know none of it is worth remembering anyway—

but if you happen to remember any of it, I would ask that you forget it. And that's all."

With that shockingly short opening, he turned and shuffled back to the defense table, exhaling deeply. As he did, his mouth hung open partway, like a cat that has found a scent. The courtroom sat hushed until Gergel called for a short break.

Truesdale couldn't believe what he'd just heard. In those moments, Roof had all of the attention he had longed for, the perfect platform to state his views—and then choked.

When Jennifer heard her name called to testify, she said a quick prayer, took a deep breath, and stood up.

She stepped away from Johnette, Kylon, and Gerald Malloy, her attorney and a Democratic Senate colleague of her late husband's, all critical supporters in her new life. She slipped down the courtroom aisle, then through the hip-high swinging door. Wearing a black suit and a coral shirt, she forced herself to walk past the spot where Roof had just delivered his opening statement so she could assume her position in the witness stand. A thick twist of soft hair framed her head, lending her a warm appearance, though she scowled and pressed her lips together.

After sitting down, Jennifer angled her body toward the jury and looked at Richardson. He wore a purple tie again today. It had been Clementa's favorite color, too.

As he began leading her through a series of warm-up questions, Jennifer described in soft tones the day she met her future husband. A friend had set them up but then ditched them, leaving her and Clementa to make awkward conversation. They had shaken hands politely but sat looking in opposite directions, mutually irritated at being put in this position. Days later, at the friend's nudging, Jennifer called him back. They talked for two hours.

"The rest is history." She smiled grimly. Her eyes caressed a photograph on the courtroom screens that showed a regal Clementa standing in front of Emanuel's pulpit, its brilliant stained glass glowing behind him. Jennifer continued, her voice quivering, "I know without a doubt that he loved me, and he knew how much I loved him."

Richardson steered her to the night of June 17, which she'd avoided for the most part ever discussing in public. The moment was unavoidable now, so Jennifer inhaled deeply and set to the task at hand.

She'd been working on a lesson plan in her husband's office that night while Malana watched cartoons and Clementa tended to Bible study, when a blast exploded from the fellowship hall. It sounded so loud, right on the other side of the thin office wall. Then she heard a sound, a grunt almost, like someone getting the wind knocked out of him. Had a generator blown? She'd hurried to the office door that looked into the fellowship hall to check, setting her hand on the knob. Then more blasts. And then more.

"What was that?" she recalled Malana asking.

"Hush, be quiet."

She described how she had quietly locked the door and grabbed Malana by the arm to ferry her six-year-old daughter into the adjoining secretary's office. She'd closed the door between the two offices, shoved Malana under the desk, and locked a second door to a side hallway a few feet away. Darkness blackened the room. They heard more gunshots. Jennifer knelt beside her little girl.

"What's that?" Malana had asked again.

"Don't say anything." Jennifer clutched the child's trembling hands and whispered that she loved her, and she loved her big sister Eliana, too. But she would need to make a run for it to get help.

As she knelt, a bullet pierced the wall just feet away and shot across the room.

Jennifer dived beneath the desk too.

"Is Daddy going to die?"

"Be quiet, Malana."

She described how she'd groped along the desktop for the phone. More gunshots. She felt the receiver, then eased it off its base and tried to dial 911. But the phone's dial pad was dark. The room was pitch-black; she couldn't see what she was doing.

As she fumbled, the phone began to beep loudly.

Jennifer described for the jury how she'd dropped the receiver back down and pressed her body against Malana under the desk more tightly while the blasts moved toward them. She set her hand over the child's mouth. Malana set her hand onto Jennifer's mouth. Both trembled. Bullets blasted from the hallway on the other side of the thin wall from them. Someone grunted. A moan. The locked office doorknob turned.

Was Clementa trying to reach them?

Then she heard a stranger's voice: "I'm not crazy. I have to do this."

Jennifer told the jury how, in those moments, she grasped for her own fleeting courage. She needed to get help. But how? Which way was safer to go? Into her husband's office near the fellowship hall, where she'd left her phone and could call 911? Or should she make a run for the side hall and the exterior doors where she'd heard the stranger's voice? And now the moaning.

Jennifer had whispered sternly to her little girl: "No matter what happens to Momma, you don't come from under this desk." Then she had pulled herself away, crawled across the dark room to Clementa's adjoining office, opened the door, and found her cell phone. She'd dialed 911.

A recording of that call then played over the courtroom speakers. The public hadn't heard it before. Neither had many of the family members listening in acute silence. Several jurors began to scribble notes.

"911, what's the address of the emergency?"

Back beneath the desk, Jennifer had blurted out a few whispered words: "I am. At. Emanuel. Mother Emanuel."

"You're at Mother Emanuel?" the operator asked.

"Yes, there's been a shooting. I'm in the office under the desk." Her words burst between such quick and shallow breaths of terror that it was hard to decipher them. But two were clear:

"Please hurry!"

Jennifer didn't know that Polly already was talking to another 911 operator from beneath a table in the fellowship hall.

After Jennifer told the jury about their eventual rescue by police, Richardson indicated that he had no further questions. Several jurors smiled at Jennifer hoping to provide her some comfort.

But Jennifer knew what would come next and dreaded it.

She'd glanced at Roof only once while testifying, preferring to center herself on Richardson's strong presence to keep her composure. And he hadn't looked at her the entire time she'd testified. Yet now, the killer rose from his chair at the defense table.

Before he stood fully straight, he blurted out: "No questions."

He quickly sat back down. Jennifer slowly exhaled.

Prosecutors barreled on, calling several people—mostly close family but also friends and colleagues—to talk about the lives and deaths of each victim.

Anthony Thompson described how shortly before her death, he and Myra had talked about buying a house in Charlotte near their grandchildren and traveling more.

"You serious?" she had asked him.

"Oh, yeah."

They'd planned to do it in January 2017. Two weeks from now.

"If she's gone, what am I here for?" he asked. Sobs began to wrack his chest, and his voice sounded like an abandoned child's. "The person I lived for is gone. I still don't know what to do."

Then came the loved ones of Sharonda Coleman-Singleton and DePayne Middleton Doctor, who had both been raising young children on their own, several of whom testified about facing their lives now without their mothers. Then, Dan Simmons' family described their love for the crusty old preacher, one more in a long march of grief.

Before turning to the remaining family members, prosecutors called Lauren Knapp, an intelligence officer with the local sheriff's department. She'd been in charge of screening Roof's mail and recalled the day he wrote a note to his sister, the first outbound letter from his cell. The two-page note, written in perfectly formed print, struck her as funny: It didn't sound like something he would write.

When Knapp had Googled the passages, she'd realized the writings were stolen from the classic novel *The Sorrows of Young Werther*, a copy of which Roof had in his cell. The book told a story of unreciprocated love that ended with the protagonist's suicide.

Jail officials, Knapp explained, had put Roof briefly on suicide watch and searched his cell. In it, they found twenty-seven pages of a notebook filled with neatly penciled words and white supremacist symbols, a journal of sorts that Roof had written about six weeks after the shooting. Its purpose was clear right off, as the jury now learned listening to Knapp read it aloud in court:

> I would like to finish writing my opinions. I was unable to finish before because I was in a hurry to get to Charleston. I would also like to make some clarifications.

Roof began these post-massacre thoughts by railing against another racial enemy, Jews:

> I would consider myself well versed on almost every issue facing white people around the world. That being said, the Jews have played a major role in literally every thing that has proved destructive to our race, culture, and society. The truth is that at the moment it is much easier to talk about blacks or muslims or hispanics to other Whites because it is easier for them to relate. I would not deny for a moment that the Jews have made many wonderful, and truly great contributions to the world. But the bad outweighs the good. Let's take Hollywood for example.

Judge Gergel, who was Jewish, listened as Knapp continued to read Roof's thoughts about Jewish people controlling media industries, thereby thwarting the realizations of white writers, musicians, and filmmakers—and thus making them the enemies of white people. Over the coming pages, Roof moved on to disparage Hispanics, Muslims, and others until he switched to reminiscing about himself and his predicament.

> Sometimes sitting in my cell, I think about how nice it would be to watch a movie, or eat some good food, or drive my car some-where, but then I remember how I felt when I did these things, and how I knew I had to do something. And then I realize it was worth it. I would rather live imprisoned knowing I took action for my race than to live with the torture of sitting idle. It isn't up to me anymore. I did what I could do, I've done all I can do. I did

what I thought would make the biggest wave. And now the fate of our race sits in the hands of my brothers who continue to live freely.

Then, Knapp read the same words that Williams mentioned in his opening statement as a hint to the jury, now in their context:

I would like to make it crystal clear. I do not regret what I did. I am not sorry. I have not shed a tear for the innocent people I killed.

As the third day of family testimony began, the picture of profound loss—of planned futures destroyed and survivors left to muster on—continued to emerge. Some were coping better than others.

Cynthia Hurd's siblings admired how she had stepped up to help their sister, Jackie Jones, diagnosed with stage three breast cancer just a couple of weeks before the shooting. Cynthia was the first person Jackie called when she got the news. "I got you," Cynthia had promised, and everyone had known that she meant it. When she agreed to stay for Bible study on June 17, Cynthia had plans to go with Jackie to meet with her doctors and discuss her treatment options the following week.

Cynthia's husband, Steve, did not testify. The jury wouldn't learn of the dark turn his life had taken after his wife's murder. How he had lost more than sixty pounds, and still spent endless hours inside the house they once shared imagining what might have happened had he not stayed on his ship a couple of weeks longer than he'd planned. He knew that he would need to return to work, to the very merchant mariner job that had kept him apart from Cynthia that night, but he seemed to be stuck. He'd always loved to tinker with things, to take them apart and rebuild them. Now, he hardly wanted to pick up a wrench anymore. When a friend recently asked for his help installing a car alternator, a simple job for him, Steve couldn't bring himself to do it. Although he'd been on the witness list to testify in the trial, nobody had seen him in court much, leaving his family to worry. It was left to Cynthia's siblings and a coworker to describe a woman who had been essential to her husband, family, and community.

Then it was time for Ethel Lance's family. After a niece testified, Sharon Risher heard her name called and rose from her seat.

Stepping into the aisle, she passed her deaf brother, Gary Washington, who looked up at her with sad, worried eyes. She touched him on the shoulder, knowing he felt the loss of their mother as acutely as anyone. Her legs wobbled as she strode by Roof's table and stepped to the witness seat, where she clutched a black handkerchief framed with lace. Her mother had given it to her almost seven years earlier, back when she was ordained. Now, her fingers rubbed the lace around its edges.

Listening to the other victims' loved ones testify about the losses to their seemingly perfect families had left her overwhelmed with regret. Tears now burned her eyes. She wanted to have a normal relationship with her youngest sister, from whom she was now so estranged. But rancor lingered, and forgiveness felt so far away. Could the jury tell that?

Looking smaller and thinner than before the shooting, Sharon sat down and leaned toward the microphone: "Good afternoon."

Richardson began by asking about her parents and becoming the first in her family to attend college. Sharon had raised two children in Charlotte until, as her daughter put it, "She caught Jesus." A picture of Sharon graduating from seminary, Ethel standing proudly at her side, popped up on the courtroom screens.

Richardson asked why that day meant so much to Ethel.

"She was an unwed teenage mother," Sharon explained. "The circumstances of my birth is not a pretty story. To be fourteen and give birth to a biracial child was just not common in 1958."

Sharon twisted the handkerchief in her lap.

Although Ethel was so young, she had raised her baby, though doing so meant she couldn't finish high school. Without a husband, she needed to work. Not long after, Ethel had married the man who raised Sharon, along with four more children, and worked hard as a custodian. Yet, Ethel always advised her girls: "A lady always—*always!*—needs to carry a handkerchief and smell good."

Sharon held up the black handkerchief in her hands.

"Now that she's gone, the last couple of years have been holes in the fabric that made our family!" She pretended to rip it apart. "There's nobody there to keep us together, to keep the pieces together. Now we have tattered pieces. And I know that would devastate her."

Richardson thanked her. She stood up slowly then, swaying as she stepped down from the witness stand, still clutching the black handkerchief.

As the sentencing phase approached its ending, South Carolina lawmakers started a new session. Some planned to try, once again, to change the state's gun laws. One was Senator Gerald Malloy, the Pinckneys' friend and attorney. As he did the previous year, he filed legislation to extend the waiting period for the FBI to complete background checks from three days to twenty-eight before gun purchases. He filed it with less hope than ever.

Republican lawmakers who controlled the legislature had other ideas. Some argued that stiffer penalties for gun law violators would serve the public better than making law-abiding citizens wait longer to purchase firearms. Others wanted to expand gun rights by letting anyone carry a concealed weapon, even without the permit now required.

They'd all soon argue their case to a new governor. Catapulted in part by her handling of the massacre, Nikki Haley was leaving South Carolina to take on her new role as President Donald Trump's ambassador to the United Nations.

Her replacement, then–lieutenant governor Henry McMaster, was an early Trump supporter and a former state Republican Party chairman and attorney general. He'd also chosen not to attend the press conference when Haley called for the Confederate flag's removal. A gun rights advocate with a 93 percent rating from the National Rifle Association, McMaster favored allowing people to carry firearms—openly or concealed—without a permit.

So, even as the families testified about the depths of their losses, the possibility of reforming gun laws felt more impossible than ever.

Felicia Sanders rose next to talk about her Aunt Susie and son Tywanza. Susie had been one of her closest friends and strongest prayer partners. Susie and her sisters were known around town for their beautiful singing voices, which they brought to church every Sunday. Faith and family, those were Susie's anchors. At one point, her relatives owned almost every house on a street behind Emanuel. Hers, a yellow classic Charleston single house, was the center of family gatherings.

Then, Felicia moved on to describe Tywanza. A picture of him at about three years old flashed on the screen. She told the jurors with a weary smile about how, to potty-train him, she had bought him Ninja Turtle underwear. She'd warned him that if he peed in them, "Then the turtle bite your you-know-what."

The courtroom howled with much-needed laughter.

Felicia described how she'd even sweet-talked Tyrone into dressing like a Ninja Turtle one year for Tywanza's birthday. A photo of Tyrone in full Ninja Turtle gear sent the audience back into fits of laughter.

"He was everybody baby," Felicia added, smiling proudly at him.

When she was diagnosed with breast cancer several years earlier, Tywanza had rushed home from college and stayed with her during a nine-hour surgery. He refused to leave. Later, he tattooed her name on his chest, and when she warned that no woman would marry him like that, he had just laughed.

That's what she missed most—a mother's bond with her baby boy.

With all nine lost lives now represented, Richardson launched into his closing argument, a two-hour, outrage-filled oratory during which he portrayed Roof as a cruel, remorseless killer.

Roof's stated goal was to incite other people to act. If allowed to live a long life behind bars, he could continue to write his racist diatribes. He could influence other inmates and people outside of prison. He could become a revered symbol to white supremacists everywhere. But with him executed, Charleston could make a statement. It could take a step away from the sins of its past.

Then, it was Roof's turn once again, a final chance to convince the jury that his life should be spared. He rose from the defense table holding a single sheet of yellow notebook paper and returned to the lectern facing the jury for the second time. Adjusting the microphone, he took a single deep breath.

"Um," he began, then swished his tongue around his mouth. "I think it's safe to say that no one in their right mind wants to go into a church and kill people. You might remember in my confession to the FBI that I told them that I had to do it. And obviously that is not really true, because I didn't have to do it. I didn't have to do anything. And no one made me do it. We already went over that. But what I meant when I said that was I felt like I had to do it.

"And I still feel like I had to do it.

"Throughout this whole trial, you've heard a lot of talk about hate and hatred and how I'm filled with it and how vast my hatred is. But again, in my confession to the FBI, they asked me, they said, 'So is it safe to say that you don't like black people?' And my response to them was, 'Well, I don't like what black people do.'"

If he was filled with so much hate, he could have just said, "Yes, I don't like black people." But he noted that he hadn't said that. "Out of all the things that I could lie about, why would I lie about that? It wouldn't make any sense."

He paused for several seconds. The courtroom listened intently as he gathered his thoughts.

"Wouldn't it be fair to say the prosecution hates me since they are trying to give me the death penalty?"

He didn't deny that lots of people hated him. "But I would say that in this case the prosecution, along with anyone else who hates me, are the ones who've been misled."

He looked down again at the paper in front of him.

"Anyone, including the prosecution, who thinks that I'm filled with hatred has no idea what real hate is. They, they don't know anything about hate. They don't, they don't know what real hatred looks like. They think they do, but they don't really. From what I've been told, I have a right to ask you to give me a life sentence, but I'm not sure what good that would do anyway. What I will say is that only one of you has to disagree with the other jurors, and I know that at least some of you during the jury selection were asked if you would be able to stand up for your own opinions in deliberation, and if you were asked that, you answered yes. Because if you said no, you wouldn't be here. That is all. Thank you."

The jurors, stone-faced, watched him shuffle back to the defense table. A female juror in back wearing a bewildered expression scratched her head.

Before the jurors headed back to their room, Gergel read his charge to them. When they began their life-and-death deliberations shortly, they would need to weigh a series of aggravating factors, including evidence of substantial planning, killing of vulnerable elderly adults, killing of multiple people, targeting a church, racial motivation, intention to incite violence, impact on loved ones, and lack of remorse. On the other hand, they also could weigh mitigating factors such as Roof's age, his lack of significant criminal or violent history, and his confession and willingness to plead guilty. It was up to each of them how much weight to give the various factors.

"You place them on a mental scale," Gergel explained.

They returned to their jury room, where they sat, yet again, around the long conference table. The room smelled of the coffee that Truesdale, the foreman, had prepared that morning, as he had every morning, a way to establish a sense of routine and normalcy.

Truesdale hadn't often sat down in here during the trial. It felt frigid and claustrophobic, so he'd mostly stood leaning against a wall or looking out one of the two floor-to-ceiling windows, where he could glimpse a historic house that he had helped to restore earlier in his career. But now, he sat in the chair at the head of the table.

He began by noting that the consequences of their coming vote were enormous. It was okay to feel overwhelmed by the burden. "I want everyone to take ten minutes, and don't say anything. Just think about it," he said.

The room fell quiet. Truesdale himself began to reflect. He wasn't a big advocate of capital punishment, and his plan to vote for a death sentence left him in agony, more than anything else he had ever decided in his life. He didn't want to vote for someone's death, not even Dylann Roof's. He'd settled on the punishment for the families, for whatever closure it offered the grief he had just witnessed. He could still feel the pain that had radiated from people like Felicia, Sharon, and Anthony as they testified just a few feet away from him. He would never forget them.

After about ten minutes, he began to speak again. Next, they would go around the table and state their votes—life in prison or death—to gauge where they stood in their opinions. The woman to his left went first, then the others.

Death. Death. Death. Death. Death.

The sixth juror, a slim white woman with long dark hair, the youngest among them at twenty-three, hesitated. She was 99 percent sure she'd vote for death. But when prosecutors played Roof's confession, she had coughed or something at the moment when an FBI agent told him he'd killed nine people. She wanted to see it again.

"Someone's life is at stake," she said.

Truesdale agreed. He wanted them all to be completely certain about their votes.

Before they addressed her question, they finished going around the room. Next went the oldest person there, a black man in his seventies, and then the other women. They ended with Truesdale.

"Death," each one said.

Now they needed to see about watching Roof's confession again. At 3:25 p.m., they asked Judge Gergel, who agreed they could view it. They returned to the jury room to wait, sifting again through the piles of boxes and envelopes that contained the evidence attorneys had offered during the trial. The room's reverent silence reminded Truesdale of sitting in church during prayer.

Standing there, he noticed the killer's Glock sitting on the table and walked over to pick it up. The grip felt cold and heavy in his hand. Chills prickled along his skin. It was as if Roof were standing right there before him watching, waiting to hear how they would vote.

Each morning during the trial, Truesdale had read a daily devotional on his phone, and that morning's passage was from Genesis, the first book of the Bible. "Whoever sheds human blood, by humans shall their blood be shed; for in the image of God has God made mankind." He'd read it with shock, its message clear. Roof had violated the sanctity of life, and now he must be held responsible in kind by a jury of his peers.

Thinking of the passage again now, Truesdale set down the gun, thankful to step away from it and feel settled in his decision.

At last, the tech crew got the confession tape playing. In the clip that the young woman wanted to see again, an FBI agent asked Roof, "So if I told you nine people died last night, how would that make you feel?"

Roof smiled. He didn't believe it. "There wasn't even nine people there!"

The sheer callousness, his smirk and utter lack of care for the lives he'd taken, felt even more heartless than before, now separated out from the rest of his confession.

The uncertain juror interrupted: "I'm good," she said.

They voted again, easily reaching a unanimous verdict. Yet, the decision felt so quick, so simple. Was it too quick? They didn't want anyone to think they hadn't taken their role seriously, so they ordered lunch to pass some time.

At 4:25 p.m., they sent a note to the judge. They had a verdict.

Again, the families returned to their seats behind the prosecutors. Roof returned to his chair at the defense table. The two rows behind him sat empty.

Last, the jury filed back in. Truesdale stood in his seat to hand the blue pages of their verdict form to the deputy clerk. She took them and, with all eyes watching, passed them up to Judge Gergel. He told Roof to stand.

The attorneys Roof had cast aside stood on either side of him as Gergel read aloud the long list of charges. After each one that carried it as a maximum sentence, he read the word:

Death.

No cries burst out from the families and survivors. Instead, a quiet sense of resolution settled over the courtroom.

As Gergel read through all thirty-three charges against Roof, some family members silently cheered the sentence. Others found it bittersweet, given the tension between their opposition to the death penalty and their gratitude that the jury had imposed the system's most severe punishment.

They adjourned for the day then. The families would have to return to the court one final time tomorrow, so that Gergel could formally impose the sentence.

As Sharon walked back to her hotel, a deep red sunset draped over the Ashley River behind it. This building had provided her a refuge during the trial, even though Roof's defense team also was staying there. She'd run into them a couple of times in the lobby. The first time, David Bruck had said hello to her, called her by name. "I just want you to know my heart goes out to you," he'd said. She had shaken his hand. Then, after the guilty verdict, she'd run into them again. Bruck said he admired her work combating gun violence. His co-counsel wished her a Merry Christmas. It helped to know they were human beings just doing their jobs, but it still felt weird to imagine them so close.

When she stepped into the lobby now, she didn't see any of them around. Instead, the smell of dinner reached out from a dining area where the hotel served complimentary dinner at six for an hour. Tonight they were serving hamburger, her dog Puff's favorite. She packed up a small container of it, a doggy bag for a dog. She took none for herself. She couldn't imagine eating.

Down a hall and to the left, room 111 waited. A cigarette and cup of coffee sure sounded good, but a network TV crew was coming to interview her, and she needed a few minutes of peace first. When she opened the door, Puff greeted her. She bent over to rub his soft white ears.

"Mommy got you a hamburger!"

She set it in her refrigerator, then sank onto a couch and ignored her phone, jangling with another text. Her voicemail filled with messages, most from reporters. Puff stared up at her. When she leaned back onto a soft cushion, he jumped up, resting two white paws onto her lap.

It didn't seem real, not yet, not Roof's guilt on all thirty-three counts, nor his death sentence for killing her mother and eight others.

But his words still stung, "I do not regret what I did."

Sharon turned on the room's large TV. Just as she did, Roof's giant mug shot popped up, his dead eyes staring right at her. It jolted her, as his image always did, although this time she quickly reminded herself that he would never know freedom again. The trial was over. He would pay for his crimes. Relief flowed in as that realization firmed. The anchor switched to a story about President Obama's final days in office and showed a press conference that the nation's first black president had held a year ago almost to the exact day to announce his executive actions to reduce gun violence. Sharon had been right there in that audience.

Exhausted, she kicked off her black boots. She'd been up since 5 a.m. Sleep hadn't come much over the past nineteen months.

The trial had opened her eyes—and lots of other people's, too, she hoped—about homegrown terrorism and the dangerous prevalence of white supremacist thinking in America. Gun violence was the mechanism Dylann Roof had chosen to commit his crimes, but racism fueled his desire to kill innocent black people. Yet, justice had been served to a group of African American victims against a white man, at least in this one case. She'd lived to see the day.

With a calm she hadn't felt since her mother's death, Sharon slipped from beneath Puff's paws and stood up to pop a frozen dinner into the room's microwave. After a few steps toward the kitchen, she suddenly halted. Standing there, something dawned inside of her. It seeped through the pain and then swept into an open space that, until now, tension and worry had filled. The sensation felt escorted by God.

Forgiveness.

Maybe it was knowing they were done with this trial. Maybe it was releasing Roof into the arms of justice. Maybe all that left enough space inside of her for God to work more fully.

"I can actually say in my heart that I can forgive you," she murmured aloud.

For several moments, Sharon stood motionless in the middle of her hotel room. The realization settled like a dove onto the nest of her thoughts. She could forgive Roof, at least right now. Forever? Time would tell. But as she stood there, the thought felt comfortable and peaceful, at home on this threshold of the next season of her life, the one when she wouldn't have to hear his name every day.

Sharon texted the network news producer. She couldn't do the interview after all. Instead, she grabbed her jacket and headed back outside into the cool night, leaving Puff behind in the hotel room. His gait was too slow, and the walk to the water too far.

The boats docked up ahead at a marina creaked as the Ashley River's ceaseless current hurried by from nearby Charleston Harbor, where an estimated 40 percent of enslaved Africans brought to America once arrived on rancid ships. Damp salty air welcomed her. Sharon stood where the water met the sulfuric scent of pluff mud and felt the steady breath of God in the breeze.

"Momma," she whispered. "Guess what happened today."

In court the next morning, Felicia stepped through the swinging door one last time, clutching her Bible. She strode firmly to a lectern positioned front and center, bringing with her the words she'd imagined saying to Roof for all these nineteen months now. She wanted to tell him about this Bible, her faith, and the things he'd tried to destroy. But had not.

Although the lectern was tilted toward Judge Gergel, she instead pivoted her body to face Roof at his table. The judge smiled kindly.

"Mrs. Sanders, you hardly need introducing."

Roof stared straight ahead as she set her Bible onto the lectern and fixed her stare onto him. He might not look at her, she figured, but he would hear her.

"I call you Dylann Roof," she began, "because you deserve respect—the respect you did not give Miss Susie, Reverend Clementa. You did not give respect to Sharonda Singleton . . ." She named them all, her sorrow building with the remembrance of each person lost so senselessly.

"And no respect for Tywanza Sanders, my baby!"

She breathed.

"But I'ma give you respect."

She couldn't stand to hear fireworks anymore, she explained, or a balloon pop, not even an acorn dropping from a tree. "And most important, I cannot shut my eyes to pray!" She couldn't let her guard down anymore, or someone else she loved might be gone that quickly.

However, Felicia said, today she had brought with her the best defense. Not a gun. Not a knife. Not her fists.

Her voice trembled as she continued. "My Bible, *abused*—abused, torn, shot up. When I look at the Bible, I see blood that Jesus shed for me. And for you, Dylann Roof." With that, she picked up her Bible, the one rescued from the fellowship hall, and held it in the air like a wand of faith. Then she pointed it at him. With her fingers, she flipped through its wrinkled, tattered, salvaged pages as if to cast the very spirit of God toward the evil man before her. Maybe one day, yet to come, grace would lead him home, as faith had rescued her.

"Yes, I forgive you," she continued. "That was the easiest thing I had to do. But you can't help someone who doesn't want to help themselves. And that's exactly what you are."

Indeed, he sat there with his same mushroom haircut, still staring straight ahead with that same blank expression he'd worn all through the trial. He wasn't going to acknowledge her now, just as he'd showed no respect, no caring or humanity at all, to the nine people he killed around her. So, she ended with words similar to those she'd spoken at the bond hearing all those months ago:

"May God have mercy on your soul."

With that, she turned away, carrying her Bible, as she stepped back through the swinging doors. When she returned to her seat, her husband's arm slipped around her shoulders.

The next three dozen people who spoke, all members of this large family of grief, showed that they weren't a single person. They weren't the homogenous group of forgiving people the world wanted them to be. Some screamed at Roof, calling him evil. Several hoped he burned in hell for eternity. They called him a coward. Satan. An animal. A monster.

Still others spoke of love and the strong bonds they had formed with one another. They were certain, as the psalmist pledged, that God was with them.

Steve Hurd had also come, and when he spoke, gaunt and bearded, his once-commanding voice was barely audible. He recalled asking Cynthia to marry him on Christmas morning and described the devastating loss of her. Sharon spoke as well, promising Roof that she would continue fighting for gun reform so that, while racism might last forever in America, a gun wouldn't allow hate to sow such devastation again.

In the end, Judge Gergel invoked a quote from Martin Luther King Jr., adopted from a nineteenth-century minister and abolitionist.

"The arc of the moral universe is long, but it bends towards justice. And justice will be done," Gergel said. "Mr. Roof, stand.

"The defendant will now pay for his crimes with his life."

Jennifer Pinckney and her sister-in-law Johnette hugged Kylon Middleton and various family members good-bye before everyone set out for their respective homes in different towns. They all smiled and laughed, finally unmoored from the weight of this trial.

Within minutes of leaving the courthouse, Jennifer merged onto the interstate she had driven that hot June night, eager to spend some time with Clementa. She drove the same car, a Toyota Highlander, although Clementa's sister now rode in the passenger seat trying to answer the deluge of calls and texts from people celebrating with them.

Johnette turned to her and smiled.

"It's over," she said.

Jennifer nodded back.

Yet, as the car's wheels hummed over the interstate, and the sun sagged in the sky ahead, an ache interrupted her joy. It wasn't the deep, gut-ripping grief for Clementa that she carried with her always. This felt softer, though it grew as she drove past endless pine trees and sleepy towns on her way home.

She realized that she'd miss the warmth of the victims' loved ones. She'd never again gather with them in the family room back at the courthouse, and it was unlikely she'd see them again anytime soon. She felt a sense of aloneness she hadn't felt since the trial began.

Before, intent on restoring normalcy to her life, she'd failed to realize how supportive the victims' families could be to one another, how they alone could understand each other's grief and the unique set of pressures this particular event had brought them all, even beyond dealing with someone like Dylann Roof or losing a loved one. One day, she hoped, they would gather again to share their grief beyond the killer's presence. Maybe she could bring Eliana and Malana to meet them all.

As they approached home, Jennifer's thoughts drifted to her girls. School had just started back after the winter holiday. No matter what happened to Dylann Roof, they still had dance classes and recitals, homework, chores, friends, church. They needed her. And she needed them. Her foot pressed the accelerator a little harder. She needed to get back to that life, the quiet one without Clementa, to continue raising their girls on her own.

EPILOGUE

Dylann Roof's sentence tied a crisp bow of justice onto the story of nine devastated families, but their sagas, the city's saga, didn't end that winter day in 2017. Two months later, Roof's friend Joey Meek was sentenced to serve two years and three months in federal prison. And, two months after that, former police officer Michael Slager pleaded guilty in federal court to violating Walter Scott's civil rights—a startling shift after he'd spent two years insisting that he shot the fleeing black man in self-defense. His sentence: twenty years in prison.

The following year, Roof's eighteen-year-old sister, Morgan, was arrested carrying a Swiss Army knife and pepper spray at her affluent Columbia-area high school. She'd been perturbed that day about the National Student Walkout over gun violence, and posted on Snapchat: "I hope it's a trap and y'all get shot we know it's fixing to be nothing but black people walkin out anyway." She pleaded not guilty.

A month later, President Trump nominated Roof's lead prosecutor, Jay Richardson, to a seat on the 4th Circuit Court of Appeals, news applauded by virtually everyone who sat in Courtroom Six. He is now Judge Richardson.

Meanwhile, those left to live with the pain Dylann Roof caused soldiered on. Anthony Thompson continued to pastor his church. Jennifer Pinckney returned to her elementary school library. Sharonda Coleman-Singleton's son, Chris, got drafted by the Chicago Cubs and welcomed a new baby boy. Sharon Risher still pushed for gun law reforms. Steve Hurd sold Cynthia's childhood home and moved to North Charleston, seeking a fresh start. Tywanza Sanders' loved ones started a foundation to carry on his legacy. So did those of Myra Thompson, Cynthia Hurd, Daniel Simmons Sr., Clementa Pinckney, and others. Reverend Pinckney's girls also began speaking out more—about guns, racism, and hopes that their loss might save other people's lives.

The city, too, strode forward. Charleston's planned International African American Museum, in the works for almost two decades, reached its $75 million fundraising goal. Construction should begin in 2019 on the site, once called Gadsden's Wharf, where thousands of African slaves arrived in Charleston.

And almost three years to the day after Roof slipped into Bible study, Charleston's City Council did something unimaginable before the massacre. Its members voted, albeit narrowly, to apologize on behalf of the city for its role in the institution of slavery. Many hailed the move as an important step toward healing. Yet, among the five councilmen who opposed it—all but one of them white men—most said they wouldn't apologize for something they hadn't done. As one former councilman asked: "Why should we do it when so much of what we'd be apologizing for happened so long ago?"

To many, it felt as if they'd chosen to ignore the fact that white supremacy remained so very alive and well in Charleston and across America. Along with the proliferation of online hate networks that molded Dylann Roof's views, President Trump's divisive rhetoric about all kinds of nonwhite people put a presidential stamp of permission onto overt displays of animosity, so clearly on the rise.

Just three years had passed since Roof's rampage when another violent white supremacist walked into a house of worship during services, this time the Tree of Life Synagogue in Pittsburgh. Moments before, like Roof, this suspected killer left a final message online. "I can't sit by and watch my people get slaughtered. Screw your optics, I'm going in." He then murdered eleven people simply because they were Jewish.

The next day, a Sunday, Reverend Eric S. C. Manning stood in Emanuel's pulpit to reassure his congregants, wounded anew by the disturbing similarities between the shootings. He also criticized the divisive speech that empowered both shooters—and surely there were others still out there feeding on the vitriol.

"The tongue has the power of life and death," he warned. "Sometimes we don't think that other people are paying attention. But they are indeed paying attention."

REMARKS BY THE PRESIDENT IN EULOGY FOR THE HONORABLE REVEREND CLEMENTA PINCKNEY

College of Charleston
Charleston, South Carolina
2:49 P.M. EDT

THE PRESIDENT: Giving all praise and honor to God.

The Bible calls us to hope. To persevere, and have faith in things not seen.

"They were still living by faith when they died," Scripture tells us. "They did not receive the things promised; they only saw them and welcomed them from a distance, admitting that they were foreigners and strangers on Earth."

We are here today to remember a man of God who lived by faith. A man who believed in things not seen. A man who believed there were better days ahead, off in the distance. A man of service who persevered, knowing full well he would not receive all those things he was promised, because he believed his efforts would deliver a better life for those who followed.

To Jennifer, his beloved wife; to Eliana and Malana, his beautiful, wonderful daughters; to the Mother Emanuel family and the people of Charleston, the people of South Carolina.

I cannot claim to have had the good fortune to know Reverend Pinckney well. But I did have the pleasure of knowing him and meeting him here in South Carolina, back when we were both a little bit younger. Back when I didn't have visible gray hair. The first thing I noticed was his graciousness,

his smile, his reassuring baritone, his deceptive sense of humor—all quali-
ties that helped him wear so effortlessly a heavy burden of expectation.

Friends of his remarked this week that when Clementa Pinckney entered
a room, it was like the future arrived; that even from a young age, folks
knew he was special. Anointed. He was the progeny of a long line of the
faithful—a family of preachers who spread God's word, a family of protesters who sowed change to expand voting rights and desegregate the South.
Clem heard their instruction, and he did not forsake their teaching.

He was in the pulpit by thirteen, pastor by eighteen, public servant by
twenty-three. He did not exhibit any of the cockiness of youth, nor youth's
insecurities; instead, he set an example worthy of his position, wise beyond
his years, in his speech, in his conduct, in his love, faith, and purity.

As a senator, he represented a sprawling swath of the Lowcountry, a
place that has long been one of the most neglected in America. A place still
wracked by poverty and inadequate schools; a place where children can still
go hungry and the sick can go without treatment. A place that needed somebody like Clem.

His position in the minority party meant the odds of winning more re-
sources for his constituents were often long. His calls for greater equity
were too often unheeded, the votes he cast were sometimes lonely. But he
never gave up. He stayed true to his convictions. He would not grow dis-
couraged. After a full day at the Capitol, he'd climb into his car and head to
the church to draw sustenance from his family, from his ministry, from the
community that loved and needed him. There he would fortify his faith,
and imagine what might be.

Reverend Pinckney embodied a politics that was neither mean, nor
small. He conducted himself quietly, and kindly, and diligently. He encouraged progress not by pushing his ideas alone, but by seeking out your ideas,
partnering with you to make things happen. He was full of empathy and
fellow feeling, able to walk in somebody else's shoes and see through
their eyes. No wonder one of his Senate colleagues remembered Senator
Pinckney as "the most gentle of the forty-six of us—the best of the forty-six
of us."

Clem was often asked why he chose to be a pastor and a public servant.
But the person who asked probably didn't know the history of the AME

Church. As our brothers and sisters in the AME Church know, we don't make those distinctions. "Our calling," Clem once said, "is not just within the walls of the congregation, but . . . the life and community in which our congregation resides."

He embodied the idea that our Christian faith demands deeds and not just words; that the "sweet hour of prayer" actually lasts the whole week long—that to put our faith in action is more than individual salvation, it's about our collective salvation; that to feed the hungry and clothe the naked and house the homeless is not just a call for isolated charity but the imperative of a just society.

What a good man. Sometimes I think that's the best thing to hope for when you're eulogized—after all the words and recitations and resumes are read, to just say someone was a good man.

You don't have to be of high station to be a good man. Preacher by thirteen. Pastor by eighteen. Public servant by twenty-three. What a life Clementa Pinckney lived. What an example he set. What a model for his faith. And then to lose him at forty-one—slain in his sanctuary with eight wonderful members of his flock, each at different stages in life but bound together by a common commitment to God.

Cynthia Hurd. Susie Jackson. Ethel Lance. DePayne Middleton Doctor. Tywanza Sanders. Daniel L. Simmons. Sharonda Coleman-Singleton. Myra Thompson. Good people. Decent people. God-fearing people. People so full of life and so full of kindness. People who ran the race, who persevered. People of great faith.

To the families of the fallen, the nation shares in your grief. Our pain cuts that much deeper because it happened in a church. The church is, and always has been, the center of African American life—a place to call our own in a too often hostile world, a sanctuary from so many hardships.

Over the course of centuries, black churches served as "hush harbors" where slaves could worship in safety; praise houses where their free descendants could gather and shout, "hallelujah!"; rest stops for the weary along the Underground Railroad; bunkers for the foot soldiers of the Civil Rights Movement. They have been, and continue to be, community centers where we organize for jobs and justice; places of scholarship and network; places where children are loved and fed and kept out of harm's way, and told that they are beautiful and smart and taught that they matter. That's what happens in church.

That's what the black church means. Our beating heart. The place where our dignity as a people is inviolate. And there's no better example of this tradition than Mother Emanuel, a church built by blacks seeking liberty, burned to the ground because its founder sought to end slavery, only to rise up again, a Phoenix from these ashes.

When there were laws banning all-black church gatherings, services happened here anyway, in defiance of unjust laws. When there was a righteous movement to dismantle Jim Crow, Dr. Martin Luther King Jr. preached from its pulpit, and marches began from its steps. A sacred place, this church. Not just for blacks, not just for Christians, but for every American who cares about the steady expansion of human rights and human dignity in this country; a foundation stone for liberty and justice for all. That's what the church meant.

We do not know whether the killer of Reverend Pinckney and eight others knew all of this history. But he surely sensed the meaning of his violent act. It was an act that drew on a long history of bombs and arson and shots fired at churches, not random, but as a means of control, a way to terrorize and oppress. An act that he imagined would incite fear and recrimination; violence and suspicion. An act that he presumed would deepen divisions that trace back to our nation's original sin.

Oh, but God works in mysterious ways. God has different ideas.

He didn't know he was being used by God. Blinded by hatred, the alleged killer could not see the grace surrounding Reverend Pinckney and that Bible study group—the light of love that shone as they opened the church doors and invited a stranger to join in their prayer circle. The alleged killer could have never anticipated the way the families of the fallen would respond when they saw him in court—in the midst of unspeakable grief, with words of forgiveness. He couldn't imagine that.

The alleged killer could not imagine how the city of Charleston, under the good and wise leadership of Mayor Riley, how the state of South Carolina, how the United States of America would respond—not merely with revulsion at his evil act, but with big-hearted generosity and, more importantly, with a thoughtful introspection and self-examination that we so rarely see in public life.

Blinded by hatred, he failed to comprehend what Reverend Pinckney so well understood—the power of God's grace.

This whole week, I've been reflecting on this idea of grace. The grace of the families who lost loved ones. The grace that Reverend Pinckney would preach about in his sermons. The grace described in one of my favorite hymnals—the one we all know: Amazing grace, how sweet the sound that saved a wretch like me. I once was lost, but now I'm found; was blind but now I see.

According to the Christian tradition, grace is not earned. Grace is not merited. It's not something we deserve. Rather, grace is the free and benevolent favor of God as manifested in the salvation of sinners and the bestowal of blessings. Grace.

As a nation, out of this terrible tragedy, God has visited grace upon us, for he has allowed us to see where we've been blind. He has given us the chance, where we've been lost, to find our best selves. We may not have earned it, this grace, with our rancor and complacency, and short-sightedness and fear of each other—but we got it all the same. He gave it to us anyway. He's once more given us grace. But it is up to us now to make the most of it, to receive it with gratitude, and to prove ourselves worthy of this gift.

For too long, we were blind to the pain that the Confederate flag stirred in too many of our citizens. It's true, a flag did not cause these murders. But as people from all walks of life, Republicans and Democrats, now acknowledge—including Governor Haley, whose recent eloquence on the subject is worthy of praise, as we all have to acknowledge—the flag has always represented more than just ancestral pride. For many, black and white, that flag was a reminder of systemic oppression and racial subjugation. We see that now.

Removing the flag from this state's Capitol would not be an act of political correctness; it would not be an insult to the valor of Confederate soldiers. It would simply be an acknowledgment that the cause for which they fought—the cause of slavery—was wrong. The imposition of Jim Crow after the Civil War, the resistance to civil rights for all people was wrong. It would be one step in an honest accounting of America's history; a modest but meaningful balm for so many unhealed wounds. It would be an expression of the amazing changes that have transformed this state and this country for the better, because of the work of so many people of goodwill, people of all races striving to form a more perfect union. By taking down that flag, we express God's grace.

But I don't think God wants us to stop there. For too long, we've been blind to the way past injustices continue to shape the present. Perhaps we see that now. Perhaps this tragedy causes us to ask some tough questions about how we can permit so many of our children to languish in poverty, or attend dilapidated schools, or grow up without prospects for a job or for a career.

Perhaps it causes us to examine what we're doing to cause some of our children to hate. Perhaps it softens hearts towards those lost young men, tens and tens of thousands caught up in the criminal justice system, and leads us to make sure that that system is not infected with bias; that we embrace changes in how we train and equip our police so that the bonds of trust between law enforcement and the communities they serve make us all safer and more secure.

Maybe we now realize the way racial bias can infect us even when we don't realize it, so that we're guarding against not just racial slurs, but we're also guarding against the subtle impulse to call Johnny back for a job interview but not Jamal. So that we search our hearts when we consider laws to make it harder for some of our fellow citizens to vote. By recognizing our common humanity, by treating every child as important, regardless of the color of their skin or the station into which they were born, and to do what's necessary to make opportunity real for every American—by doing that, we express God's grace.

For too long—

AUDIENCE: For too long!

THE PRESIDENT: For too long, we've been blind to the unique mayhem that gun violence inflicts upon this nation. Sporadically, our eyes are open: When nine of our brothers and sisters are cut down in a church basement, twelve in a movie theater, twenty-six in an elementary school. But I hope we also see the thirty precious lives cut short by gun violence in this country every single day; the countless more whose lives are forever changed—the survivors crippled, the children traumatized and fearful every day as they walk to school, the husband who will never feel his wife's warm touch, the entire communities whose grief overflows every time they have to watch what happened to them happen to some other place.

The vast majority of Americans—the majority of gun owners—want to do something about this. We see that now. And I'm convinced that by acknowledging the pain and loss of others, even as we respect the traditions and ways of life that make up this beloved country—by making the moral choice to change, we express God's grace.

We don't earn grace. We're all sinners. We don't deserve it. But God gives it to us anyway. And we choose how to receive it. It's our decision how to honor it.

None of us can or should expect a transformation in race relations overnight. Every time something like this happens, somebody says we have to have a conversation about race. We talk a lot about race. There's no shortcut. And we don't need more talk. None of us should believe that a handful of gun-safety measures will prevent every tragedy. It will not. People of goodwill will continue to debate the merits of various policies, as our democracy requires—this is a big, raucous place, America is. And there are good people on both sides of these debates. Whatever solutions we find will necessarily be incomplete.

But it would be a betrayal of everything Reverend Pinckney stood for, I believe, if we allowed ourselves to slip into a comfortable silence again. Once the eulogies have been delivered, once the TV cameras move on, to go back to business as usual—that's what we so often do to avoid uncomfortable truths about the prejudice that still infects our society. To settle for symbolic gestures without following up with the hard work of more lasting change—that's how we lose our way again.

It would be a refutation of the forgiveness expressed by those families if we merely slipped into old habits, whereby those who disagree with us are not merely wrong but bad; where we shout instead of listen; where we barricade ourselves behind preconceived notions or well-practiced cynicism.

Reverend Pinckney once said, "Across the South, we have a deep appreciation of history—we haven't always had a deep appreciation of each other's history." What is true in the South is true for America. Clem understood that justice grows out of recognition of ourselves in each other. That my liberty depends on you being free, too. That history can't be a sword to justify injustice, or a shield against progress, but must be a manual for how to avoid repeating the mistakes of the past—how to break the cycle. A roadway toward a better world. He knew that the path of grace involves an open mind—but, more importantly, an open heart.

That's what I've felt this week—an open heart. That, more than any particular policy or analysis, is what's called upon right now, I think—what a friend of mine, the writer Marilynne Robinson, calls "that reservoir of goodness, beyond, and of another kind, that we are able to do each other in the ordinary cause of things."

That reservoir of goodness. If we can find that grace, anything is possible. If we can tap that grace, everything can change.

Amazing grace. Amazing grace.

[Sings; all join in]—*Amazing grace, how sweet the sound, that saved a wretch like me; I once was lost, but now I'm found; was blind but now I see.*

Clementa Pinckney found that grace.

Cynthia Hurd found that grace.

Susie Jackson found that grace.

Ethel Lance found that grace.

DePayne Middleton Doctor found that grace.

Tywanza Sanders found that grace.

Daniel L. Simmons Sr. found that grace.

Sharonda Coleman-Singleton found that grace.

Myra Thompson found that grace.

Through the example of their lives, they've now passed it on to us. May we find ourselves worthy of that precious and extraordinary gift, as long as our lives endure. May grace now lead them home. May God continue to shed his grace on the United States of America.

END
3:28 P.M. EDT

ACKNOWLEDGMENTS

I wrote this book to convey the sheer scope of devastation that mass tragedies sow in the lives of everyday people. Given the enormity of hurt this particular one caused, and the sheer number of people I relied on to portray that, I cannot thank all of those to whom I owe debts of gratitude. First and foremost, I extend my deepest thanks to Felicia Sanders, Polly Sheppard, and Jennifer Pinckney for describing what happened in the fellowship hall that night and the devastation they are left to live with. My most heartfelt thanks also to the victims' loved ones who shared their journeys with me, especially Anthony Thompson, Sharon Risher, Nadine Collier, Daniel Simmons Jr., Arthur Stephen Hurd, Melvin and Malcolm Graham, Sheila Capers, Kevin Singleton, Aja and Brandon Risher, Bethane Middleton-Brown, and the late Esther Lance.

This isn't a story only about scope. I also sought to express the deeply personal pain that people suffered, and I am forever grateful to my insightful editor, Tim Bartlett, who never met a scene or character that couldn't be enhanced with another detail, more precise description, or improved analysis. Thank you for making me a better writer and this book a better read.

The idea for this project came from my agent, Albert Lee, whose tireless enthusiasm kept us on task throughout. I couldn't ask for a more dedicated and encouraging advocate.

My thanks also to the wonderful staff at St. Martin's Press who embraced this story from day one. Alice Pfeifer for helping this first-time author in countless ways throughout the process. Production editor Alan Bradshaw for the care and attention he brought to the manuscript. Copy editor Jennifer

Simington for polishing it. Susan Walsh created the elegant interior design, and Jon Bush designed a memorable jacket. Last but not least, the publishing team who conveyed from the beginning that this book was important to them: publisher Jennifer Enderlin, associate publisher Laura Clark, publicist Rebecca Lang, and marketer Martin Quinn.

Here in Charleston, just one mile away from Mother Emanuel, I work in a newsroom of incredibly dedicated reporters, photographers, editors, designers, and others who have covered this tragedy since the dark hours of June 17, 2015. My deepest thanks to *Post and Courier* publisher P. J. Browning and executive editor Mitch Pugh, who supported this project, which often took me away from newspaper work, because they believed in the greater public service of telling the story of what happened in our city. This book bears my name but relies on reporting and institutional knowledge from our entire newsroom, none more so than my immeasurably talented editor Glenn Smith and reporting colleague Andrew Knapp. Thank you also to Doug Pardue, Brian Hicks, Adam Parker, Robert Behre, Abigail Darlington, Andy Shain, Schuyler Kropf, Cynthia Roldan, Hanna Raskin, and many others. As the images in this book demonstrate, our photojournalists also are among the nation's best. Their coverage of this tragedy made them Pulitzer Prize finalists, and deservedly so. Thanks to Matthew Fortner, Grace Beahm Alford, Brad Nettles, Leroy Burnell, Paul Zoeller, Michael Pronzato, Lauren Prescott, and Wade Spees, who took the elegant cover jacket photograph. Design desk chief Chad Dunbar created the now-iconic tribute to the nine victims using palmetto roses, a quintessential symbol of Charleston's complex racial history. Managing editor Autumn Phillips also shared with me her brilliant writer's eye in the final stages. I'm honored to have worked with all of you.

Many people whose names appear only briefly or not at all on these pages provided critical guidance and shared memories, letters, notes, emails, voicemails, video recordings, and photographs to re-create scenes I did not witness and provide context to those that I did. Thanks for particular insight from Kylon Middleton, Andy and Cheryl Savage, Nikki Haley, Rob Godfrey, Greg Mullen, John Lites, Jennie Antonio, Valerie Jarrett, Gerald Truesdale, Emily Barrett, Markland Johnson, Gerald Malloy, Joseph Darby, Althea Latham, Brenda Nelson, Elnora Taylor, Jean Ortiz, Eric S. C. Manning, William and Linda Toney, Liz Alston, Cress Darwin, Spike Coleman, Margaret Seidler, Mullins McLeod, and Mickey Bakst. Special thanks also to my dear friend Sharon Putman, who provided early and important criticism and whose father, Robert Williamson, shared his deep knowledge of Confederate flag history.

As any writer knows, the real economy of writing is time, and no one makes greater sacrifice on that front than a writer's family. Without the support of mine, I would not have been able to write this book, or much else worth reading. Alan, Lauren, and Wesley, I love you.

INDEX

African Methodist Episcopal (AME)
Church
call and response tradition of
preaching, 202
Emanuel AME Church as South's
oldest, ix, 3
hierarchical nature of, 142
history and calling of, 288–290
meeting and election of bishops
(Philadelphia, 2016), 206–207
Mount Zion AME, 202
purple and black liturgical colors, 89
Roof's choice of as target, 182–183,
245
two hundredth anniversary of,
206–207
See also Emanuel African Methodist
Episcopal Church
al-Marri, Ali, 124
American Civil War
centennial celebrations, 98–99, 105
and Charleston, 7, 34–35, 92, 227
first shots of, 35
and Heritage Act, 97
as War Between the States, 97, 109
as War of Northern Aggression,
109
See also Confederate flag
Anglin, Andrew, 83
Antonio, Jennie, 36, 140–141
apartheid, 66, 182
Army of Northern Virginia Battle Flag,
85. *See also* Confederate flag
Aurora, Colorado, movie theater
shooting, 53, 114

Ballenger, James, 219
Baltimore protests, 30, 75, 78
Bamberg, Justin, 222, 226
Bamberg, South Carolina, 65, 93–94,
109–110
Barbier, Deborah, 187
Beard, Danny (boyfriend of Amy Roof),
250
Benjamin, Cleo, 165, 198
Bernat, Dan, 61–62
Biden, Jill, 117
Biden, Joe, 117, 162
Binghamton immigration center
shooting, 114
Black Liberation Theology, 91
bomb threat, 40–43
Boston Marathon bombing, 41,
190
Bright, Lee, 105, 106
Brown, Caleb, 182
Brown v. Board of Education, 209
Bruck, David (attorney for Dylann
Roof), 189–190, 220, 231–233,
237–238, 255–256, 264, 279–280
Bundy, Ted, 220
Burns, Ken, 199
Burris, Joe, 62, 63

Calhoun, John C., 4, 32–33, 107
Capers, Sheila (Steve Hurd's sister),
127
CCC (Council of Conservative
Citizens), 82, 248–249
Charleston, South Carolina
America Street, 42

Charleston, South Carolina (cont'd)
    and American Civil War, 7, 34–35, 92,
        227
    Arthur Ravenel Jr. Bridge, 91
    Calhoun Street, 4, 11, 24, 28, 32, 40,
        50, 88, 115, 149, 174, 196
    cemetery district, 176
    City Council's vote to apologize for
        city's role in slavery, 286
    College of Charleston, 12, 27, 52, 115,
        203
    Emanuel AME Church Cemetery,
        176–178
    Four Corners of Law, 208, 221
    furniture showroom fire (2007),
        30–31, 138
    Gadsden's Wharf, 286
    and gentrification, 5, 125, 176
    Hanging Tree, 34
    Holy Trinity Reformed Episcopal
        Church, 27, 261
    International African American
        Museum, 286
    John C. Calhoun Monument, 4,
        32–33
    Magnolia Cemetery, 176
    Marion Square, 32–33, 41, 44, 115,
        124, 198
    Medical University Hospital, 26–27,
        40, 49–50
    Meeting Street, 19, 32, 36, 39, 41, 115,
        227
    The Mills House, 227
    Neck area, 176
    reasons chosen by Roof, 7, 245
    Second Presbyterian, 125–126, 142,
        150, 155–156, 173–175, 190–191,
        201–203, 206
    Vesey's planned slave uprising, ix, 34,
        138, 156, 206, 261
Charleston Gaillard Center
    circle of trees memorial, 198
    as command post, 40–41, 64
Citizens' Councils of America, 82
Civil War. See American Civil War
Clark, Betty Deas (AME pastor),
    170–175, 190–194, 205
Clinton, Hillary, 117, 184, 214
Clyburn, Jim, 100–101, 102, 126, 127,
    174
Coakley family, 129

Coates, Ta-Nehisi, 92
Cobb, Jelani, 199–200
Coleman, Spike, 31–32
Coleman-Singleton, Sharonda, 10, 119,
    260, 289, 294
    family of, 270, 285
    funeral of, 126
    night of the shooting, 10, 12, 23, 24
    Roof found guilty of death of (count
        one), 260
Collier, Nadine (Ethel Lance's
    daughter), 38, 79, 177–178, 202,
    206–207, 253–254
    meeting with Barack Obama, 119
    notified of Ethel's death, 49–50
    remarks at bond hearing, 74, 77–78,
        89, 202
Columbine shooting, 53, 161
command post (Charleston Gaillard
    Center), 40–41, 64
Cone, James, 91
Confederate flag, 66
    flags and symbols displayed by Roof,
        7, 47, 60, 85, 93
    General Assembly's legislation to
        remove flag from State House,
        104–113
    Haley's calling for removal of,
        93–102
    history of on State House grounds,
        85, 95, 98–99
    moved from State House dome to
        flagpole (2000), 85, 95
    Ravenel's defense of, 91
    reactions to Haley's press conference,
        103–104
    symbolism of, 7, 85, 98–102, 105–113
Council of Conservative Citizens
    (CCC), 82, 248–249
Cross, Frazier Glenn, 220
Curnell, Denzel, 42–43

Daily Stormer (website), 83, 249
Darby, Joseph, 113, 200
Darwin, Cress (pastor of Second
    Presbyterian)
    and Felicia Sanders, 142–143, 150, 155,
        173–174, 202, 206
    and funerals for Tywanza Sanders
        and Susie Jackson, 125–126
    at the trial, 229, 234

death penalty
  and competency, 210
  opposed to by Roof's attorney,
    189–190, 240, 255
  religious objections to, 188, 254, 259,
    279
  and Roof's closing argument, 276
  and Roof's federal indictment,
    188–189
  Roof's sentence of, 279, 283
  self-representation in death penalty
    cases, 224
  in South Carolina, 189
  and speedy trials, 189–190
Delaney, Andrew, 21
Denmark Vesey's Garden (Kytle and
  Roberts), 92
Doctor, DePayne Middleton. See
  Middleton Doctor, DePayne
Duncan, Jeff, 100

Emanuel African Methodist Episcopal
  (AME) Church (Mother Emanuel)
  anniversary remembrance of
    shooting, 197–204
  architecture of, 5
  civil rights history of, 5–6, 9, 12,
    182–183, 190
  donations sent to, 127, 131–137,
    151–155, 171, 190–192, 206
  fellowship hall (after the shooting),
    87, 126–127, 131, 132, 139, 146, 148,
    155–156
  fellowship hall (night of the
    shooting), 6, 8, 10–19, 22, 24, 40,
    43, 234, 240, 244
  layout of, 6, 21, 25–26, 88, 244,
    268–269, 282
  quarterly conference held on the
    night of the shooting, 6, 8–10, 43
  reasons chosen by Roof, 7, 245
  security cameras, 45, 52
  South's oldest AME church, ix, 3
  watch night church service, 262–263
Emanuel AME Church Cemetery,
  176–178
Emanuel Nine, 111–112, 119, 127, 132,
  133, 261, 294
  donations sent to Emanuel AME for,
    127, 131–137, 151–155, 171, 190–192,
    206

Hope Fund for, 133, 151
  See also Coleman-Singleton,
    Sharonda; Hurd, Cynthia Graham;
    Jackson, Susie; Lance, Ethel;
    Middleton Doctor, DePayne;
    Pinckney, Clementa; Sanders,
    Tywanza; Simmons, Daniel L.;
    Thompson, Myra
Embassy Suites (meeting place in
  shooting's aftermath), 34–44
  building's history, 34–35
  coroners' announcements at,
    47–50
  Haley's visit to, 64
  Mullen's visit to, 42–44
  Neal's visit to, 111
  staff of, 35–36, 157
empathy, x, 288

Faith & Politics Institute, 174
federal trial of Dylann Roof
  death penalty verdict, 279
  footage of Roof's initial interview
    with Shelby police, 242–247
  guilt phase, 233–256
  guilty verdict, 259–261
  indictment, 188–190
  jury deliberations for guilt phase,
    257–259
  jury deliberations for penalty phase,
    277–279
  lead prosecutor (Jay Richardson), 189,
    229, 231, 233–235, 237, 260–261,
    267–269, 273–275, 285
  penalty phase, 265–283
  pre-sentencing competency hearing,
    264
  pre-trial competency hearing,
    210–211, 219–222
  Roof's attorney (David Bruck),
    189–190, 220, 231–233, 237–238,
    255–256, 264, 279–280
  Roof's closing argument in penalty
    phase, 276–277
  Roof's opening statement in penalty
    phase, 266–267
  Roof's request to represent himself,
    220
  Roof's request to represent himself
    for sentencing phase only,
    223–224

federal trial of Dylann Roof (*cont'd*)
   sentencing of, 282–283
   See also Gergel, Richard
Ferguson unrest, 30, 65, 75, 78
forgiveness
   as "deep spiritual resistance," 91
   families' expression of forgiveness at
     bond hearing, 74–76
   Goff's sermon on, 89–91, 170
   and Haley's meeting with Sanders
     family, 143–145
   Obama's decision to focus on, 76,
     114–115, 189
   remarks by Felicia Sanders at
     sentencing, 282–283
Fort Hood shooting, 114
Frady, Todd, 59–60
Friendship Nine, 99

Gates, Henry Louis, Jr., 199
gentrification, 5, 125, 176
Gergel, Belinda, 209
Gergel, Richard (U.S. District Judge
   presiding over Roof's trial)
   career of, 208–209
   delays trial for competency hearing,
     209–211
   grants Roof's request to represent
     himself, 220
   grants Roof's request to represent
     himself in penalty phase only,
     223–224
   Roof declared competent by, 219–220,
     264
   sentencing by, 282–283
   and trial's guilt phase, 233, 234, 237,
     238, 240, 247, 254, 257, 260
   and trial's penalty phase, 271, 277–279
Giffords, Gabrielle, 161
Gilliard, Wendell, 108
Glee, Willi, 126–127
Glock pistol, 7, 15, 18, 63, 67, 183, 252,
   278
Goff, Norvel (Emanuel AME presiding
   elder and interim pastor), 145–150,
   168
   and donations to families and
     Emanuel AME, 133–135, 137,
     152–153
   Father's Day forgiveness sermon,
     89–91, 170

   financial questions regarding,
     152–154
   firing of Althea Latham, 137
   and funeral for Clementa Pinckney,
     117, 118
   as interim pastor, 64, 86–87, 123, 139,
     142
   letter from Felicia Sanders to, 145–147
   night of the shooting, 8, 9, 11
   prayer with families at Embassy
     Suites, 43–44
   press conference by, 153–155
   as Reid Chapel pastor, 152–154
   replaced by Betty Deas Clark, 170
   run for bishop, 170, 206–207
Gosnell, James, 72–75
Gowdy, Trey, 100
Graham, Lindsey, 99–100, 117
Graham, Malcolm (brother of Cynthia
   Graham Hurd), 127–128
Graham, Melvin (brother of Cynthia
   Graham Hurd), 50–51, 119,
   157–159
Greenberg, Reuben, 42
Gregorie, William Dudley, 130
Gullah culture, 156
gun violence
   background checks, 162
   Glock pistol, 7, 15, 18, 63, 67, 183, 252,
     278
   gun control, 54, 145
   gun laws, 163, 274, 285
   gun rights, 108, 274
   hollow-point bullets, 7, 15
   lone wolf type of killer, 67, 85
   mass shootings, 21, 41, 53, 76, 140,
     161–162, 193, 286
   White House event, 161–163

Haley, Nikki, 118, 163, 291
   appointed ambassador to the United
     Nations, 274
   body camera legislation signed by, 54
   call for removal of Confederate flag
     from State House, 95–102
   childhood of, 65, 93–94, 109–111
   at Father's Day Emanuel AME
     service, 89
   at funeral for Clementa Pinckney, 117
   at funeral for Cynthia Graham Hurd,
     126

influence of shooting on views of,
95
legislation to remove flag from State
House signed by, 112
meeting with Felicia and Tyrone
Sanders, 143–145
notified of shooting, 53–55
Order of the Palmetto presented to
Norvel Goff by, 170
pleas for calm in the aftermath of
Slager mistrial, 225
racial profiling story shared with
State House Republicans, 109–111
reaction to call for removal of
Confederate flag, 103–104, 107
remarks at joint press conference
announcing Roof's arrest, 64–66
Republican response to Obama's
State of the Union address
delivered by, 164
Hamrick, Scott, 62–63, 67
hate crime, 45, 188
Henderson, Doug, 56–57
Henderson, Edward, 21, 25
Heritage Act, 97
hollow-point bullets, 7, 15
Holy Trinity Reformed Episcopal
Church, 27, 216
Hope Fund, 133, 151
Horne, Jenny, 111–112, 174
Hurd, Arthur Stephen "Steve" (husband
of Cynthia Hurd), 73
and Cynthia's funeral, 127–128
lawsuit filed by, 152–153, 171, 191
life after shooting and funeral,
130–131, 158–160, 167–168, 272,
283, 285
mother of, 38
night of the shooting, 37–38, 50–51,
56–57
remarks at sentencing, 283
Hurd, Cynthia Graham, 89, 119,
128, 130–131, 171, 283, 285, 289,
294
burial of, 176
family's testimony at trial, 272
funeral of, 126–128
night of the shooting, 9–10, 235
See also Graham, Malcolm; Graham,
Melvin; Jones, Jackie
Hurd, Steve. See Hurd, Arthur Stephen

iconography and symbols
Confederate flag, 85, 98–102, 105–113
Gadsden flag, 250
Rhodesian flag, 66, 182, 250
Roof as potential symbol, 221,
275
Roof's penchant for, 7, 66–67, 85, 93,
105, 182, 250, 271
tragedies as symbols, 123
of white supremacy, 7, 66, 84–85, 93,
98–102, 105–113, 182, 250, 271
Ifill, Gwen, 199–200
Illumination Project, 200–201

Jackson, Susie, 59, 89, 119, 174, 282, 289,
294
burial of, 176
family notified of death of, 48–49
family's testimony at trial, 274–275
joint funeral for Tywanza Sanders
and, 123–126, 142, 144
as matriarch of Emanuel AME, 10
night of the shooting, 6, 10, 16, 20,
23–24, 236–237, 241, 265
See also Sanders, Felicia; Sanders,
Tyrone
Januchowski, Craig, 67, 69–70, 242,
243–244, 246–247
Jarrett, Valerie, 114
Jim Crow laws, 3, 290, 291
Johnson, James, 224
Johnson, Wilbur, 134
Jones, Jackie (sister of Cynthia Graham
Hurd), 272

Keel, Mark, 53
King, Bernice, 198
King, Coretta Scott, 198
King, Martin Luther, Jr., 6–7, 165, 182,
198, 283, 290
KKK. See Ku Klux Klan
Knapp, Lauren, 270–272
Kniess, Justin, 21
Ku Klux Klan (KKK), 5, 82–84, 93, 96,
183, 248–249
Kytle, Ethan J., 92

Lance, Jon Quil (grandson of Ethel
Lance), 39
Lance, Esther (daughter of Ethel Lance),
77, 177–178, 231

Lance, Ethel, 119, 289, 294
  absence of will left by, 79, 178
  burial of and headstones for, 176–178,
    253–254
  death of daughter (Terrie
    Washington), 77
  family notified of death of, 49–50
  family's testimony at trial, 273–274
  funeral for, 126
  night of the shooting, 10
  See also Collier, Nadine; Lance, Esther;
    Risher, Sharon; Washington, Gary;
    Washington, Terrie
Latham, Althea (Emanuel AME
  secretary), 8, 45, 86–87, 132–133,
  137, 145
Lee, Robert E., 107–108, 112
Lites, John, 22–26, 43
lone wolf type of killer, 67, 85
Lord's Prayer, The, 88, 203,
  261
Lynch, Loretta, 189

Made in Britain (film), 66
Malloy, Gerald, 106, 166, 267,
  274
manhunt for Roof, 31–32, 44–45
Mann, Paige (stepmom of Dylann
  Roof), 185
Manning, Eric S. C., 263, 286
Martin, Larry, 105–106
Martin, Trayvon, 82, 248
Martinez, Johnette Pinckney, 227–228
mass shootings, 21, 41, 53, 76, 140,
  161–162, 193, 286. *See also individual*
  shootings; gun violence
May, John Amasa, 98–99
McAllister-Wilson, David, 165
McMaster, Henry, 100, 274
Meek, Joey, 46–47, 66–67, 181–183,
  185–187, 285
Metze, Tony, 185
Middleton, Kylon (AME minister), 106,
  136, 176, 202
  and anniversary service, 202–204
  Bible study led by on anniversary of
    shooting, 201–202
  night of the shooting, 36–37, 48
  and the trial, 230, 259, 267, 284
Middleton Doctor, DePayne, 49, 119,
  289, 294

  family of, 260, 266, 270
  night of the shooting, 9–10, 235
"Miseducation of Dylann Roof"
  (Southern Poverty Law Center),
  249
Moore, JA (brother of Myra Thompson),
  196
Mother Emanuel. *See* Emanuel African
  Methodist Episcopal Church
Moving Forward Fund, 127, 131–137,
  151–155, 171, 190–192, 206
Mullen, Greg (police chief)
  at bond hearing, 76
  and Illumination Project, 200–201
  initial press conference, 44–45
  manhunt run by, 52–53, 55, 60
  night of the shooting, 30–31, 40–45
  notified of the shooting, 30–31
  press conference to announce Roof's
    arrest, 64–65
  visit to Embassy Suites, 42–44
Mulvaney, Mick, 100

NAACP, 89, 91, 99, 113, 200
National Action Network, 224
National Rifle Association, 163, 274
Neal, Joe, 111
Need to Identify sheet, 53
Nelson, Brenda, 135
neo-Nazis, 5, 7, 249. *See also* white
  supremacy
Norris, Richard Franklin, 117, 152, 170,
  205, 207
Norris, Wesley, 108

Obama, Barack, 164, 249, 261, 280
  "Amazing Grace" sung by, 118, 196,
    294
  decision to focus on families'
    forgiveness, 76, 114–115, 189
  eulogy for Clementa Pinckney,
    114–115, 117–119, 287–294
  letter congratulating seminary
    graduates, 165–166
  White House gun violence event,
    161–163
Obama, Michelle, 117, 119–120, 192
Orlando shooting, 193

Parable of the Sower, 13–14, 193–195
Peeler, Harvey, 105, 105

Pinckney, Clementa
  altar chair draped in black robe, 89
  education scholarship in name of,
    133
  family notified of death of, 47–48
  family's testimony, 267–270
  father of, 259
  funeral for, 114–119, 126, 196
  funeral program for, 116
  night of the shooting, 7–12, 15, 18, 53,
    55, 235–236, 238–239, 241–242
  posthumous Doctorate of Ministry
    degree, 164–166
  remarks by Barack Obama in eulogy
    for, 114–115, 117–119, 287–294
  Roof welcomed to Bible study by,
    12–13
  Senate chair draped in black, 104
  shooting of, 15
  as state senator, 37, 53–56, 104,
    107–111
Pinckney, Eliana (daughter of Clementa
    Pinckney), 55–56, 197–198, 239,
    268, 284, 286, 287
  at Clementa's funeral, 116
  at Clementa's posthumous
    commencement, 165–166
  receives Clementa's hood, 166
  told of Clementa's death, 48
Pinckney, Jennifer (wife of Clementa
    Pinckney)
  and Clementa's funeral and eulogy,
    114–117
  death of mother, 198
  decision not to attend anniversary
    remembrance, 197–198
  and legislation to remove Confederate
    flag from State House, 105–107
  letter of apology from Joey Meek to,
    187
  life after the shooting and trial,
    135–137, 164, 284, 285
  mentioned in Barack Obama's
    eulogy, 287
  morning after the shooting, 55–56
  night of the shooting, 8, 10, 16, 25–26,
    36–37, 47–48, 87
  911 call by, 25, 268–269
  notified of Clementa's death, 47–48
  at posthumous Doctorate of Ministry
    degree for Clementa, 164–166

  testimony at trial's penalty phase,
    267–270
  at the trial, 227–230, 233–241, 247,
    255, 259–260, 265, 267–270, 284
  at White House gun violence event,
    161–163
Pinckney, Johnette (sister of Clementa
    Pinckney), 227–228, 230, 234,
    238–239, 259–260, 267, 284
Pinckney, Malana (daughter of
    Clementa Pinckney), 197, 239, 284,
    286, 287
  at Clementa's funeral, 116–117
  at Clementa's posthumous
    commencement, 165–166
  Grasshopper (nickname), 8, 116
  night of the shooting, 8, 10–11, 16,
    25–26, 37, 47–48, 241, 268–269
  receives Clementa's diploma, 166
Pitts, Michael, 108–112
Post and Courier, The, ix, 148, 152,
    206–207
Priebus, Reince, 101
Pulse nightclub shooting, 193

Quarles, Denise (daughter of Myra
    Thompson), 129, 259–260

racial profiling, 82, 110
Randhawa, Ajit (father of Nikki Haley),
    94, 110
Randhawa, Raj (mother of Nikki
    Haley), 65, 94
Reid Chapel (Columbia, South
    Carolina), 152–154
Rice, Tom, 100
Richardson, Jay (lead prosecutor)
  nominated to 4th Circuit Court of
    Appeals, 285
  pre-indictment conference call,
    189
  trial's guilt phase, 229, 231, 233–235,
    237, 260–261
  trial's penalty phase, 267–269,
    273–275
Riley, Joseph, Jr., 42, 44, 64, 101, 117,
    125–127, 151, 290
Risher, Sharon (daughter of Ethel
    Lance), 39, 77–79, 171, 176–178, 188,
    279–281, 285
  remarks at sentencing, 283

Risher, Sharon (daughter of Ethel
    Lance) (cont'd)
  testimony at trial's penalty phase,
    273–274
  at the trial, 231, 240, 253–254, 259
  and White House gun violence event,
    161, 262
Roberts, Blain, 82
Rogers, Kyle, 82–83
Romney, Mitt, 96
Roof, Amy (mother of Dylann Roof),
    184–186, 211–212, 215–218, 233,
    249–250
Roof, Benn (father of Dylann Roof),
    66–67, 184–186, 211–217, 239
Roof, Dylann Storm
  in Bible study, 12–15
  bond hearing, 72–76
  capture and arrest in North Carolina,
    60–63
  charges against, 188
  at Charleston County detention
    center, 71, 80–81
  childhood of, 184–186
  drive to Emanuel AME, 7–9
  enters Emanuel AME, 11–12
  extradition to South Carolina, 70
  Glock owned by, 2, 15, 18, 63, 67, 183,
    252, 278
  hours following the shooting, 45–47,
    53, 59–60
  and iconography, 7, 66–67, 85, 93, 105,
    182, 250, 271
  interrogation of, 67–70, 242–247
  jail visit by parents, 211–218
  and Joey Meek, 46–47, 181–183, 185–187
  manhunt for, 31–32, 44–45, 52–53
  manifesto of, 81–82, 93, 98, 183,
    242
  night of the shooting, 4–5, 7, 8–9,
    11–19
  notes to parents, 45–46
  photographs of, 84–85, 250–251
  shooting by, 15–19
  spotted by Debbie Dills, 59–60
  website of, 4–5, 81–83
  websites visited by, 82–83, 85,
    248–249
  See also federal trial of Dylann Roof
Roof, Joseph (grandfather of Dylann
    Roof), 239–240

Roof, Lucy (grandmother of Dylann
    Roof), 239–240
Roof, Morgan (half-sister of Dylann
    Roof), 185, 285
Roof, Paul (uncle of Dylann Roof),
    203–204

San Bernardino shooting, 161, 162
Sanders, Felicia (mother of Tywanza
    Sanders)
  attendance at every court hearing
    and trial, 187, 241
  and Betty Deas Clark, 171–174,
    190–192, 205–206
  Bible of, 3, 17, 139–141, 282–283
  first visit to Second Presbyterian,
    142
  forgiveness extended to Roof by,
    282–283
  friendship with Andy Savage, 58–59,
    142, 190
  and joint funeral for Tywanza and
    Susie Jackson, 123–126
  letter from Joey Meek to, 187
  letter to Goff from, 145–146
  meeting with Nikki Haley, 143–145
  and Moving Forward Fund, 153–155,
    191–192
  night of the shooting, 3–6, 9–10,
    14–17, 20–24, 29, 31–32, 35, 49
  opening Tywanza's bedroom, 147
  photography visit to Emanuel AME,
    148–150
  remarks at bond hearing, 75, 78
  remarks at sentencing, 282–283
  at removal of Confederate flag from
    State House, 112
  represented by Andy Savage, 59, 171,
    190, 224
  in reserved seating at Emanuel AME
    memorial service, 139
  return to service at Emanuel AME,
    172–173
  and Second Presbyterian, 173–175,
    201–202, 206–207
  spiritual struggle of, 138–139, 141–147,
    155–156, 173–175, 201–202
  testimony at trial's guilt phase,
    234–238
  testimony at trial's penalty phase,
    274–275

at the trial, 209, 228–230, 234–238, 240, 241, 255, 259, 260
Sanders, Tyrone (father of Tywanza Sanders and nephew of Susie Jackson), 3–4, 58, 89, 119
  at Goff's press conference, 153–155
  life after shooting and trial, 89
  meeting with Nikki Haley, 143–145
  and Moving Forward Fund, 153–155, 191
  in Ninja Turtle costume for Tywanza's birthday, 275
  notified of shooting, 23–24
  opening Tywanza's bedroom, 147
  photography visit to Emanuel AME, 148–150
  in reserved seating at Emanuel AME memorial service, 139
  return to service at Emanuel AME, 172–173
  at Second Presbyterian, 174
  at the trial, 229, 234, 241, 245, 255
Sanders, Tywanza, 75, 143–145, 147, 285, 289, 294
  bedroom of, 147
  burial of, 176
  childhood of, 275
  death of, 23
  family's testimony at trial, 275
  Instagram page, 14, 147
  joint funeral for Tywanza Sanders and Susie Jackson, 123–126, 142, 144
  and Meek's letter of apology, 187
  night of the shooting, 4, 10, 14, 16–18, 20–23, 48, 59, 187, 236–237, 241
  "Reasons Why I Lock People Out," 147
  shooting of, 16–17
  Snapchat recordings, 14
  Wanza (nickname), 10, 147
Sandy Hook Elementary shooting, 41, 114, 161–162
Sanford, Mark, 100
Savage, Andy, 58, 124, 142, 171–172, 190, 224, 231, 234
Savage, Cheryl, 172, 190, 202, 229, 259
Savage, Michael, 81
Scott, Anthony, 225
Scott, Tim, 89, 99–102, 117, 126, 174

Scott, Walter, 30, 54, 58, 65, 71, 81, 101, 200
  attorney for, 124 (see also Savage, Andy)
  news coverage of shooting of, ix
  public opinion of race relations following shooting of, 199
  Slager's guilty plea for violating civil rights of, 285
  trial of Michael Slager for murder of, 190, 208, 221–225
Scriven, Christon, 181–182
shared experience, x
Sheheen, Vincent, 105
Sheppard, Polly, 113, 141, 174, 187, 202, 209
  at funeral for Cynthia Graham Hurd, 126–127
  meeting with Barack Obama, 119
  night of the shooting, 10, 12–13, 17–18, 20–22, 24, 29, 31–32, 35, 49, 269
  911 call by, 18, 20
  photography visit to Emanuel AME, 148–150
  represented by Andy Savage, 124, 171
  at the trial, 229, 240, 259, 260
Simmons, Daniel L., Jr., 89
Simmons, Daniel L., Sr., 119, 123, 153, 285, 289, 294
  arrives at hospital, 27
  Dapper Dan (nickname), 14
  death of, 27
  family's Hate Won't Win movement, 119–120
  family's testimony, 270
  night of the shooting, 9, 10, 13–16, 18, 22–24, 26–27, 59, 87, 235, 238, 240
  shooting of, 15–16
  as usual Bible study leader, 9, 235
Singleton, Chris (son of Sharonda Coleman-Singleton), 285
16th Street Baptist Church bombing (Birmingham, Alabama), 127
skinheads, 5, 66, 82, 84, 248. See also white supremacy
Slager, Michael
  guilty plea for violating Walter Scott's civil rights, 285
  in jail cell adjacent to Dylann Roof, 71, 81

Slager, Michael (*cont'd*)
 jury for, 230
 lawyer for (Andy Savage), 58, 124
 mistrial declared for, 225–226
 trial of, 190, 208, 221–226, 231
slavery
 Emancipation Proclamation, 262–263
 Hanging Tree, 34
 and John C. Calhoun Monument, 4,
 32–33
 slave trade, 92, 95
 Vesey's planned slave revolt, 34, 138,
 156, 206, 261
 and watch night church services,
 262–263
 See also American Civil War;
 Confederate flag
Smith, Susan, 190
Southern Cross, 95. *See also* Confederate
 flag
Southern Poverty Law Center, 82, 83,
 249
Stansbury, Michael, 69–70, 242–247
Stewart, David, 21
Stormfront (website), 83, 249, 251
Styers, Matt, 68–69
symbols. *See* iconography and symbols

Tea Party, 96, 110, 250
Temoney, Herbert, 47–49
Thompson, Anthony (husband of Myra
 Thompson)
 Advent service led by, 261–262
 anniversary Bible study led by,
 192–196
 and Betty Deas Clark, 171, 192–193
 life after shooting and trial, 128,
 168–169, 285
 marriage of, 128–130, 193–194
 night of the shooting, 27–30, 31–32,
 35, 49
 notified of Myra's death, 49
 and Parable of the Sower, 193–194
 and pre-indictment conference call,
 188
 remarks at bond hearing, 74–75, 130
 testimony at trial's penalty phase,
 270
 at the trial, 240, 259–260
Thompson, Myra, 74–75, 119, 171, 285,
 289, 294

Bible study led by, 9–10, 12–14,
 193–194, 235
"bugaboo" (nickname), 14, 235
childhood and family of, 129
family's testimony at trial, 270
first sermon of, 251
funeral for, 129–130
marriage of, 128–130, 193–194,
 270
night of the shooting, 8–10, 12–14, 20,
 24, 27–30, 35, 49, 235
and Parable of the Sower, 13–14,
 193–194
 See also Moore, JA; Quarles, Denise
Thurmond, Paul, 101
Thurmond, Strom, 101
trial of Dylann Roof. *See* federal trial of
 Dylann Roof
Truesdale, Gerald, 257–260, 265–267,
 277–279
Trump, Donald, 214, 261
 announces candidacy for president, 83
 endorsed by Andrew Anglin, 83
 nomination of Jay Richardson to
 4th Circuit Court of Appeals, 286
 rhetoric of, 286
 supporters of, 100, 164, 184, 274
Tsarnaev, Dzhokhar, 190
Tucson shooting, 114, 161

Verdin, Danny, 106
Vesey, Denmark, 34, 138, 156, 206, 261
Virginia Tech shooting, 53

Waring, J. Waties, 209
Washington, Booker T., 5
Washington, Gary (son of Ethel Lance),
 177, 273
Washington, Terrie (daughter of Ethel
 Lance), 77
white nationalism, 81, 85, 248
white supremacy
 and Confederate flag, 93, 95–96
 Council of Conservative Citizens, 82,
 248–249
 Daily Stormer (website), 83, 249
 and Dylann Roof, 4–5, 66–67, 82–85,
 93, 95, 182, 208, 230, 248–251, 258,
 270–271
 Ku Klux Klan, 5, 82–84, 93, 96, 183,
 248–249

Overland Park Jewish Community
  Center shooting, 220
prevalence of, 281, 286
and Red Bank (Lexington suburb), 46
Roof as potential symbol for, 221, 275
16th Street Baptist Church bombing,
  127
Stormfront (website), 83, 249, 251
symbolism and iconography, 7, 66,
  84–85, 93, 98–102, 105–113, 182,
  250, 271
Tree of Life Synagogue shooting, 286
websites and online networks, 4–5,
  81–83, 85, 248–249, 286
Williams, Nathan, 254, 265
Wilson, Joe, 100
Wilson, Scarlett, 188, 222, 225
Wright, Jonathan Jasper, 209